Martin Luther King Jr. and the Morality of Legal Practice

This book seeks to reframe our understanding of the lawyer's work by exploring how Martin Luther King Jr. built his advocacy on a coherent set of moral claims regarding the demands of love and justice in light of human nature. King never shirked from staking out challenging claims of moral truth, even while remaining open to working with those who rejected those truths. His example should inspire the legal profession as a reminder that truth telling, even in a society that often appears morally balkanized, has the capacity to move hearts and minds. At the same time, his example should give the profession pause, for King's success would have been impossible absent his substantive views about human nature and the ends of justice. This book is an effort to reframe our conception of morality's relevance to professionalism through the lens provided by the public and prophetic advocacy of Dr. King.

Robert K. Vischer is professor of law and associate dean for academic affairs at the University of St. Thomas School of Law in Minneapolis. He is the author of *Conscience and the Common Good: Reclaiming the Space between Person and State* (2010). His scholarship explores the intersection of law, religion, and public policy, with a particular focus on the religious and moral dimensions of professional identity.

Martin Luther King Jr. and the Morality of Legal Practice

Lessons in Love and Justice

ROBERT K. VISCHER

University of St. Thomas School of Law

CAMBRIDGE
UNIVERSITY PRESS

CAMBRIDGE
UNIVERSITY PRESS

32 Avenue of the Americas, New York NY 10013-2473, USA

Cambridge University Press is part of the University of Cambridge.

It furthers the University's mission by disseminating knowledge in the pursuit of education, learning and research at the highest international levels of excellence.

www.cambridge.org
Information on this title: www.cambridge.org/9781107429161

© Robert K. Vischer 2013

First published 2013
First paperback edition 2014

A catalogue record for this publication is available from the British Library

Library of Congress Cataloguing in Publication data
Vischer, Robert K.
    Martin Luther King Jr. and the morality of legal practice : lessons in love and justice / Robert K. Vischer.
        p.   cm.
    Includes index.
    ISBN 978-1-107-03122-7 (hardback)
    1. King, Martin Luther, Jr., 1929–1968   2. Lawyers–United States–
    Biography.   3. Law–Moral and ethical aspects–United States.   I. Title.
    KF373.K523V57   2012
    174'.30973–dc23   2012033807

ISBN 978-1-107-03122-7 Hardback
ISBN 978-1-107-42916-1 Paperback

For *Sophia, Lila, and Ava*

Contents

Acknowledgments

This book benefited from comments generously offered by Deborah Cantrell, Scott Cummings, Marc DeGirolami, Kate Kruse, David Luban, Lisa Schiltz, Susan Stabile, Amy Uelmen, Brad Wendel, and Alice Woolley, as well as feedback I received from presenting portions of the book at Catholic University, Notre Dame, Pepperdine, the University of St. Thomas, Stanford, and Sophia University (Italy). I am also grateful for the institutional support provided by the University of St. Thomas and Blackfriars Hall (Oxford). I am, as always, profoundly grateful to my wife, Maureen, for her support. This book is dedicated to my daughters – Sophia Marie, Lila DeNell, and Ava May. Fatherhood provides a daily reminder that my own integration of love and justice is a work in progress, and I appreciate their patience.

Acknowledgments

I am grateful for the permission to include portions of my earlier work in this book. Much of Chapter 1 was published as *How Do Lawyers Serve Human Dignity?*, Univ. of St. Thomas L.J. (2012). Part of Chapter 2 was published as *Big Law and the Marginalization of Trust*, 25 Geo. J. Legal Ethics 165 (2012). Small portions of Chapter 3 and Chapter 4 were included in *Legal Advice as Moral Perspective*, 19 Geo. J. Legal Ethics 225 (2006). My classroom experience with competing moral perspectives, mentioned in the Introduction and Conclusion, was also included in *Professionalizing Moral Engagement*, 103 N.W. L. Rev. Colloquy (2009), and *Moral Engagement without the "Moral Law": A Post-Canons View of Attorneys' Accountability*, 2008 Prof'l Lawyer 213 (2008).

Introduction

Several years ago in my legal ethics class, I wanted to see how far I could push my students in their embrace of the notion that the moral evaluation of conduct depends on the professional role one occupies. I asked students to imagine that they were medical researchers in Nazi Germany and that the authorities took them to a concentration camp, inviting them to experiment on live human subjects. Would they, as scientists, proceed with the experiments? The first three students I called on answered that they would do the experiments if it would advance the research. One explained that morality is constructed by society, and in that particular society, the experiments would not be considered immoral. Another wondered why, if their deaths were assured through no fault of the scientists, we would not take the opportunity to advance the greater good. The third insisted that the job of the researcher is to expand scientific knowledge, and the job of the government is to define the limits of that research. Absent government prohibition, the researcher has no moral reason not to proceed.

These students, I am confident, did not believe what they were saying. They were engaging my question according to the rules of good lawyering, as they perceived them – figuring out a way around any and all obstacles standing between the actor and a given course of conduct. Indeed, much of the blame for their answers belongs with the implicit messages they receive about the values of the legal profession: that cleverness is valued over wisdom, and that the law is simply a problem to be solved, rather than an inescapably moral endeavor.

More pointedly, the third student's answer was an extreme example of the common conception that professional identity is premised on the actor's capacity to stay within his or designated role, and to treat as irrelevant any moral considerations that distract from the role's primary function. The primary function, when it comes to lawyers, is to attain the client's stated objectives to the extent permitted by law. The dominant view, which holds that lawyers are not morally accountable for these objectives,[1] presumes that

---

[1] *Model Rules of Prof'l Cond. R.* 1.2(b) ("A lawyer's representation of a client … does not constitute an endorsement of the client's political, economic, social or moral views or activities."), cmt 2

lawyers are able and willing to disconnect their own moral convictions from their evaluation of the causes and clients they are asked to represent.

In comparison to the era when the American Bar Association, via the 1908 *Canons of Professional Ethics*, could confidently instruct lawyers to "impress upon the client and his undertaking exact compliance with the strictest principles of moral law,"[2] today we are more skeptical about the existence of any "moral law," much less that it could or should be impressed upon the client. Recognizing the variability of moral convictions and complexity of moral analysis has understandably made lawyers reluctant to judge their clients by moral standards not reflected in positive law. But this reluctance to judge seems also to have produced a reluctance to engage the client on moral terms. The resulting technocratic view of law is evidenced far beyond the walls of my classroom. A refusal to acknowledge the moral dimension of legal practice has contributed to several of the leading lawyer-fueled scandals of recent years, as well as to the broader malaise that has afflicted the profession for some time.[3] Nevertheless, the prospect of putting morality onto the table of legal representation is unsettling to many.

("[L]awyers usually defer to the client regarding such questions as the expense to be incurred and concern for third persons who might be adversely affected.").

[2] *ABA Canons of Prof. Ethics*, Canon 32.

[3] Patrick J. Schiltz, *On Being a Happy, Healthy, Ethical Member of an Unhappy, Unhealthy, Unethical Profession*, 52 VAND. L. REV. 871 (1999) (collecting statistics from various studies of attorney well-being).

Introduction

Lawyers are in a position to help bring their clients' consciences into play by bringing the moral dimension of the representation to the surface. This may strike nonlawyers as an obvious conclusion, but it unfortunately runs counter to some mainstream interpretations of the lawyers' obligations. For example, Stephen Pepper has famously compared a lawyer's client to "someone who stands frustrated before a photocopier that won't copy," and who needs "a technician ... to make it go." The technician is ordinarily not concerned with "whether the content of what is about to be copied is morally good or bad."[4] At one level, this analogy tells us something important about what lawyers do: lawyers provide citizens with access to a machine that they would not know how to work on their own. Just as we do not want the photocopier technician telling us that he will only fix our machine if we promise not to use it to copy pornography or radical political literature, we do not want the lawyer restricting an individual's legally available options based on the lawyer's own moral convictions.

The legal profession is rightfully concerned about access to law if the lawyer's conscience operates as a trump card – that is, if the lawyer is primarily concerned about "resolving" whatever moral questions are presented by the representation. But the opposite extreme – the lawyer as

[4] Stephen L. Pepper, *The Lawyer's Amoral Ethical Role: A Defense, a Problem, and Some Possibilities*, 1986 AM. B. FOUND. RES. J. 613, 624.

a photocopier technician – is equally problematic. The law is not like a photocopier. When I copy something, I know exactly what I am putting in, and I know exactly what I get back, even if I do not understand everything that happens in between. By contrast, legal advice is neither self-contained nor self-defined. In terms of "input," legal advice does not derive exclusively from application of black-letter law to the client's stated objective. Extralegal norms – including, especially, moral considerations – are part of the equation, whether they arise from the lawyer's own moral perspective, the lawyer's perception of the client's (often unstated) moral perspective, or the lawyer's application of the profession's moral perspective.[5] Further, the "output" is not an exact reproduction of the input – that is, pursuing the client's objectives may have consequences beyond the attainment of those objectives. Those consequences – such as collateral effects on the client's public standing or moral integrity, harms to the opposing party or third parties, damage to the reputations of the lawyer or her colleagues – may not be readily apparent to the client. It is not difficult to appreciate what one hath wrought through the use of a copy machine; the same cannot be said for one's use of a lawyer.

It is not the lawyer's job to resolve the moral questions that clients face. To do so infringes on client autonomy, particularly if clients are not empowered to participate in the

[5] *See generally* Robert K. Vischer, *Legal Advice as Moral Perspective*, 19 GEO. J. LEG. ETHICS 225 (2006).

resolution. In this regard, we do need lawyers to make sure that clients are aware of the moral questions that are often embedded in the legal questions raised by the representation. Especially in cases where the governing law is indeterminate, lawyers need to be able to engage their clients in a moral dialogue, which requires some familiarity with, and sensitivity to, moral reasoning. But lawyers' capabilities in this regard should not be deployed in order to resolve the moral questions; rather, they should be deployed in order to *assist the client* in resolving the moral questions.

Unless the lawyer can refuse the representation in the first place or withdraw early enough so as not to harm the client's interests, critics understandably are troubled by the prospect of a lawyer refusing to defer to her client's moral judgment. A lack of deference has the potential to impede a client's exercise of autonomy in choosing among legally permissible courses of conduct. But what often goes unnoticed is that the lawyer's failure to engage the client in moral terms also threatens a client's autonomy by failing to alert the client to the full scope of what is at stake in the representation.

To the extent that lawyers approach the client's objectives as fully formed and fixed and limit their own role to identifying the most effective technique for pursuing those objectives within the channels provided by law and counseling the client as to how the attainment of those objectives might impact the client's legal interests, they are implicitly making one of two presumptions. The lawyer might be presuming that the client is not interested in questions beyond the maximization of her own legal interests – that is, that legal permissibility, not moral accountability, is the only question that matters to the client. Alternatively, the lawyer might be presuming that the client will work through, and resolve any concerns regarding, the nonlegal implications of a chosen course of conduct without the lawyer's help.

Either one of these presumptions is problematic. The first portrays human nature in a way that is unrecognizable, or at least severely inadequate, in light of the lived experiences of most human beings. Our self-interest is rarely just about the self. Our own flourishing is wrapped up with others' flourishing – not primarily in the tactical sense in which we mean that the consideration of each other's interests is to our mutual advantage, but in the ontological sense in which we mean that others' interests are actually part of our own. We are not islands by nature – even Robinson Crusoe was waiting for Friday – and it is rare that a person can define his or her well-being in strictly rights-maximizing terms or in isolation from a broader social context.

If the true scope of a person's interests goes beyond the law's narrow lines of individual rights and privileges, the lawyer is making a dangerous gamble by leaving those interests unacknowledged and unexplored. Perhaps the client is able to analyze the relationship between her broader interests and the course of the legal representation without the lawyer's assistance. In many cases, though, the client will lack the ability to navigate the domain of law with a competence that would permit her to draw connections between legal and moral considerations. In some cases, it might not be a question of competence, but of inclination. A lawyer's finding of legal permissibility can function as an overarching seal of approval on the course of conduct under consideration, and the lawyer's failure to signal the narrowly technical nature of her conclusion may make it unhelpfully easy for the client to disregard bigger questions that remain beneath the surface. In either case, the client may be better served by a broader conversation with her lawyer.

The leading alternative model to the lawyer-as-amoral-technician paradigm does not capture this type of moral engagement between lawyer and client. The "cause lawyering" movement has inspired lawyers across a range of fields to invest themselves in the substantive ends of the representation.[6] Whether these lawyers advocate for an expansion of antidiscrimination laws, environmental justice, tenant rights, or the defense of private property, they have made themselves morally accountable for the identity of the clients and causes on whose behalf they labor. Cause lawyers "reconnect law and morality" by "using their professional work as a vehicle to build the good society."[7] The

[6] *See generally* Austin Sarat & Stuart Scheingold, *The Cultural Lives of Cause Lawyers* (2008); Austin Sarat & Stuart Scheingold, *Cause Lawyers and Social Movements* (2006).

[7] Austin Sarat & Stuart Scheingold, "Cause Lawyering and the Reproduction of Professional Authority," in *Cause Lawyering: Political Commitments and Professional Responsibilities,* ed. A. Sarat & S. Scheingold (1998), 3, 3.

problem is that the cause lawyering movement does not necessarily equip lawyers to reach a deeper level of moral engagement with *the client*. A sense of moral accountability for the ends of the representation may, in fact, reduce the depth and quality of engagement between the lawyer and client. As Derrick Bell recognized in the context of school desegregation work, there can be real tension between the interests of the clients and the lawyers' pursuit of systemic change.[8] Paying attention to the moral dimension of legal practice may lead a lawyer to be more deliberate about the type of cases she accepts without being more deliberate about the type of relationship she cultivates with clients.

Another well-known attempt to broaden the lawyer's vision of the interests implicated by a given representation falls short of authentic moral engagement. Nearly a century ago, Louis Brandeis encountered significant turbulence during his Supreme Court confirmation hearings when he labeled himself a "counsel for the situation."[9] Brandeis was attempting to justify his work in a bankruptcy case that appeared to involve his representation of conflicting

---

[8] Derrick A. Bell Jr., *Serving Two Masters: Integration Ideals and Client Interests in School Desegregation Litigation*, 85 YALE L.J. 470 (1976) (explaining that the lawyers' "determination to implement *Brown* using racial balance measures ... involves great risk for clients whose educational interests may no longer accord with the integration ideals of their attorneys").

[9] *See The Nomination of Louis D. Brandeis to Be an Associate Justice of the Supreme Court of the United States: Hearing before the Subcomm. of the S. Comm. on the Judiciary*, 64th Cong. 287 (1916).

interests. He insisted that a good lawyer can help produce a more favorable outcome for all concerned by helping mediate among multiple interests in a given matter. Brandeis came closer to capturing the relational dimension of lawyering than today's profession does, but he had a different focus. He was concerned with the ability to counsel clients whose interests are competing, if not conflicting; the relational dimension arose from the context – for example, a bankruptcy matter involving several related parties – rather than from human nature itself. Put differently, while Brandeis broadened his professional view to include the relationships presented by "the situation," I am interested in broadening the view to include the relationships presented by the client herself.

This is not to suggest that encouraging lawyers to raise the client's relational interests to the surface of the representation is an entirely novel approach. Tom Shaffer, a pioneer in the academic study of legal ethics, complained of the "radical individualism" reflected in the modern profession's ethics codes.[10] Shaffer gave an example of a husband and wife who retain a lawyer to draft their wills. If one spouse were to disagree with the other spouse's wishes on designating beneficiaries, the profession's reflexive recommendation is for the lawyer to withdraw and recommend that the couple each retain their own counsel. In Shaffer's view, this

---

[10] Thomas L. Shaffer, *The Legal Ethics of Radical Individualism*, 65 TEX. L. REV. 963 (1987).

mistakenly views the client as two individuals who happen to be married, rather than as a family. The lawyer should not abandon the family – much less encourage the individuals who compose the family to "lawyer up" – simply because the messy reality of family life may require messy conversations that go far beyond the technical boundaries of estate planning.

In many ways, this book builds on Shaffer's insights. Family law is the most obvious area where lawyers need to recognize that the client's self-interest is not just about the self. The principle is much more broadly applicable, though. The fact that our social nature may be most apparent within the family does not mean that our social nature goes no further than the family. Our relational accountability and its implications for the lawyer's work spring from who we are as people, not just from the particular relational context in which the lawyer happens to find us. The lawyer's failure to engage the client along the lines of relational accountability is a failure just as likely to be found in the corporate boardroom as in family court.

The lawyer is not simply a technician; nor is she a moral arbiter. As legal advisers, lawyers are partners in a dialogue that is brimming with moral significance, whether they acknowledge the significance or not. Ignoring the potential for interpersonal moral engagement in the course of an attorney's work comes at a significant cost. To the extent that an attorney approaches the client as a bundle of legal interests to be maximized, the client's true interests may often remain out of view and unprotected. The surrounding community loses as well, for the reflexive maximization of the client's legal interests tends to push a broader social accountability to the margins, even in cases where that accountability matters to the client. In other words, while some bad actors will ignore the common good no matter what a lawyer tells them, do some well-intentioned actors ignore the common good because of what their lawyer never bothers to mention?

There is also a cost to the attorney, as the lack of moral engagement can exacerbate the perceived incoherence of her life, widening the gap between her professional role and her understanding of social justice, moral truth, and the common good. The segmentation of a lawyer's personal and professional identities can be profoundly unsettling for the lawyer herself, especially if the lawyer has deeply held beliefs that do not speak only to the nonprofessional aspects of her existence. To borrow from Camus's thoughts on the feeling of absurdity, such segmentation constitutes a "divorce between man and his life, the actor and his setting," creating an existence in which "man feels an alien, a stranger."[11] The capacity to motivate lawyers turns on our ability to identify their deeply held values and translate those values into professionally relevant language, allowing them to transcend the lowest common denominator approach of a one-size-fits-all

---

[11] Albert Camus, "An Absurd Reasoning," in *The Myth of Sisyphus and Other Essays* (1991), 453.

ethical regime. Acting as a partner in a moral dialogue with the client might allow the lawyer to introduce a deeper sense of responsibility and meaning to her work.

Improving lawyer morale is not what drives this project, though. The aim is to connect the lawyer's work more closely with the reality of the human experience. And that experience is inescapably social, giving rise to interests that defy perfect alignment with the law's framework of individual rights and privileges. A broader conversation between lawyer and client is often in order. Recognizing the need for moral engagement is one thing; actually pulling it off in a manner consistent with the client-centered norms on which the profession is based is quite another. The profession's struggle in this regard should not be surprising. Our society more broadly is struggling mightily to find the resources to maintain meaningful but respectful moral engagement. However problematic the lack of such resources is for society at large, the void presents an identity crisis for lawyers, who make their living among members of various moral communities, crossing boundaries routinely as both advocates and counselors. Do the divergent worldviews and ideologies embraced by the lawyer's clients preclude any meaningful dialogue beyond the political community's best attempt at a common normative language – that is, law – or is there a deeper possibility for meaningful moral engagement emanating from our very nature?

This book hopes to begin tracing the contours of an approach that takes both the need for moral engagement and the fear of moral paternalism seriously. The approach is not reducible to bullet points or new ethics rules, but is exemplified in the complexities and tensions of a particular life. More than forty years after his death, Martin Luther King Jr. maintains his hold on the American imagination as a modern-day prophet who captivated consciences across ideological, racial, and religious lines by embracing, rather than avoiding, substantive moral claims. His success in articulating a moral worldview that resonated deeply and broadly with human experience holds lessons for today's legal profession, in terms of both the manner of his moral engagement and the substantive vision that served as the impetus for that engagement. The book is an effort to reframe our conception of morality's relevance to professionalism through the lens provided by the public and prophetic advocacy of Dr. King.

King's lessons along these lines are not just relevant to lawyers, of course. As an intensely and unabashedly pluralistic society, we have grown less willing (and increasingly ill equipped) to introduce substantive moral claims into the various nonprivate settings we navigate every day, whether as citizens, as professionals, or even as consumers of popular culture. On the cable news channels, "moralizing" tends to resemble "bullying" and culminate in shouting matches between participants from opposite sides of the ideological divide. When cooler heads do prevail, the default position tends to be a sort of unspoken moral libertarianism, eschewing whenever possible the need for substantive moral engagement across boundaries. Our moral convictions may reign in our personal lives, but our shared social space has become not only less amenable to moral consensus, but also less amenable to a commitment to cultivate moral consensus, and thus the introduction of moral claims as a source of guidance beyond our own decision making is often taken as an imprudent interference with another's autonomy. This dynamic is particularly corrosive within the legal profession because, more than in other fields, winnowing the lawyer's services down to the strictly technical eviscerates her potential value to both the client and society.

A second reason to focus on the legal profession is one of practical necessity. While King's lessons have an unmistakably broad reach, tracing their real-world implications requires a narrower focus on the state of the field to which they are applied. King, as a theologian of action, did not settle for articulating big-picture ideas; he was intensely concerned with the relationship between the ideas and the situation on the ground.[12] Accordingly, this book explores King's ideas while depicting the situation on the ground in a specific context: the legal profession. Other professions

[12] See Timothy P. Jackson, "Martin Luther King Jr.," in *The Teachings of Modern Christianity: On Law, Politics & Human Nature*, vol. I (2006), 473 (noting that King "embodied, above all, the 'uses' of the law and theology, rather than their innovation or scholarly analysis"); Anthony E. Cook, *Beyond Critical Legal Studies: The Reconstructive Theology of Dr. Martin Luther King, Jr.*, 103 HARV. L. REV. 985, 1013 (1990).

could stand to learn a thing or two from King, but at least at this stage of our history, lawyers need to hear from him more than others do. Perhaps more than any other figure, King, as an advocate and counselor, was able to navigate American pluralism without bracketing his moral commitments, resorting to heavy-handed paternalism, or presuming that serving others means maximizing their autonomy as individuals.

King burst into the public consciousness as the leader of the Montgomery bus boycott in 1955, but his relevance as a model of moral engagement begins much earlier, for his ministry is really an outgrowth of a life steeped in moral claims. Without a self-conception grounded in a broader narrative that included an account of human nature and the social good, King would not have stood at the front lines of the civil rights movement. As the son and grandson of prominent pastors in Atlanta, King was raised in the black church, learning stories of God's deliverance that would shape his conviction that "the moral arc of the universe is long, but it bends toward justice."[13] After attending college at Morehouse, he spent three years at Crozer, the predominantly white seminary in Pennsylvania, then earned his doctorate at Boston University. As we will see, his formal education was essential for exposing King to the intellectual traditions that would provide much of the language and nuance – though not the fundamental orientation – of his

[13] Martin Luther King Jr., *Strength to Love* (1963).

prophetic work. He accepted the pastorate at Dexter Avenue Baptist Church in Montgomery the year before Rosa Parks triggered the landmark bus boycott, and from that point on, King modeled the tactics of moral engagement that emerged naturally and inescapably from the content of the moral vision that he had embraced over the course of his lifetime.

King's moral formation did not stop when he began living out his worldview on a public stage, of course. His commitment to nonviolence, for example, only came into sharp relief as an integral element of his ministry after he became a student of Mahatma Gandhi's legacy later in the 1950s. And the implications of his worldview continued to unfold throughout his life. It was not until relatively late in life that he realized – to the frustration of many – that his commitment to justice must include antiwar and antipoverty initiatives, not just race. He also began to see the limits of law, noting ruefully that the legislative victories he had labored so hard to achieve had done little to change the lives of poor blacks. Throughout his ministry, King employed a robust theological framework for expressing the means and ends of the work that lay before him. He never allowed the thickets of theory to obscure the human person on whose behalf he advocated. He trafficked in the world of ideas, but his gaze stayed at ground level.

In one sense, King's lessons for lawyers are far from obvious. King, after all, was not constrained by any fiduciary duty toward a single client; prophets have considerable discretion to tell the truth no matter whose ox ends up gored.

But his relevance becomes more apparent once we contextualize the lawyer's fiduciary duty in light of basic truths about human nature. Lawyers' narrow focus on the client's individual self-interest emerges from largely unfounded presumptions about the client's nature. To the extent that a client's gaze naturally extends beyond herself, the lawyer's narrower gaze does not authentically serve the client's interests. Further, lawyers' myopia in this regard may obscure from the client's view the implications the matter has for the surrounding community. Much professional rhetoric is based on a purportedly categorical tension between the client and the community.[14] King did not call for whites to sacrifice their power and privilege for the betterment of their black neighbors; he called for the restoration of relationships in order to make both blacks and whites whole again. King served real human interests by serving human nature.

King was a religious leader, make no mistake, and there is no point in trying to separate him, or any aspect of his

---

[14] The classic (and hyperbolic) example is Lord Brougham's centuries-old description of the advocate as one who "in the discharge of his duty, knows but one person in the world, and that person is his client. To save that client by all means and expedients, and at all hazards and costs to other persons, and, among them, to himself, is his first and only duty; and in performing this duty he must not regard the alarm, the torments, the destruction which he may bring upon others. Separating the duty of a patriot from that of an advocate, he must go on reckless of consequences, though it should be his unhappy fate to involve his country in confusion." Geoffrey C. Hazard, *The Future of Legal Ethics*, 100 YALE L.J. 1239, 1244 (1991) (quoting Trial of Queen Caroline).

public leadership, from his faith.[15] Yet we are somehow comfortable as a nation celebrating King as a hero of our secular legal order, not just as a noteworthy religious figure. Herein lies one of the keys for lawyers who aim to take moral engagement seriously: King's moral framework was not a vacuous, process-driven template for reaching resolution in a pluralistic society; nor did he search out the lowest common denominator between his own faith and the American public writ large. King was not running from who he was or what he believed. Instead, he relied on the full dimension of his own expansive religious and moral commitments to distill the essence of a foundational truth about the human condition. In focusing on the restoration of relationships – on what he referred to as the "beloved community" – King appealed to a widely accessible moral vision that was not dependent on any particular religious revelation or political agenda. It was a basic reminder not to ignore what we know about ourselves: we are social creatures whose accountability does not begin and end with ourselves.

That the moral inquiry begins with an anthropological question – what is the nature of the human person? – is hardly an insight unique to King. Nor is the resulting

---

[15] We cannot help but shake our heads at the reporter covering King's funeral who somberly reported that "today there was a memorial service for the slain civil rights leader, Dr. Martin Luther King, Jr. It was a religious service, and it is fitting that it should be, for, after all, Dr. King was the son of a minister." Richard John Neuhaus, *The Naked Public Square: Religion and Democracy in America* (1984), 97–8.

conclusion that we are oriented toward relationship. King worked out a distinctively robust vision of what our social nature could and should mean in the modern world – as subsequent chapters will detail – but his underlying anthropological premise is shared across religious traditions. Even among philosophers and political theorists who resist King's religious narrative, their approaches suggest that the human person's social orientation remains central to the moral inquiry.[16] As King famously put it, "we are all caught in an inescapable network of mutuality, tied into a single garment of destiny."[17] Though the normative conclusions King draws from the fact of our social nature are widely disregarded in our day-to-day moral lives, the degree to which his starting point resonates truthfully with our human experience forces us to take his conclusions seriously once we are called to account for the gap.

King's convictions regarding the reality of human nature provided a metaphysical grounding for his commitment to human dignity. Instead of serving a solely autonomy-based conception of dignity devoid of substantive content, King's commitment to the social nature of the human person gave

---

[16] See, e.g., Bertrand Russell, "A Free Man's Worship," in *Why I Am Not a Christian,* ed. Paul Edwards (1957), 104, 116 ("United with his fellow men by the strongest of all ties, the tie of a common doom").

[17] Martin Luther King Jr., "Letter from Birmingham City Jail"(1963), in *A Testament of Hope: The Essential Writings of Martin Luther King Jr.*, ed. James M. Washington (1986), 289, 290.

him a starting place at which to anchor his resistance to –
indeed his very discernment of – injustice. The truth telling
at the center of his prophetic ethics required a commitment
to truth claims that arose outside, and prior to, the positive
law or social convention.[18]

By this point, many lawyers have undoubtedly started
to squirm. Talk of extralegal truth claims raises the specter
of paternalism, of lawyers hijacking the representation in
a way that subverts the client's lawful pursuit of a lawful
objective. King's prophetic ethics, imported to the legal profession, raise understandable concern for the client-directed
nature of legal work. But again, moral engagement does not
equate to moral paternalism. A client may reject the premises on which her lawyer's moral claims are based, even if
the claims are as widely agreed to as King's. The question
for lawyers is, Will they begin from a premise that rejects
the substance of King's moral claims? In other words, will
lawyers assume that the client rejects a conception of the
human person as relational and accountable in ways that
transcend narrowly construed self-interest?

---

[18] Richard Wayne Wills Sr., *Martin Luther King and the Image of
God* (2009), 24–5 ("The image of God provided the question of civil
rights with an ontological reason for reinforcing the meaning and
experience of just political and judicial affairs.... A conversation
concerning rights and the political documents that prescribed
them necessarily backed into a conversation about that which
preceded sociopolitical reality, and ultimately defined how King
understood human nature by establishing the theological relationship between moral and social experience.").

The accessibility of King's anthropological claim – that is, the social nature of the human person – is magnified by the fact that King did not require agreement "all the way down" in order to join in the struggle to see the moral implications of the anthropological claim lived out. King worked out those implications within a particular worldview, and the theological and philosophical sources of King's worldview are not as widely accessible as the resulting claims themselves. This does not make the sources marginal to King, for his moral claims could not have been formed in a vacuum, apart from those sources. But King did not ask his listeners to embrace all of his sources (though many did); he asked listeners to embrace the moral claims themselves. Whether or not someone in the 1960s would have shared King's admiration for Walter Rauschenbusch's interpretation of the Old Testament prophets, for example, they could have understood, appreciated, and (in most cases) affirmed King's resulting exhortation to resist Sheriff Bull Connor's violent suppression of peaceful protests in Birmingham. In this regard, King's moral claims were embodied in action.

To illustrate Christians' tendency to pay only lip service to justice, he told a story about visiting an imaginary city where no one wore shoes even though it was cold and snowy. He asks a local resident why no one wears them:

"But what is the matter? Don't you believe in shoes?"
"Believe in shoes, my friend! I should say we do. That is the first article of our creed, shoes. They are indispensable to the well-being of humanity."

"Well, then, why don't you wear them?" said I, bewildered.

"Ah," said he, "that is just it. Why don't we?"

After I checked in the hotel I met a gentleman who wanted to show me around the city ... [and pointed to a huge brick structure] "You see that?" said he. "That is one of our outstanding shoe manufacturing establishments!"

"A what?" I asked in amazement. "You mean you make shoes there?"

"Well, not exactly," said he, "we talk about making shoes there, and believe me, we have got one of the most brilliant young fellows you have ever heard. He talks more thrillingly and convincingly every week on the subject of shoes.... Just yesterday he moved the people profoundly with his exposition of the necessity of shoe wearing. Many broke down and wept. It was really wonderful!"

"But why don't you wear them?" said I, insistently.

"Ah," said he, "that is just it. Why don't we?"[19]

In tracing King's intellectual legacy, it is important not to lose sight of the fact that his was a theology of action. He was not interested primarily in theology as a theoretical inquiry or systematic explication. King's passion was a rigorous exploration of theology *as applied*. History's narrative did not call for his cognitive assent; it called for his active participation. In most situations, King's moral worldview

---

[19] Martin Luther King Jr., "A Religion of Doing," sermon at Dexter Avenue Baptist Church (July 4, 1954, Montgomery), in *The Papers of Martin Luther King Jr.*, vol. VI, 170, 173.

was discernible primarily through the courses of conduct he embarked on directly or recommended to his audience; he did not spend much time in his ministry debating the fine points of philosophical or theological theory. King cared less about how a person arrived at her commitment to justice as long as she arrived at it somehow. Because action follows from commitment, the path of commitment matters greatly to the actor herself, but King never espoused a particular path as a litmus test for participating in the struggle for justice. The protest march photos of King locked arm in arm with leaders from various religious and political traditions bear witness to this fact.

By the same token, lawyers are not hired to opine on prevailing currents in academic thought; if their worldview is going to matter, it has to matter in the world of concrete action items. For example, the mammoth (and now defunct) energy futures trading company Enron focused relentlessly on share price – to the exclusion of any more fulsome measure of corporate well-being and accountability. This narrow conception of self-interest stands in tension with a variety of moral truth claims and traditions. From whatever perspective Enron's lawyers would have approached the problem, though, it was important for them to flag for management the concern that the company was neglecting its broader responsibility to constituents. The lawyer's moral framework is both more efficacious and more accessible to the extent that it expresses itself in the world of action. King is a powerful model on that front.

This book seeks to reframe our understanding of the lawyer's work by exploring how Martin Luther King Jr. built his public advocacy on a coherent set of moral claims regarding the demands of love and justice in light of human nature. That King maintains his heroic stature today among conservatives and progressives, religious believers and non-believers, and citizens of all races is remarkable. It is especially remarkable because King never shirked from staking out challenging claims of moral truth, even while remaining open to conversation with those who rejected those truths. He proposed without imposing, and he never let disagreement derail his pursuit of relationship. His example should inspire the legal profession as a reminder that truth telling, even in a society that often appears morally balkanized, has the capacity to move hearts and minds. At the same time, his example should give the profession pause, for King's success would have been impossible absent his substantive views about human nature and the ends of justice. To the likely consternation of many lawyers, King's prophetic ethics were primarily about substance, not about process. This book, then, will focus primarily on the substance, though as we will see, the process – that is, the tactics – of King's advocacy are largely a function of his substantive claims, so once one knows the substance of those claims, certain attributes of the corresponding process naturally follow.

Chapter 1 takes up the ubiquitous but frequently unhelpful concept of human dignity. The legal profession still insists that its primary service is to the cause of human dignity, though its inability to identify – much less reach any semblance of consensus regarding – meaningful content for the term has led "dignity" to function primarily as a stand-in for "individual autonomy." This means that lawyers serve dignity essentially by serving as extensions of their client's will, points of access to the legal system, mouthpieces for those who would otherwise be rendered silent under the law. As important as this function is, portraying it as the fullest embodiment of the lawyer's role is hardly inspiring for lawyers, whose own moral agency is thereby extinguished, or at least greatly circumscribed, as their role becomes primarily technical. Further, it offers no resources by which lawyers are encouraged (or even permitted?) to resist client demands for which there is an arguable legal justification. Lawyers at the center of many of our recent corporate and government scandals can readily claim fidelity to their clients' autonomy, but they are harder pressed to defend their work as a vindication of human dignity. In many cases, it is not even clear that the client's autonomy is authentically served, for to the extent that the attorney fails to engage the client in a richer dialogue about the potential tensions between the client's actual interests and the maximization of her legal interests, it is a superficial sense of autonomy that prevails in the representation.

This superficial sense of autonomy feeds into the legal profession's one-dimensional conception of dignity. In the field of bioethics, by contrast, autonomy merely provides the floor of human dignity – failure to obtained informed consent, for example, violates the requirements of human dignity. But dignity also carries more aspirational content: the fact that a person desires a new technology does not answer the ultimate question about the wisdom of the technology. That question requires deeper reflection about human fallibility and the compatibility of particular innovations with the essence of the human condition. Is the enhancement of individual choice invariably good, or in certain contexts does it threaten to distort what it means to be human? Similarly, King stood not just for enhanced individual choice, but for empowerment to make choices consistent with the dignity that flows from the reality of our created nature – that is, he stood for the affirmation of relationship. Autonomy was the beginning, but by no means the end, of the journey. As a core part of his work on behalf of human dignity, King asked his listeners to face the impact that their choices have on those with whom they are, or should be, in relationship. Such questions are largely absent from the legal profession's ongoing conversation about human dignity and the lawyer's role.

Chapter 2 looks at agape, which was the concept by which King's commitment to human dignity was lived out. Put simply, agape is love without self-interest, love for the other's sake. Agape was a hallmark of the civil rights movement, as King's advocacy called for blacks to love their white oppressors, not to meet hatred with hatred. King mined a rich biblical and theological legacy on agape, relying especially on the work of Anders Nygren for the radical notion that love for neighbor must not discriminate according to how one is treated by the neighbor. Many lawyers will bristle at any suggestion that they are to "love" their clients, but it is more difficult to reject the relevance of agape once the emotional and affectionate components of love are stripped away (as King did), leaving agape's core: commitment to another's well-being. Agape requires the lawyer to live out her social nature by recognizing her accountability to the good of her client.

Because agape is an active love that seeks out the good of the client, however, a lawyer who aspires to agape will need to rediscover – or discover for the first time – her own status as a moral subject. Agapic love is inconsistent with a vision of the lawyer as mouthpiece. While showing proper deference to the client-centered nature of the undertaking, lawyers must not avoid speaking the truth to clients. As this chapter explains, though, this function is under increasing pressure because market forces and regulatory changes are making attorneys more like any other service providers, thereby marginalizing the relational trust that has traditionally marked the attorney-client relationship. For this reason, agape may become an even more elusive practice among lawyers.

In Chapter 3, the focus turns to personalism, the philosophical tradition that drew King to Boston University for his graduate studies. Personalists emphasize the sacredness and relationality of the human person. King famously captured the personalist mindset with his "Letter from a Birmingham City Jail," in which he observed that "we are all caught in an inescapable network of mutuality, tied into a single garment of destiny," and thus "whatever affects one directly, affects all indirectly."[20] To the extent that King's advocacy for the expansion of legal rights was driven by his desire to restore relationship between the oppressor and the oppressed, his was a healing work. King firmly believed that human beings were created for relationship, and this conviction shaped his work. While agape teaches lawyers to treat their clients (and themselves) as subjects, personalism teaches lawyers not to presume that their clients exist as atomized individuals with strictly self-regarding interests. In other words, while agape bears witness to the relational accountability between lawyer and client, personalism speaks to the lawyer's view of the client's own relational accountability. This chapter will also explore the potential tension between personalism's expansive consideration of human well-being and the lawyer's devotion to a particular client's interests. Without jeopardizing the client-directed nature of legal representation, the personalist lawyer will push back against the individualist premises underlying much of the profession's narrative.

Justice as a defining element of King's prophetic ethics takes center stage in Chapter 4. King's pursuit of justice blended together several themes from his theological

[20] Martin Luther King Jr., *supra* note 17.

worldview, most notably exploring justice's relationship with love. The social gospel movement, exemplified by the work of Walter Rauschenbush, gave impetus to King's theology of action. Perhaps most relevant for lawyers, King frequently spoke of justice requiring the airing of conflict. Against his critics, he insisted that superficial peace was no peace at all, and that an advocate for justice must bring tensions to the surface in order to achieve a peace based on the restoration of relationships. The lesson here is about more than the potential value of litigation, though litigation is undoubtedly an important component of the lawyer's facilitation of justice. But justice for King was not only about giving voice to the voiceless, as though facilitating individual autonomy exhausts justice's call.

Instead, King returned to the human person's social nature as the benchmark for justice; restoring breaches in the human community, thereby making possible "the beloved community," aligned his efforts with the intrinsic nature of the created universe. The restoration of relationships provided the ends of his work, but it also provided the means. The beloved community cannot be built on violence or hatred. To give in to such impulses is to demean the human person on whose behalf he labored. King's model of nonviolent resistance may help check the lawyer's tendency toward succumbing to "an internal violence of spirit" as she works in an adversarial system. At a minimum, King provides a rich and substantive understanding of justice that may spark deeper and more ambitious conversations within the profession about the lawyer's role.

Finally, in Chapter 5, we look to Christian realism, a tradition dating back to St. Augustine but most rigorously developed in the modern era by Reinhold Niebuhr, whose emphasis on human sinfulness functioned as a needed corrective to the prevailing confidence in the unwavering progress of human enlightenment. Though King and Niebuhr disagreed about the wisdom of nonviolence, they both decried the naiveté reflected by liberals of the era who believed that whites would welcome blacks into the community as education and social progress took their natural courses. Christian realism prevented King from believing in the inevitability of justice and thereby precluded passive acquiescence as an option. King knew that the reality of collective evil required active resistance, and that the reality of individual sinfulness required humility and self-restraint in any exercise of power.

In this regard, lawyers might claim the realist label as a justification for checking their own moral commitments at the office door. Fearful of limiting a client's access to the law by imposing extralegal considerations on the representation, lawyers, on this account, fulfill their roles by showing fidelity to the law. Expecting the lawyer to focus exclusively on the client's legal entitlements to the exclusion of his or her broader interests, however, replaces a holistic view of the client as person with a one-dimensional view of the client as citizen. Neither Niebuhr nor King allowed the human incapacity to achieve ideal justice to excuse us from pursuing relative justice; nor did they permit our limited grasp of reality to obscure what we could recognize about the social nature and corresponding needs of the human person. We are not freestanding bundles of legal rights; we are relational beings whose nature calls them, as Niebuhr put it, toward "fulfillment in the lives of others."[21] At a minimum, lawyers who purport to face reality unflinchingly should not *presume* that their clients defy their own relational nature.

So what does Martin Luther King Jr. have to say to my students, who seemed to equate the lawyer's work with a willingness to set aside their moral intuitions and create technically colorable but hopelessly myopic justifications for a proposed course of conduct? At bottom, King encourages my students to widen their gaze, to remember that law serves the well-being of the human person, and thus the person must remain at the center of their work. Lawyers must be technically competent, to be sure, but they also must remain cognizant of the fact that a client's best interests are not always served by the maximization of his or her legal interests. This is a difficult message for the students to carry into a profession that often appears to have lost sight of what makes it a profession in the first

---

[21] Reinhold Niebuhr, "Children of Light and Children of Darkness," in *The Essential Reinhold Niebuhr: Selected Essays and Addresses,* ed. Robert McAfee Brown (1986), 160, 170.

place. Without some understanding of human nature and the relational needs that spring from that nature, lawyers are indeed photocopier technicians, and the profession is rightly dismissed as a cartel wielding its monopoly power to keep out the competition. Current competitive and regulatory pressures are solidifying this view, as we will see. King reminds lawyers of a higher purpose: lawyers stand where state power meets everyday life, where our collective norms for resolving disputes gain real-world traction, and where questions of permissibility can function as either the end or the beginning of conversations that will impact both the client and the myriad relationships in which the client is situated. In short, King asks us to recognize that, even in a client-centered vocation, lawyers play a central role in building the beloved community. This book gives an account of that role.

1

Human Dignity

Lawyers as (More Than) Technicians

Martin Luther King's ministry is the most widely acknowledged American example of a socially transformative personal commitment to human dignity. Even avowed proponents of dignity may struggle to articulate its substantive content, much less reach consensus about that content, but virtually no one denies that King was the embodiment of dignity's public relevance. As such, he stands out as the most powerful rejoinder to those who dismiss invocations of dignity as easy sloganeering. As the old joke about infant baptism goes, not only do we believe in human dignity, we have seen it done! King's example is especially powerful because we do not have to speculate about the relationship between his on-the-ground ministry and his underlying normative commitments. As a theologian, King laid out the relationship for us, providing both the content and the implications of his dignity-based truth claims.

In pursuing his commitments, of course, King was not constrained by any legal or ethical duty to favor the interests of one person over another. He did not owe fiduciary obligations to anyone in particular. He was free to follow the demands of dignity, wherever they led. Put simply, King did not have a client. For lawyers, then, perhaps King's ministry is a reminder of the limitations that accompany their chosen professional role. Unless dignity's implications overlap with the client's interests, they are irrelevant to – and perhaps a dangerous distraction from – the lawyer's work. Or so the argument goes.

Despite dignity's conceptual elusiveness, no one wants to forgo its ennobling banner completely. Even lawyers routinely unfurl it, insisting that they serve the cause of dignity by serving the interests of their clients. The conception of human dignity that prevails within the legal profession, though, is roughly interchangeable with individual autonomy. That is, lawyers serve the cause of dignity by facilitating the client's autonomy. In this regard, the legal profession's dignity discourse lacks the nuance and depth that are found in the discourse occurring in other fields, bioethics in particular. As far as it goes, autonomy is a key component of individual dignity, but autonomy does not exhaust the nature or implications of dignity, particularly the narrow conception of autonomy employed widely within the legal profession. The conversation needs to be expanded.

Venturing further down the path of human dignity rhetoric is not a journey without peril, however. As more substantive moral claims come within dignity's province, dignity becomes as sharply contested as the underlying claims themselves. Aside from its contested content, the sheer number of claims gives rise to the charge that dignity is hopelessly indeterminate. On the other hand, to the extent that dignity is narrowly circumscribed to function as a stand-in for autonomy, it appears to be utterly superfluous. It is no wonder that even prominent ethicists have deemed human dignity "a useless concept."[1] To redeem the concept of human dignity for lawyers, then, requires the reclamation of the concept more broadly.

I. Human Dignity in the Lawyer's Narrative

To begin, the centrality of individual autonomy to the lawyer's pursuit of human dignity warrants a bit of unpacking. Counterintuitively, lawyers portray their contributions to human dignity as a function of their willingness to suspend their own moral agency. Provided that their clients' objectives are legal, lawyers are to remain neutral regarding

---

[1] Ruth Macklin, "Dignity Is a Useless Concept," *BMJ* 327 (2003): 1419–1420.

the moral status of those objectives. The legal profession's ethics code makes clear that "[a] lawyer's representation of a client, including representation by appointment, does not constitute an endorsement of the client's political, economic, social or moral views or activities."[2] William Simon identifies this principle of neutrality – requiring the lawyer to "remain detached from his client's ends" – as one of the two foundational principles of the ethics of legal advocacy, as traditionally understood.[3] Under this view, lawyers serve human dignity by helping to empower their clients to pursue their chosen ends, not by choosing their ends for them. There is a danger that neutrality's requirement of detachment from the client's ends often leads to a lack of engagement with, and exploration of, the full breadth and depth of the client's ends.

The second foundational principle, according to Simon, is partisanship, which "prescribes that the lawyer work aggressively to advance his client's ends," and "employ means on behalf of his client which he would not consider proper in a non-professional context even to advance his own ends."[4] Not only is the lawyer's moral agency suspended as to the client's choice of objectives, it remains suspended as to the client's pursuit of those objectives. The lawyer is expected to prefer, and to favor aggressively, the client's

---

[2] *ABA Model Rules of Prof'l Conduct* R. 1.2(b).

[3] William Simon, *The Ideology of Advocacy*, 1978 WISC. L. REV. 29, 36.

[4] *Id.*

interests over others' interests, and to allow that favoring to shape the lawyer's behavior during the representation, even leading the lawyer to disregard the interests of others. The ethics code goes so far as to provide that "lawyers usually defer to the client regarding such questions as ... concern for third persons who might be adversely affected" by the representation.[5] Lawyers serve human dignity not only by deferring to their clients' chosen ends, but by doing whatever they can within legal bounds to maximize the likelihood that those ends will be met. To the extent that partisanship is interpreted to imply a single-minded focus on the client's interests, as though her interests are not wrapped up with the interests of others, there is a danger that partisanship does not always account for the client's well-being, authentically and fulsomely understood.

Defenders of the traditional approach see danger in the prospect of a lawyer identifying with the client more personally. Norman Spaulding, for example, asserts that the practice of law is "grounded in a logic of service, not identification," and thus the lawyer should be "willing to diligently represent a client irrespective of any personal, moral, or ideological affinity between them."[6] In providing access to law, lawyers must show "uninhibited orientation of their faculties towards the realization of their clients' lawful objectives."[7]

---

[5] *ABA Model Rules of Prof'l Conduct* R. 1.2 cmt. 2.
[6] Norman Spaulding, *Reinterpreting Professional Identity*, 74 U. COLO. L. REV. 1, 6 (2003).
[7] *Id.*

More intense identification perverts the service norm, according to Spaulding, by making the attorney's self-realization an object of the representation.[8] The concern for maintaining the primacy of client autonomy is a common refrain among legal ethicists.[9]

Whether we consider the lawyer's own moral agency to be an exercise of self-realization or a component of professional judgment may depend on our view of moral claims more broadly. Spaulding (and many others) believe that allowing a lawyer's moral judgment to limit client autonomy "presupposes that the moral costs of facilitating autonomy can be accurately and decisively weighed – that a lawyer who screens clients will make choices we can agree are 'right' and 'good.'"[10] Given the reality of moral pluralism, such consensus is illusory. As such, the lawyer needs some other basis for justifying the intrusion of her moral judgment into the representation. Stephen Pepper fears that such intrusion would lead to "rule by an oligarchy of lawyers."[11]

Under these terms, the lawyer serves human dignity by maximizing the client's legal interests and suspending her

---

[8] *Id.*

[9] *See also, e.g.*, Stephen Ellman, *Lawyers and Clients*, 34 U.C.L.A. L. Rev. 717 (1987); Marcy Strauss, *Toward a Revised Model of Attorney-Client Relationship: The Argument for Autonomy*, 65 N.C. L. Rev. 315 (1987).

[10] Spaulding, *supra* note 6, at 79.

[11] Stephen L. Pepper, *The Lawyer's Amoral Ethical Role: A Defense, a Problem, and Some Possibilities*, 1986 Am. B. Found. Res. J. 613, 617.

own moral judgment regarding the client's underlying goals. This approach poses some complications, though, for it is no easy feat for the lawyer to discern the client's goals, which "are subjective and peculiar to the individual," for "any speculation by the lawyer would reveal merely the interference of the lawyer's own biases or ends."[12] The client cannot easily articulate her goals on her own, apart from the lawyer's knowledge of the information that is (and is not) legally relevant. Some conversation that takes the lawyer outside the seemingly comfortable bounds of moral detachment appears necessary. But the profession has tended to avoid that path. As observed by the authors of a leading text on legal ethics, "The lawyer's strategy for dealing with this dilemma is to impute certain basic ends to the client, and then to work to advance these ends, even though this weakens the premise of the absolute individuality of the client's ends."[13]

Nevertheless, the legal profession's human dignity narrative begins from an individualist premise. I do not mean to suggest that the profession's commitment to dignity as autonomy is consciously antisocial. The profession is agnostic as to the client's ends, social or not. Some clients may have relational goals that they can articulate in a way that permits the lawyer to incorporate them into the representation. In these cases, even the lawyer as mouthpiece can serve a fulsome sense of human dignity because there is harmony

[12] Geoffrey C. Hazard Jr., Susan P. Koniak & Roger C. Cramton, *The Law and Ethics of Lawyering* (3d ed. 1999), 33.

[13] *Id.*

between the client's expressed wishes and her social nature. But it is a harmony by happenstance.

By disregarding the extent to which the client's interests include relational accountability, not just the maximization of legal rights or economic gain, a lawyer may facilitate anti-social decision making by clients in three types of cases. First, in some cases, the client may not be in a position to discern, much less articulate, how his or her relational interests may be implicated by the legal representation. When the Catholic Church's lawyers adopted a no-holds-barred approach to contesting sexual abuse lawsuits, including opposing reasonable discovery requests and forbidding contact or apologies between bishops and victims, arguably the lawyers were exacerbating the damage that had already been done to relationships that are part of the church's mission and institutional identity, but it is questionable whether the bishops were able to see the connection between the chosen litigation strategy and those relationships.[14]

Second, in some cases, the lawyer will be trained to push the relational interests to the background of the representation, elevating an individual autonomy that, under the circumstances, may be an artificial construct. Tom Shaffer's example of a married couple encountering disagreement in the drafting of their wills falls into this category. Rather than helping the husband and wife sort through their differences as a family, the lawyer's inclination often will be to

---

[14] This example is discussed further in Chapter 3.

engage her clients strictly as individuals, washing her hands of the "conflict" and encouraging each spouse to retain his or her own lawyer.[15]

Third, in some cases, the client may want to avoid facing relational interests that may prove insurmountable if acknowledged, but are more easily eluded if the lawyers themselves provide a sort of cover by ducking the issues in their legal analysis. For example, when the Department of Justice lawyer John Yoo provided the Bush administration with a legal memorandum justifying aggressive interrogation techniques that, in the eyes of many, amounted to torture, his skirting of the moral issues – more pointedly, his dressing up of the moral issues as legal issues – permitted administration officials to invoke the memo as a license for the practices.[16]

Serving autonomy in this "thin" sense – that is, acting on the client's presumed interests without delving into the messy moral considerations that may actually constitute their interests – causes different types of harm to the client, the public, and the lawyer herself. One common thread to these harms is the lawyer's failure to broaden her view of the interests relevant to the representation. At least part of the blame may lie with the codification and bureaucratization of lawyers' ethics. Richard Greenstein argues that lawyers' ethical obligations have been simplified and narrowed

---

[15] This example is discussed in the Introduction.
[16] This example is discussed further in Chapter 4.

toward two goals: first, the protection of client interests, "to the increasing exclusion of other interests," and, second, the protection of lawyers "from unforeseeable or unavoidable ethical missteps," which is made more difficult "in an increasingly diverse society that lacks fine-grained consensus on standards of professional conduct."[17] Greenstein sees this simplification facilitated by what he calls "the rule of partiality," meaning that the client be given ethical priority, coupled with the "no remainder" principle, which refers to the "tenet that following the rule of partiality exhausts the professional's ethical responsibility."[18]

Limiting the professional implications of human dignity to the facilitation of client autonomy represents an unduly narrow conception of dignity. The narrowness is exacerbated by lawyers' failure to invest in the dialogue necessary to pursue a fully relational sense of client autonomy, rather than a simplistic autonomy of individual self-interest secured through the maximization of legal rights and privileges. In reality, there are multiple layers of human dignity, not all of which are centered on individual autonomy. There has been a tendency to pick a single understanding of dignity and push alternatives to the margins. As conversations about dignity proceed, though, there may be a deepening sense that human dignity is multifaceted in its

[17] Richard K. Greenstein, *Against Professionalism*, 22 GEO. J. LEGAL ETHICS 327, 328–9 (2009).
[18] *Id.*

sources, definitional content, and implications. This sense can be seen in recent bioethics literature in particular. Like law, the practice of medicine is an essential support for the lived reality of human dignity.[19] Expanding the discourse on human dignity within the legal profession along similar lines may help reconcile some of the perceived tensions within the lawyer's role.

II. Dignity as Autonomy

One reason why discussions of dignity are so muddled is that we mean to communicate different ideas by the term. It is helpful to distinguish between human dignity as a quality or attribute that a person can have in greater or lesser degrees – for instance, "he comported himself with dignity under very trying circumstances" – and human dignity as the ground of every human being's moral status –for example, "treating any person in that manner violates their

---

[19] Daniel Sulmasy explains: "Health is ... a fundamental condition for attributions of value, either reflexively by an individual, or by the attribution of others. To see this, one need only reflect on the ways in which illness and injury assault the attributed dignity of human beings. Those who are ill are robbed of their stations in life. They lose valued independence. They often become disfigured. They lose their social productivity. They lose esteem in the eyes of others and may even begin to question their own value. If there are any duties to build up the attributed dignities of human beings, surely health care is one of the primary means of doing so." Daniel Sulmasy, *Dignity and Bioethics: History, Theory, and Selected Applications* 469, 486–7.

human dignity."[20] For the most part, the legal profession sticks to the latter meaning. If the law embodies human dignity by granting every citizen equal standing before the law and equal access to its framework of rights and privileges, it is understandable that the profession's view of dignity is grounded in intrinsic equality, rather than any comparative evaluation of conduct. Lawyers honor dignity by honoring their clients' equality, which requires, under this view, deference to their chosen ends. If dignity is intrinsic and not contingent on the quality of the client's choices, lawyers serve dignity by implementing their clients' choices, not by questioning or seeking to shape those choices.

Defenders of this notion of dignity point to Immanuel Kant's insistence that a person be treated as an end, never as a means.[21] It is a deeply mysterious idea, both because of the contestability and elusiveness of its source(s), and because of its seeming impracticality given conflicting economic and social pressures to treat certain people instrumentally or even as expendable. Defenders of this conception of dignity may not reject out of hand the notion that "dignity" is

---

[20] *See generally* Nick Bostrom, "Dignity and Enhancement," in *President's Council on Bioethics, Beyond Therapy: Biotechnology and the Pursuit of Happiness* (2003) 173, 175.

[21] "Now I say that man, and in general every rational being, exists as an end in himself, not merely as a means for arbitrary use by this or that will: he must in all his actions, whether they are directed to himself or to other rational beings, always be viewed at the same time as an end." Immanuel Kant, *Groundwork of the Metaphysic of Morals* (trans. H. J. Paton 1948) (1964), 95.

a characteristic to be cultivated, but they would insist that seeing dignity as inherently variable among persons is a dangerous idea.

If everyone has equal moral standing, and everyone is an end in herself, rather than a means to someone else's ends, then the facilitation of a person's ends can be an obvious way of honoring her dignity. This is why lawyers correctly see autonomy as an important value. Further, lawyers correctly see that autonomy is not a self-executing proposition; it usually requires assistance from others. As Martha Nussbaum puts it, "Human capacities require support from the world (love, care, education, nutrition) if they are to develop internally, and yet other forms of support from the world if the person is to have opportunities to exercise them (a suitable material and political environment)," and thus "we need a picture of human dignity that makes room for different levels of capability and functioning and that also makes room for unfolding and development."[22] By providing access to the privileges and rights afforded under law, lawyers are important contributors to this process of unfolding and development. Lawyers can invoke Nussbaum's pronouncement that respect for human dignity requires more than "a reverential attitude" – it requires the creation of "conditions favorable for development and choice."[23]

---

[22] Martha Nussbaum, "Human Dignity and Political Entitlements," in *Human Dignity and Bioethics: Essays Commissioned by the President's Council on Bioethics* (2008), 351, 357 (hereinafter, *Human Dignity and Bioethics*).

[23] *Id.* at 359.

The human being's capacity for development and choice is not a new theme in the articulation of dignity. In the fifteenth century, Pico della Mirandola emphasized self-definition as a distinctive mark of human dignity:

> We have given to thee, Adam, no fixed seat, no form of thy very own, no gift peculiarly thine, that thou mayest feel as thine own, have as thine own, possess as thine own the seat, the form, the gifts which thou thyself shalt desire. A limited nature in other creatures is confined within the laws written down by Us. In conformity with thy free judgment, in whose hands I have placed thee, thou art confined by no bounds; and thou wilt fix limits of nature for thyself.... Thou, like a judge appointed for being honorable, art the molder and maker of thyself; thou mayest sculpt thyself into whatever shape thou dost prefer. Thou canst grow downward into the lower natures which are brutes. Thou canst again grow upward from thy soul's reason into the higher natures which are divine.[24]

Herbert Spiegelberg explains that Pico's originality was in locating dignity in the human's "'chameleon'-like freedom to mould and make himself into lower or higher natures."[25] Of course, while this "may give man a remarkable ontological

---

[24] Pico della Mirandola, "On the Dignity of Man" (trans. Paul Miller 1940), in *On the Dignity of Man, On Being and the One, Heptaplus* (1965), 4–5.

[25] Herbert Spiegelberg, "Human Dignity: A Challenge to Contemporary Philosophy," in *Human Dignity: This Century and the Next,* ed. Rubin Gotesky & Ervin Laszlo (1970), 39, 48.

distinction," is it "enough of a reason for paying him our respects in a moral sense?"[26] From a theological perspective, according to Kendall Soulen and Linda Woodhead, the novelty of Pico's approach is the emphasis on humanity's natural powers and radical freedom, which places human dignity "on a purely internal basis (properties integral to 'human nature') rather than on an external basis (the God who creates and redeems humanity)."[27] As a consequence, dignity "becomes more individualistic, as humanity is seen to consist in distinct agency rather than in membership in the body of Christ."[28]

While the tendency to equate dignity with autonomy has a long history, in the legal profession (as elsewhere), we may have gradually "thinned out" the conception of autonomy to the point where it resembles a distinctly atomistic individualism. Even Kant, often derided as the source of this individualist line of moral thought, portrayed dignity and autonomy as relational. Autonomy, in Kant's work, consists of a person's subjection to self-made law, and thus dignity flows from our awareness "that one is morally obliged and therefore morally accountable."[29] Autonomy, then, is not

---

[26] *Id.* at 48.

[27] Soulen and Woodhead, *Introduction: Contextualizing Human Dignity,* in *God and Human Dignity,* ed. R. Kendall Soulen & Linda Woodhead (2006), 1, 10.

[28] *Id.*

[29] Susan M. Shell, "Kant on Human Dignity," in *In Defense of Human Dignity: Essays for Our Times* (Robert P. Kraynak & Glenn Tinder, eds.), 53, 57. *See* Immanuel Kant, *Conflict of the Faculties,* VII 87n.;

some sort of infinitely malleable and self-defined freedom of choice; it is grounded in human nature – in particular, in "our shared capacity to obey the law of which we are ourselves the author."[30] As Kant puts it, it is the human will that "has as nature's purpose for it the function of making universal law."[31]

A key contribution of Kant is his grounding dignity in our (shared) human nature, specifically in our faculty of rational freedom.[32] Further, this freedom is dialectical, leading "us to make demands upon the world that ultimately devolve upon ourselves," and our dignity "derives from our capacity to act upon the dictates of our own reason."[33] For this reason, Kant's moral anthropology is about more "than the reciprocal freedom of consenting adults," for "it also imposes limits

157n. ("No being endowed with freedom is satisfied with the enjoyment of life's comforts that are apportioned to him by another.... What matters is rather the principle according to which he provides it for himself.").

[30] *Id.* at 74.

[31] Immanuel Kant, *Groundwork of the Metaphysic of Morals,* trans. H. J. Paton (1948), 100.

[32] Soulen & Woodhead, *supra* note 27, at 11 (noting three key contributions by Kant: "First ... there is Kant's virtual identification of human dignity with a single preeminent faculty: (rational) freedom. Second, there is Kant's elevation of human dignity to a central – indeed, foundational – normative principle for ethical reflection. Last, there is Kant's profound conceptual linkage of the concept of human dignity with corresponding and specific rights inherent in and belonging to the human person.").

[33] Susan M. Shell, *Kant's Concept of Human Dignity as a Resource for Bioethics,* 333, 338–9.

on the uses to which one may put one's own capacities."[34] The Kantian emphasis on autonomy is not premised on a notion of moral judgment as a sort of internalized "black box," lying beyond the reach of interpersonal engagement. The capacity for moral judgment on which human dignity depends requires that an agent look beyond herself to what is true, not only for herself, but for others.

In practice, the notion of autonomy as a sort of "moral self-definition" is misleading. As Peter Lawler explains, the notion that "we must free our minds from the authority of parents, country, tradition, nature, God, and so forth" ignores the fact that "the individual human mind is anxious, disoriented, and paralyzed if it has to work all by itself," and thus "the pretense of radical doubt ... eventually leads the individual to lose confidence both in the soundness of his mind and in the personal foundation of his dignity."[35] In this regard, autonomy requires "a social dimension: consciousness necessarily is knowing with others."[36] While "the solitude of radical freedom makes effective human thought and

---

[34] *Id.* at 339 ("Now I say that man, and in general every rational being, exists as an end in himself, not merely as a means for arbitrary use by this or that will: he must in all his actions, whether they are directed to himself or to other rational beings, always be viewed at the same time as an end.") Quoting Immanuel Kant, *Groundwork of the Metaphysic of Morals* (trans. H. J. Paton 1948) (1964), 95.

[35] Peter Augustine Lawler, "Modern and American Dignity," in *Human Dignity and Bioethics, supra* note 22, at 229, 245–6.

[36] *Id.* at 246.

action impossible," the sharing of self-knowledge, thought Kant, provides "a rational standard that we can genuinely have in common."[37]

The self-defining individual poses a problem for human dignity to the extent we struggle to discern "where the self-defining individual is supposed to get the point of view, the character or virtue, the genuinely inward life or conscience required to resist degrading social or scientific conformity."[38] In the focus on avoiding the "tyrannical moralism of others," we cannot neglect the "necessarily social, natural, and personal sources of the moral resolution of the dignified 'I.'"[39] Accounting for this danger is not just a project for abstract philosophizing; the resolution is lived out in our relationships. In fact, our dignity, under Lawler's view, flows from the combination of the human person's social instincts with our self-consciousness, represented starkly in "our ability to know and love – and to be known and loved by – other, particular persons."[40]

Today we tend not to focus on the relational aspects of Kant's autonomy – as captured in his emphasis on duty – instead seeing autonomy as equivalent to freedom of choice.[41] The difference is "between autonomy as self-

[37] *Id.*

[38] *Id.*

[39] *Id.*

[40] *Id.* at 249.

[41] Ruud H. J. ter Meulen, "Towards a Social Concept of the Person," in *Personhood and Health Care,* ed. David C. Thomasma et al. (2001),

legislative (Kant) and autonomy as self-determination."[42] As Ruud ter Meulen puts it, "Individuals are not so much directed by rational decisions as they are by the image of themselves," and thus autonomy, authentically understood, "means in practice that you identify yourself with your own practice."[43] In health care, for example, the person afflicted with chronic disease becomes dependent on others, but this dependency is not inconsistent with autonomy, for what the dependent needs is "support by his environment to find again or to adjust his identity," so that he can identify with the choices he makes.[44] As Charles Taylor has so painstakingly demonstrated, our identities are inescapably social, as "[a] self can never be described without reference to those who surround it."[45]

III. Dignity Grounded in Reality

Perhaps autonomy's ubiquity as a rhetorical tool has marginalized its usefulness to the extent that the term has been reduced to a simplistic slogan lacking the nuance of human

129, 130 ("While Kant sees the freedom of the person constitutive of acting from duty, in health care ethics freedom is merely seen as a freedom to decide about one's own body and mind, without any reference to a universal duty.").

[42] *Id.* at 130.

[43] *Id.* at 132–3 (citing work of George Agich).

[44] *Id.* at 133.

[45] Charles Taylor, *Sources of the Self: The Making of the Modern Identity* (1989), 35.

experience. Whether or not a more authentically relational conception of autonomy can be reclaimed, it is important to articulate how the human orientation toward relationship can help provide substantive content to the elusive concept of human dignity. With the widespread adoption of informed consent requirements, for example, individual autonomy provides the minimum threshold of dignity in the field of bioethics, but the fact that a procedure comports with individual choice does not end the inquiry. Many bioethicists are grappling with deeper questions about the compatibility of a procedure or technology with the essence of the human condition and our accountability to one another in light of our shared vulnerability. Martin Luther King Jr. also resisted the equation of dignity with autonomy. He stood for individual empowerment, to be sure, but he worked to empower individuals to make choices consistent with the dignity that flows from the reality of our created nature. King honored human dignity by working to repair the relationships for which we are created.

Individual autonomy is an important component of bioethics, as it is in legal ethics. But the conversation in bioethics also encompasses considerations beyond the protection of patient choice. Leon Kass contrasts "the basic dignity of human being" with "the full dignity of being (actively) human, of human flourishing."[46] The first type is "intended – and needed – to restrain the strong in their dealings with

[46] Leon R. Kass, "Defending Human Dignity," in *Human Dignity and Bioethics, supra* note 22, at 297, 299.

the weak."[47] The second type is needed, though, "when we turn from concerns with abuse of power that the strong inflict upon the weak to concern with ethically dubious uses of power that the strong – indeed, most of us – will choose to exercise for and on ourselves."[48] Connecting dignity to the notion of human flourishing need not result in the ranking of individuals in terms of the dignity with which they lead their lives, for as Kass explains, "we are not comparing individuals against each other; we are measuring them against a standard of goodness."[49] Even when we identify conduct by others that reflects dignity better than our own conduct does, most of us "do not feel ourselves diminished by it."[50]

Daniel Sulmasy provides an example of how individual autonomy – wrapped into the concept of basic dignity – is the beginning, not the end, of conversations about one of the more difficult issues in bioethics, euthanasia:

> Proponents … argue that [euthanasia] ought to be permitted because the assaults that illness and injury mount upon the attributed dignities of human beings can be so overwhelming that some patients might be led to attribute no more worth or value to themselves, thus making euthanasia a reasonable option.[51]

[47] *Id.* at 301.

[48] *Id.*

[49] *Id.* at 310.

[50] *Id.*

[51] Daniel P. Sulmasy, "Dignity and Bioethics: History, Theory, and Selected Applications," in *Human Dignity and Bioethics, supra* note 22, at 469, 487.

Opponents of euthanasia need not deny that illness can assault the attributed dignities of human beings, but a commitment to human dignity can have other implications as well:

> The argument from inflorescent dignity suggests ... that the value of the human is expressed most fully (i.e., flourishes) in the ability to stand up to such assaults with courage, humble acceptance of the finitude of the human, nobility, and even love. To kill oneself in the face of death or to ask to be killed, on this view, is precisely the opposite of what it means to face death with dignity.... The argument from intrinsic dignity suggests that the fundamental basis for the duty to build up the inflorescent dignity of sick human beings – the root of any motivation to attribute dignity to them – is the intrinsic value of the human, the value human beings have by virtue of being the kinds of things that they are ... no circumstances can eliminate that intrinsic dignity.... Thus, while one might, out of human sympathy, suggest that a duty to build up attributed dignity legitimizes euthanasia ... this cannot be permitted because it undermines the fundamental basis of morality itself – respect for intrinsic dignity.[52]

However persuasive one finds these arguments in the context of euthanasia, for our purposes it is important to see how bioethicists are able to make substantive, intellectually coherent claims about human dignity's implications for the

[52] *Id.* at 487–8.

physician-patient relationship. Further, these claims are, at bottom, about what it means to be human. The claims are thus widely accessible and suited for interpersonal engagement.

Whether or not these claims are of a type that should ultimately be reflected in the law is immaterial for our inquiry into the role of lawyers. I am taking background legal norms as a given and asking whether lawyers should go beyond those norms in counseling their clients. Nevertheless, it bears noting that there have been glimpses outside bioethics of a legally cognizable dignity that goes beyond individual autonomy. In France, the Conseil d'Etat upheld a ban on dwarf tossing contests even though the dwarfs consented to participate in the activity.[53] There was no threat of physical harm, as the contests occurred along padded corridors and the dwarfs wore harnesses with handles on their backs. The French authorities deemed the activity to violate the dwarfs' dignity, even if the dwarfs did not recognize it as such. The case exemplifies the inalienability of human dignity.[54] In some contexts, we do not permit the individual to reject the implications of her own dignity.

Human dignity was also the operative concept underlying the South African Constitutional Court's decision upholding a ban on prostitution against a challenge that the

---

[53] Conseil d'Etat, Ass., October 27, 1995, Commune de Morsang sur Orge, Recueil Lebon at 372 (cited in Jeremy Waldron, *Dignity, Rights, and Responsibilities*, 43 ARIZ. ST. L.J. 1107, 1130 (2011)).

[54] *See* Waldron, *supra* note 53.

statute violated the prostitute's dignity by depriving her of economic liberty. The Court reasoned:

> [An aspect of human dignity] is the fundamental dignity of the human body which is not simply organic. Neither is it something to be commodified. Our Constitution requires that it be respected. We do not believe that [the law banning prostitution] can be said to be the cause of any limitation on the dignity of the prostitute. To the extent that the dignity of prostitutes is diminished, the diminution arises from the character of prostitution itself.[55]

In law and elsewhere, it is important not to allow a new awareness of higher dignity to obscure the importance of basic dignity, or vice versa. As Fraser Watts puts it, we need to remain open to "the dignity that we have already as a gift, and the fuller dignity that we are promised and toward which we are called."[56] Dignity is not simply a fixed property of the human being – there is a personal and relational unfolding of dignity in a human life that must pervade our respect for dignity. At the same time, we must be careful not to lose our conviction that dignity "is already in some basic sense present," or "there would be no constraints on current indignities."[57]

---

[55] *Id.* at 1131–2 (quoting Constitutional Court of South Africa, October 9, 2002, Case CCT31/01, *Jordan v. the State* per O'Regan and Sachs, J. J., concurring [majority agreed with this portion of concurrence]).

[56] Fraser Watts, "Human Dignity: Concepts and Experiences," in *God and Human Dignity, supra* note 27, at 247, 251.

[57] *Id.*

Gilbert Meilander captures the distinction in two seemingly contradictory statements about murderers by Thomas Aquinas and Pope John Paul II. According to Aquinas, "A man who sins deviates from the rational order, and so loses his human dignity," but John Paul II insisted that "not even a murderer loses his personal dignity."[58] Meilander explains that they are talking about two different types of dignity – human and personal. Human dignity, the type underlying Aquinas's statement, "has to do with the powers and limits characteristic of our species," and dignity in this sense "would be diminished or lost if we were utterly to transcend the limits of our bodies (and become something more like a god) or if we were to think of our bodies not as a place of personal presence but (as for beasts) things to be manipulated for purposes entirely external to them."[59] By contrast, personal dignity, according to Meilander, "has to do not with species-specific powers and limits but with the individual person, whose dignity calls for our respect whatever his or her powers and limits may be."[60] This type of dignity is more closely tied to human equality. So slavery, for example, can violate the human dignity of the slave even though nothing can deprive the slave of his personal dignity.[61]

---

[58] Quoted in Gilbert Meilander, *Neither Beast nor God: The Dignity of the Human Person,* 7.

[59] *Id.* at 8.

[60] *Id.*

[61] *See id.* at 83.

In practice, the basic (personal) and the higher (human) senses of dignity will be integrated by the fact that we live as embodied beings, able to reflect on and evaluate our own behavior and attitudes. This is a defining attribute of humans, categorically separating us from animals. Further, our awareness of, and respect for, the similar capacity of other human beings binds us with others in a shared knowledge of our distinctive dignity.[62] Our innate capacity is not coextensive with the exercise of such capacity, though. The living out of dignity is "a dialectic of reflection and action."[63] Put more simply, humans have dignity because they are "able to entertain the concept of dignity (and to acknowledge dignity by way of respect, recognition, courtesy)."[64] Using the higher sense of dignity in a way that invites comparative assessment acknowledges that "some of us flourish

[62] Holmes Rolston explains:

Animals do not have a sense of mutual gaze in the sense of joint attention, of "looking with." ... They do not negotiate the presence of an existential self, interacting interpersonally with other such agents, in the process of thinking about and pursuing goals in the world. Animals do see others in pursuit of the food, mates, or territories they wish to have; but they do not know that other minds are there, much less other spirits. This capacity for referencing others as distinct, intentional, existential selves like ourselves gives rise to an enhanced sense of the worth of such fellow humans, parallel to our own worth.

Holmes Rolston III, *Human Uniqueness and Human Dignity: Persons in Nature and the Nature of Persons,* 129, 146.

[63] *Id.* at 147.

[64] *Id.*

more than others, showing in our lives what human beings at their best can be," though basic dignity "provides protection" by affirming our equal dignity.[65]

But if we are to assess the degree to which conduct comports with human dignity, rather than just enshrining the individual's choices as inherently reflective of dignity because of the actor's intrinsic dignity, by what criteria are we to judge? Because lawyers' services cross religious, philosophical, and ideological lines, it is especially important that the operative criteria for judging their support of human dignity be grounded in the empirical reality of the human experience. The provider should at least begin from the premise that her services support observable truths about human nature, rather than an artificial construct of the profession's own devising. Leon Kass offers one example of the distinction between a professional serving human nature and mastering it:

> When a physician intervenes therapeutically to correct some deficiency or deviation from a patient's natural wholeness, he acts as a servant to the goal of health and as an assistant to nature's own power of self-healing, themselves wondrous products of evolutionary selection. But when a bioengineer intervenes for nontherapeutic ends, he stands not as nature's servant but as her aspiring master, guided by nothing but his own will and serving ends of his own devising.[66]

[65] Meilander, *supra* note 58, at 87.
[66] Kass, in *Human Dignity and Bioethics*, *supra* note 22, at 324–5.

The problem is not just the unintended consequences that can result, according to Kass, but also the false picture of the naturally given world from which it derives: "The root of the difficulty seems to be both cognitive and moral: the failure properly to appreciate and respect the 'giftedness' of the world."[67] While it is not obvious how to separate the "gifts" that should be accepted from those that should be improved or opposed, it is important to consider whether the "proposed improvements might impinge upon the nature of the one being improved."[68] The danger of hubris in the designer is the degradation of the designed.[69]

One important "given" feature of the human condition is our shared vulnerability. This is a familiar theme in political theory,[70] but it can also provide a key criterion for discerning the extent to which human dignity is expressed in our social interactions. David Weisstub and David Thomasma explain that social interaction "creates minute and major vulnerabilities, corrected for by both personal and social commitments that ascribe honor and dignity to the other individual," and that personhood thus arises, at least in part, from "the extent to which we protect the vulnerable from harm."[71] This takes us squarely into the conception of

---

[67] *Id.* at 324–5.

[68] *Id.* at 325–6.

[69] *Id.*

[70] *See* Thomas Hobbes, *The Leviathan*.

[71] David N. Weisstub and David C. Thomasma, "Human Dignity, Vulnerability, Personhood," in *Personhood and Health Care* (2001), 317, 330.

human dignity as a relational attribute. Jurgen Habermas has embraced this understanding, rejecting the notion that dignity is "a property like intelligence or blue eyes, that one might 'possess' by nature." Instead, it "indicates the kind of 'inviolability' which comes to have a significance only in interpersonal relationships of mutual respect, in the egalitarian dealings among persons."[72] Moral behavior, then, is "a constructive response to the dependencies rooted in the incompleteness of our organic makeup and in the persistent frailty (most felt in the phases of childhood, illness, and old age) of our bodily existence."[73] And autonomy, far from being a freestanding property of individuals, "is a precarious achievement of finite beings who may attain something like 'strength,' if at all, only if they are mindful of their physical vulnerability and social dependence."[74]

George Harris has mined the relationship between dignity and vulnerability for important insights about why we admire human character. He explains:

> Among the virtues of a stone from the perspective of diamond lovers is its strength.... Among the virtues of wine from the perspective of wine lovers is its fragility. If a liquid has dispositional properties such that its character would not break down under certain conditions, it is not wine and cannot be admired as such. The admiration of human character is both like the admiration of diamonds

[72] Jurgen Habermas, *The Future of Human Nature* (2003), 34.
[73] *Id.*
[74] *Id.*

and like the admiration of good wine. This is to say that we admire human character both for its strength and for its fragility.[75]

For example, according to Harris, we place value "on the human capacities that render people of good character vulnerable to the devastating effects of grief."[76] A person impervious to grief would not be admirable and we would consider her to be "some sort of emotional monstrosity."[77] Individuals' vulnerability to grief is "is part of what we respect in them; it is a constitutive element of their dignity-conferring qualities," at least in part because the vulnerability stems from their willingness to love others in a way that renders them vulnerable.[78] Vulnerability is not the only attribute that we admire in a person, but Harris points out that we do not respect a person because of her invulnerability; nor do we find any source of dignity in it.[79]

This focus on shared vulnerability as a dignity-conferring quality roots dignity firmly in the human experience. Put differently, moral accountability based on our shared vulnerability premises our commitment to human dignity on the observed reality of the human condition. The philosopher Gabriel Marcel, writing in the early 1960s,

[75] George W. Harris, *Dignity and Vulnerability: Strength and Quality of Character* (1997), 6.
[76] *Id.* at 68.
[77] *Id.*
[78] *Id.*
[79] *Id.* at 69.

faulted communism for its spirit of abstraction – that is, its "inability to treat a human being as a human being," instead substituting "a certain idea, a certain abstract designation."[80] Marcel also returned to human vulnerability as the centerpiece of this reality, arguing that "dignity must be sought at the antipodes of pretension and rather on the side of weakness."[81] Marcel, a Christian existentialist,[82] traced dignity to the fact of human mortality, noting that mortality's practical implication for how we live is not a paralyzing sense of insignificance, but resistance. And significantly for our purposes, this resistance "is founded, not on the affirmation of the self and the pretensions it exudes, but on a stronger consciousness of the living tie which unites all men."[83] By linking herself to her neighbor, the individual frees herself from herself,[84] at the same time placing hope in the neighbor, resisting the temptation to "enclose them in what strikes us as their nature" based on "their conduct which almost always begins by bruising or disappointing us."[85] Can lawyers prevent the law's protective function

---

[80] Gabriel Marcel, *The Existential Background of Human Dignity* (1963), 122–3.

[81] *Id.* at 134.

[82] While Marcel initially embraced this label (affixed to him by Jean-Paul Sartre), he eventually rejected it. *See* "Gabriel Marcel," *Stanford Encyclopedia of Philosophy* (http://plato.stanford.edu/entries/marcel/).

[83] Marcel, *supra* note 80, at 134–5.

[84] *Id.* at 147.

[85] *Id.* at 147–8.

from leading to an individualist account of well-being that short-circuits the capacity for placing hope in one's neighbor and proving worthy of such hope in return?

IV. Lawyers and Human Dignity

The legal profession's exclusive reliance on dignity as an equal and intrinsic property of a human being is inadequate to the justificatory task assigned it by the profession. If we lack the language – much less the will – to assess the quality of dignity embodied in a particular decision or course of conduct, our commitment to dignity will have practical import primarily on questions of process. Process, as a mechanism for recognizing our basic equality before the law and giving voice to the otherwise voiceless, is essential to dignity's realization. But questions of process do not lend themselves to the sort of deeper substantive inquiries found in current bioethics discussions and King's advocacy. Few people, lawyers included, would identify "equality before the law" as the sole implication of one's commitment to human dignity. Lawyers might defend such equality as the sole implication that is relevant to their work as lawyers, but that is eminently debatable.

Take Martha Nussbaum's explanation that respect for human dignity requires the creation of "conditions favorable for development and choice" because our internally developed capacities require external support if we are to have opportunities to exercise them.[86] To the extent that the actual stakes of a client's choices are not reflected in her conversations with her attorney about those choices, the support for her exercise of her internally developed capacities may be inadequate. As discussed earlier, the lack of moral engagement may be a disservice to the client's autonomy by tending to push relational accountability to the periphery.

Dignity as a relative attribute and as the ground of our intrinsic moral status both depend on acting consistently with our shared human nature. We still face choices to act with more dignity or less, but the "dignity" label is tied to something more fundamental about what it means to be human. In bioethics, this aspect of the debate focuses on the need for humility and respect for the "given" nature of our world. Of course, one person's emphasis on humility may strike someone else as a justification of passivity in the face of suffering, and respect for the "given" may come across as support for the status quo. Lawyers, whose clients rely on the legal system as a bulwark against state power and as a path toward greater social equality, are unlikely to look to the "given" as an unqualified good. But the question remains whether even lawyers are compelled by the dictates of dignity to respect, or at least to act with cognizance of, certain qualities and conditions that are distinctively human.

Human dignity is a formless void if unhinged from a conception of the human person. The legal profession's failure

[86] Nussbaum, *supra* note 22, at 357.

to make moral engagement a part of the lawyer's role tends toward an operative conception of the person as an atomistic individual. Again, this is not – or at least does not appear to be – the result of any concerted or deliberate rejection of the social nature of the person. But for the reasons set forth previously, the lawyer's failure to invite the client to consider the relational interests implicated by a course of conduct functions in some circumstances as an invitation not to consider such interests. That is not to say that a client will never choose to ignore the social dimension of the human experience, only that the profession should not begin with that possibility as the default premise for the attorney-client relationship. How often do a lawyer's "hardball" litigation tactics further strain a client's relationships without inviting the client to reflect on alternative approaches to advocacy? How often do lawyers serve to push the well-being of their organizational client's constituents from view by focusing exclusively on the organization's legal interests? And how often does a lawyer communicate her finding of legal permissibility in a way that signals the end of the inquiry into the wisdom of a proposed course of conduct, rather than the beginning? If dignity is an attribute cultivated by a greater awareness of our social nature – and the shared vulnerability that is a product of that nature – do lawyers truly contribute to the project by suppressing their moral agency in favor of a detachment-based neutrality and interest-narrowing partisanship?

Along with Tom Shaffer, David Luban is perhaps the most notable exception to the profession's tendency to disregard the relational accountability at the core of human dignity. He argues that "human dignity should best be understood as a kind of conceptual shorthand referring to relations among people, rather than as a metaphysical property of individuals."[87] In other words, human dignity "designates a way of being human, not a property of being human."[88] More specifically, according to Luban, "agents and institutions violate human dignity when they humiliate people, and so non-humiliation becomes a common-sense proxy for honoring human dignity."[89]

Nonhumiliation is not the same as the maximization of individual choice, and Luban readily perceives the limitations of a respect focused on the facilitation of individual autonomy:

> Autonomy focuses on just one human faculty, the will, and identifying dignity with autonomy likewise identifies human dignity with willing and choosing. This, I believe, is a truncated view of humanity and human experience. Honoring someone's human dignity means honoring their being, not merely their willing. Their being transcends the choices they make. It includes the way they experience the world – their perceptions, their passions and sufferings, their reflections, their relationships and commitments, what they care about.... What I care about is central to who I am, and to honor my human dignity is to take my

[87] David Luban, *Legal Ethics and Human Dignity* (2007), 6.
[88] *Id.* at 66.
[89] *Id.*

cares and commitments seriously. The real objection to lawyers' paternalism toward their clients is not that lawyers interfere with their clients' autonomous choices, but that they sometimes ride roughshod over the commitments that make the client's life meaningful and so impart dignity to it.[90]

Luban mines the case of Ted Kaczynski ("the Unabomber") for insight on this distinction. Kaczynski believed that the apocalyptic warnings he offered to modernity were valid and true, and he did not want to seek the protection of an insanity defense, even if it could mitigate his punishment. His lawyers successfully invoked the defense against his will. The primary harm to Kaczynski was not the deprivation of his free choice (though he lost that too), but the fact that his lawyers "made nonsense of his deepest commitments, of what mattered to him and made him who he was."[91] To claim insanity made his self-conception incoherent and his work pointless. According to Luban, this was his lawyers' "sin against human dignity," and "autonomy has little to do with it."[92]

Katherine Kruse also adds nuance to our understanding of autonomy's utility as a justification for the lawyer's role. She does not reject its value, but she emphasizes its relational dimension – a dimension usually ignored in our

[90] *Id.* at 76.
[91] *Id.* at 79.
[92] *Id.* at 79.

construction of the client within legal ethics discourse.[93] Kruse explains:

> The obsession in legal ethics with the problems of zealous partisanship dates back to a preference of early legal ethics scholars, most of whom were philosophers, to focus on conflicts between professional role morality and ordinary morality. To generate these conflicts, legal ethics scholars had to construct clients as "cardboard clients" – one-dimensional figures interested only in maximizing their legal and financial interests. Implicit assumptions also led these ethicists to propose the problematic solution that lawyers should act as moral consciences for their clients. The "lawyer-statesman" model that emerged as an alternative professional ideal rests on the morally elitist assumption that lawyers are better situated than clients to exercise moral judgment and carries the danger of moral overreaching when lawyers and clients disagree about morality.[94]

A more pressing problem for the profession is "legal objectification," which refers to lawyers' tendency to "'issue-spot' their clients as they would the facts on a blue book exam, overemphasizing the clients' legal interests and minimizing or ignoring the other cares, commitments, relationships, reputations, and values that constitute the objectives clients

---

[93] Katherine R. Kruse, *Beyond Cardboard Clients in Legal Ethics*, 23 Geo. J. Legal Ethics 103 (2010). Even Luban, Kruse thinks, uses "cardboard" clients to make his points. *Id.* at 114.

[94] *Id.* at 103.

bring to legal representation."[95] She proposes an "ideal of professionalism for 'three-dimensional clients' based on helping clients articulate and actualize their values through the law."[96]

That said, Kruse remains leery of drawing lawyers' own values into the representation. "Moral activist counseling," she asserts, "has an inherent tendency to veer in the direction of moral elitism."[97] To defend such an approach, "one has to explain why lawyers are better situated than their clients to exercise responsible moral judgment in legal representation."[98] Otherwise, "the chances of advancing the public good by pursuing the client's moral choices would seem to be just as great as the chances of advancing the public good by shaping client objectives according to the lawyer's moral choices."[99] By treating clients as three-dimensional and respecting a particular client's values – not presuming that the client's only concern is the maximization of her legal or financial interests – the lawyer will include moral considerations in the representation while avoiding the dangers of moral overreaching. Note, however, that even under this more nuanced understanding of autonomy, the lawyer tends to recede into the background. Lawyers, in Kruse's view, are "channels through which clients can access the law."[100]

[95] *Id.*
[96] *Id.*
[97] *Id.* at 120.
[98] *Id.* at 120–1.
[99] *Id.*
[100] *Id.* at 121.

As Kruse's cautious approach to lawyers' moral agency reflects, an authentic conception of human dignity requires more than the recognition that we are social beings; we also must grapple with the destructive capacity of human pride. Glenn Tinder explains that we are reluctant to acknowledge our finitude and even more reluctant to acknowledge that we are morally flawed.[101] This pride leads human beings to trust in our own power, which makes us "vulnerable not merely to miscalculation, but to [our] own malicious impulses."[102] The opposite risk, though, is when pride "gives way altogether"; then "the end sought becomes, in place of inordinate expansion of the self, the virtual eradication of the self," and people give up not only "power and domination, but all responsibility."[103] Avoiding these dual impulses is to remain human, to maintain the dignity of the human condition.[104]

[101] "Glenn Tinder, Against Fate: An Essay on Personal Dignity," in *In Defense of Human Dignity, supra* note 29, at 11.

[102] *Id.*

[103] *Id.* at 18.

[104] John Witte (2003) makes a similar point in Lutheran terms: "[In Luther's view] we are at once sinners and saints; we are at once lords and servants. We can do nothing good; we can do nothing but good. We are utterly free; we are everywhere bound. The more a person thinks himself a saint, the more sinful in fact he becomes. The more a person thinks herself a sinner, the more saintly she in fact becomes. The more a person acts like a lord, the more he is called to be a servant. The more a person acts as a servant, the more in fact she has become a lord. This is the paradoxical nature of human life. And this is the essence of human dignity."

If the polar extremes of pride and self-abandonment are risks embedded within the human condition, how should this reality impact an attorney's relationship with her client? The profession seems to be well aware of an attorney's capacity to impose her will on the client – which could be understood as a consequence of the attorney's pride – but safeguarding against that possibility by erecting a vision of the attorney as a mouthpiece may not only amount to a sort of self-abandonment on the attorney's part; it may also facilitate the client's own self-aggrandizement or self-abandonment by failing to provide a meaningful check on, or opportunity for meaningful reflection about, the client's assumptions. The attorney's passivity may contribute to a client's failure to act consistently with her nature as a finite, flawed, but responsible and accountable moral agent – that is, to act consistently with her human dignity. Far from being the paradigmatic defenders of human dignity, lawyers sometimes may contribute to the client's disregard of her own dignity even when they have honored her stated wishes.[105]

John Witte, Jr., "Between Sanctity and Depravity: Human Dignity in Protestant Perspective," in *In Defense of Human Dignity: Essays for Our Times*, ed. Robert Kraynak & Glenn Tinders, 119, 127.

[105] "'Losing one's dignity' in the sense of becoming deprived of it and of losing it by doing something which is beneath it refer to two different kinds of losing: in the first case to being henceforth without dignity, something which the thesis of universal human dignity considers impossible; in the second case, to do something which

Concern regarding moral overreaching by lawyers contributes to the view that the only legitimate expression of a client's relational accountability is the law. As long as the attorney faithfully guides the client within the boundaries set by law, critics of my thesis will argue, she is honoring an understanding of dignity that is grounded in the reality of our social nature. As we will discuss further in Chapter 5, though, the language of legal entitlement and permissibility does not include any level of relational accountability beyond that of citizen. The law does not reflect partial loyalties, obligations, or any other measure of accountability beyond those enacted by the political community. "Citizen" only begins to capture our social nature, and law only begins to capture a sense of the moral accountability based on the shared vulnerability that marks the human condition. There is some capacity for this accountability to be reflected in private ordering, as the law will (usually) enforce contracts, but a minuscule portion of the relationships that constitute our day-to-day well-being and worldview are ever distilled into a legal document. Our shared legal framework is an essential bulwark in the cause of human dignity to the extent that it makes possible the protection of individual autonomy, but it does not come close to exhausting the breadth and depth of real human flourishing.

is in conflict with the demands of his own dignity, which remain unaffected by such 'loss.' What is lost is merely the kind of attitude, the 'composure,' demanded by dignity itself." Spiegelberg, *supra* note 25, at 54–5.

Martin Luther King's worldview has not been the center-piece of this chapter, as it will be through the rest of the book. The chapter has sought to contextualize King's relevance to this project by framing the current debate about human dignity in terms that lay bare the understandable attractiveness, but ultimate inadequacy, of the notion of human dignity as individual autonomy. The legal profession's failure to encourage moral engagement between attorney and client magnifies this inadequacy by effectively enshrining, in many cases, the maximization of individual legal interests as the default objective of the representation.

Human dignity's contribution to the work of the attorney is to help provide a starting point for dialogue that is broad enough to encompass basic insights about human nature, not just one-dimensional professional constructs of client interests. Dignity is relational. More particularly, the relational quality of dignity requires interpersonal space for reflection, dialogue, and accountability. Dignity requires the constant effort to explore and narrow the gap between the ideal and the real: "we cannot realize our dignity" without ethics.[106] Science, according to Holmes Rolston, "not only struggles to understand how amoral nature evolved the moral animal, but finds itself incompetent to analyze how even now *Homo sapiens* has duties, how to set up and resolve that reflective tension between real and ideal."[107] If attorneys are to serve

---

[106] Rolston, *supra* note 62, at 150.
[107] *Id.*

the dignity of their clients (and their own), they need to make space for ethical reflection; a mouthpiece does not contemplate such space; nor do increasingly narrow and technical disciplinary regulations that serve as the profession's "ethics" codes.[108] Aspirational ethics codes, by contrast, are widely derided now as impractical and indeterminate, but they can perhaps more helpfully be understood as demarcating the space for such reflection. And in the end, if this reflection is premised on the reality of human dignity, it must be aimed – cannot help but be aimed – toward the social. While "a deer can be fully a deer without being conscious of the deer population of the earth or of the problem commonly affecting deer," "not so a human being."[109]

Admittedly, bioethicists may appear better situated for grappling with questions that implicate "high" dignity, facing dilemmas that lend themselves to being addressed at a level of generality that does not work as easily for lawyers. Bioethical inquiries that go beyond questions of autonomy to questions of human flourishing – controversies regarding the end of life, technological enhancements, genetic screening, and assisted reproduction, for example – are at least potentially amenable to engagement as categorical questions. By contrast, lawyers' engagement with questions of human flourishing remains highly contextual. We can debate a categorical ban on human cloning; it makes little

---

108 *See ABA Model Rules of Professional Conduct: ABA Model Code of Professional Responsibility.*

109 Rolston, *supra* note 62, at 48.

sense to discuss attorney-client confidentiality, or the attorney's duty of loyalty, or the scope of the attorney's counseling responsibilities without delving into the specific circumstances that will determine the scenario's implications for dignity. An attorney's commitment to dignity always plays itself out in the context of a particular representation.

Further, once we recognize that a commitment to human dignity is more than a commitment to individual autonomy, we still face a messy task in working out the content of that commitment. Grounding dignity in the shared vulnerability of the human person is a start, but it does not take the lawyer very far, particularly if the lawyer finds herself working in a legal system that is premised on role-differentiated behavior as an antidote to the vulnerability of individual citizens. If vulnerability leads only to a systemic commitment to empower everyone to "lawyer up," we still have some work to do.

King looms large in this inquiry, even at this stage. He grounded his defense of human dignity in reality, arguing that our social nature is not just an aspirational goal to be theorized, but an empirical truth to be recognized. This stance was not costless for King. His categorical affirmation of human relationship meant disavowing the winning of power for power's sake. King encouraged the African American community to reject the suggestion that white power should be replaced with black power; he insisted that black empowerment was in the white community's interests as well, for our nature calls us to relationship, not subjugation. This insistence cost King credibility in the wake of more pessimistic analyses offered by figures such as Malcolm X and Stokely Carmichael. King's contrary stance is captured in his espousal of Martin Buber's "I-Thou" moral admonition –that is, we recognize our mutual dignity by recognizing one another as subjects in relationship, rather than in the "I-It" language of objectification.

Regarding the gap between categorical dignity-based pronouncements and contextual dignity-based decision making, King's ministry serves as a bridge. King wrote at a very high level of generality in articulating the meaning of human dignity – particularly a meaning that provided a more robust basis for his ministry than individual autonomy ever could – but he was careful to connect that articulation to the decisions he made on the ground. His sometimes sweeping pronouncements can be traced to specific actions, made on behalf of specific people, at specific times, in specific places. In other words, King employed the rhetoric of universality as the foundation for his ministry of particularity.

King's intellectual legacy also makes clear that human dignity is not a freestanding or self-contained concept. Human dignity, as an overarching belief, provided King with a certain orientation toward the world around him, but it did not provide a comprehensive account of that world, the nature of its inhabitants, or the moral obligations that flow from this reality. Human dignity is not a worldview; it is a starting premise on which a worldview can be built. King was of course not unique in this: no one who possesses a coherent moral identity can derive it from a single value. King invested his commitment to human dignity with real-world power, not by dropping it into his surroundings like a quick-start impetus for moral action, but by treating it as an integral part of his account of reality. It is the content of that account to which we now turn.

2

Agape

Lawyers as Subjects

If the recognition of human dignity served as an animating value of King's ministry, agape was the vehicle by which that value became operational in his daily work. Lawyers who seek to follow King's example by practicing agape will need to eschew some of today's most ubiquitous conceptions of the lawyer's role. In a nutshell, they will act as subjects, not as objects. In other words, agapic love makes a lawyer an active participant in a dynamic relationship, not a passive vessel or conduit for client demands. Lawyers give voice to their clients, to be sure, but a lawyer who loves is more than a mouthpiece. A lawyer who loves cares about the client in a way that does not presume to equate the client's well-being with the maximization of her independence and autonomy. In loving the client, the lawyer's own being is involved, and thus the lawyer's devotion to the client's well-being will inescapably implicate the lawyer's beliefs regarding human nature and the conditions on which human flourishing depends.

I. King and Agape

Tracing the connection between King's practice of agape and this view of lawyering is not possible until we have a firm grasp on King's understanding of agape's demands. King called love "the supreme unifying principle of life."[1] Throughout his work, King emphasized the need for African Americans to embrace their "somebodiness," through which they could gain a "new determination to achieve freedom and human dignity at any cost."[2] According to King, nonviolent resistance empowered African Americans to become "somebody" and gave them "the courage to be free," but it did not do so by facilitating self-absorption or self-aggrandizement. Rather, nonviolent resistance transformed those "who subordinate themselves to its disciplines, investing them with a cause that is larger

---

[1] "Kenneth B. Clark Interview" (1963), in *A Testament of Hope: The Essential Writings and Speeches of Martin Luther King Jr.*, ed. James M. Washington, 1986, 331, 334 (hereinafter *A Testament of Hope*).

[2] Martin Luther King Jr., "The Case against Tokenism" (1962), in *A Testament of Hope, supra* note 1, at 106, 109.

than themselves." [3] King's agape was not simply about supporting the individual and her preferences as a fixed set of predetermined objectives for the relationship. King's agape was a dynamic encounter with another, challenging the other to look beyond herself.

King regularly offered agape as the model for engaging a world that was hostile to the goals of the civil rights movement. *Agape* is the term used in the Bible to denote sacrificial love, in contrast to *phileo*, which focuses more on the lover's feelings for another, rather than on how the lover can meet the other's needs. The clearest illustration of the distinction is an exchange between Jesus and Peter:

> When they had finished eating, Jesus said to Simon Peter, "Simon son of John, do you truly [agape] me more than these?"
>
> "Yes, Lord," he said, "you know that I [phileo] you." Jesus said, "Feed my lambs."
>
> Again Jesus said, "Simon son of John, do you truly [agape] me?"
>
> He answered, "Yes, Lord, you know that I [phileo] you." Jesus said, "Take care of my sheep."
>
> The third time he said to him, "Simon son of John, do you [phileo] me?" Peter was hurt because Jesus asked him the third time, "Do you [phileo] me?" He said, "Lord, you know all things; you know that I [phileo] you." Jesus said, "Feed my sheep."[4]

[3] "Playboy Interview: Martin Luther King Jr. (1965)," in *A Testament of Hope, supra* note 1, at 340, 349.

[4] John 21:15–17 (NIV). *See, e.g.,* Ed Hindson & Ergun Caner, The Popular Encyclopedia of Apologetics (2008), 333.

When we love those "who oppose us," according to King, we speak of agape. Agape "means nothing sentimental or basically affectionate; it means understanding, redeeming good will for all men, an overflowing love which seeks nothing in return." Agape "is the love of God working in the lives of men," and thus "when we love on the agape level we love men not because we like them, not because their attitudes and ways appeal to us, but because God loves them."[5] The key, for King, was that agape is a "disinterested love" in the sense that "it is a love in which the individual seeks not his own good, but the good of his neighbor," and does not discriminate "between worthy and unworthy people" or on the basis of "any qualities people possess."[6] As Karl Barth put it, agape means "identification with [the neighbor's] interests in utter independence of the question of his attractiveness."[7] The importance of these demands for the civil rights movement is obvious, and King made it explicit, asserting that "the best way to assure oneself that love is disinterested is to have love for the enemy-neighbor from whom you can expect no good in return, but only hostility and persecution."[8]

---

[5] Martin Luther King Jr., "Nonviolence and Racial Justice" (1957), in *A Testament of Hope, supra* note 1, at 5, 8–9.

[6] Martin Luther King Jr., "An Experiment in Love" (1958), in *A Testament of Hope, supra* note 1, at 16, 19.

[7] Karl Barth, *Church Dogmatics* IV/2, trans. G. W. Bromiley (1958), 745.

[8] "I'm very happy that [Jesus] didn't say like your enemies, because it is pretty difficult to like some people. Like is sentimental, and it is

By "disinterested," then, King means that agapic love does not seek gain for self. Even though the love is not contingent on any quality of the person loved, King does not mean that the one loving is disinterested in the person loved, as though it is a nonspecific sentiment that extends to the world without cognizance of its object's particular nature and needs. Indeed, the one loving takes a pronounced interest in the person loved, for agape itself "springs from the need of the other person." Because the white man's "personality is greatly distorted by segregation, and his soul greatly scarred," he "needs the love of the Negro" to "remove his tensions, insecurities, and fears."[9]

King's articulation of agape derived in significant part from the work of the Swedish theologian Anders Nygren and his landmark book *Agape and Eros*.[10] Nygren argued that Christianity departed from prevailing philosophies by defining "the question of the Good" in terms of social

---

pretty difficult to like someone bombing your home; it is pretty difficult to like somebody threatening your children; it is difficult to like congressmen who spend all of their time trying to defeat civil rights. But Jesus says love them, and love is greater than like. Love is understanding, redemptive, creative, good will for all men. And it is this idea, it is this whole ethic of love which is the idea standing at the basis of the student movement." Martin Luther King Jr., "Love, Law, and Civil Disobedience," in *A Testament of Hope, supra* note 1, at 43, 47.

9 Martin Luther King Jr., "An Experiment in Love," in *A Testament of Hope, supra* note 1, at 16, 19.

10 *See* Ira G. Zepp, *The Social Vision of Martin Luther King Jr.* (1989), 109 (demonstrating that King quoted Nygren without citation).

relationships, rather than from the perspective of "the isolated individual."[11] Nygren criticized human love as measured against the standard of divine love, for human love tends to be "only a form of natural self-love, which extends its scope to embrace also benefactors of the self."[12] Laying out themes that echoed in King's work, Nygren noted that "man's natural attitude is a reflection of his neighbor's attitude to him: love is met with love, hate with hate," but Christian love must reflect God's love, so "to isolate neighborly love from love towards God, allowing only the latter to have a religious basis, is therefore entirely wrong."[13]

Nygren found no place in the Christian life for self-love. He condemned the more intimate form of love, "eros" as "acquisitive love" and "egocentric love"[14] because it "does not seek the neighbor for himself," but so "it can utilize him as a means for its own ascent." Citing Plato, Nygren characterized eros as "not concerned with its immediate object," but rather "always detaching itself from its object and using it as a stepping-stone to higher things."[15] Agape is different, according to Nygren, for it is "directed to the neighbor himself, with no further thoughts in mind and no side-long

---

[11] Anders Nygren, *Agape & Eros,* 1982 ed. (1953), 45.

[12] *Id.* at 96–7.

[13] *Id.* at 97.

[14] *Id.* at 175.

[15] *Id.* at 214.

glances at anything else."[16] (As C. S. Lewis puts it, "In love we escape from our self into one other.")[17]

Not only does agape focus on the neighbor himself, but it also must be radically unmotivated and spontaneous in order to reflect divine love. Nygren explains that "when it is said that God loves man, this is not a judgment on what man is like, but on what God is like."[18] Indeed, agape is a value-creating principle, not a value-recognizing principle, for "God does not love that which is already in itself worthy of love, but on the contrary, that which in itself has no worth acquires worth just by becoming the object of God's love."[19] Applying this to Christian love of neighbors, he goes so far as to assert that "if my love for my neighbor is not concerned with him himself, but with a supposed Divine kernel or essence within him, then my love is very far from being unmotivated," and that this misses the whole point of agapic love, a love "that otherwise seems to elude all rational explanation."[20]

Nygren's work provided exhaustive historical and logical support for the argument that our practice of agapic love must not discriminate on the basis of how we are treated by the neighbor, and this argument was central to King's

---

[16] *Id.* at 215.

[17] C. S. Lewis, *An Experiment in Criticism* (1961), 138.

[18] Nygren, *supra* note 11, at 75–6.

[19] *Id.* at 78.

[20] *Id.* at 98.

theological justification for nonviolent resistance. But King did not accept Nygren's more controversial assertion – that our practice of agapic love does not recognize value or worth in the neighbor. King believed that value is inherent in the human soul, and that a person's value does not derive solely from her relationship to God.[21] This is an important deviation from Nygren. Nygren's approach is vulnerable to the development of an impersonal love. If there is nothing about the person that motivates our love – if we are simply passive conduits for God's love – it is not much of a jump to begin conceptualizing agape as a love that is desensitized to the objectives of love in light of the neighbor's nature and needs. In other words, if there is nothing about the neighbor that motivates our love, will there be nothing about the neighbor that shapes our love?

As noted previously, King resisted this temptation by insisting that agapic love must account for the neighbor's needs and be directed toward the neighbor's well-being. Crucially, the neighbor's needs and the criteria for her well-being may not even be recognized, much less acknowledged, by the neighbor herself. Agapic love, as envisioned and practiced by King, does not passively take the shape of the neighbor's own stated preferences. It is premised on an understanding of human nature. King explained:

---

[21] Zepp, *supra* note 10, at 111 ("King opts for the 'values of the human soul' as inherent, rather than the more radical Biblical idea that men have value in terms of their relationship to God").

Agape is not a weak, passive love. It is love in action. Agape is love seeking to preserve and create community. It is insistence on community even when one seeks to break it. Agape is a willingness to go to any length to restore community.[22]

King cast further doubt on the viability of a passive and impersonal agape when he rejected pity, which "may arise from interest in an abstraction called humanity," and emphasized the importance and efficacy of sympathy, which "grows out of a concern for a particular needy human being who lies at life's roadside." Sympathy "is fellow feeling for the person in need – his pain, agony, and burdens," and the "expression of pity devoid of genuine sympathy" will lead "to a new form of paternalism which no self-respecting person can accept."[23] On one hand, then, there is the danger of paternalism that accompanies love that is too far removed from the lived experience of the neighbor; on the other hand, though, stepping into the neighbor's shoes does not mean that we reflexively adopt the neighbor's subjective understanding of her own best interest. Sympathy for the neighbor gives agape its real-world traction, but agape's implications cannot be defined solely by the neighbor's lived experience. Agape pushes the lover and the loved to look beyond themselves.

In this regard, King's practice of agapic love seems more akin to the philosopher Josef Pieper's understanding. Pieper

---

[22] Martin Luther King Jr., "An Experiment in Love," in *A Testament of Hope, supra* note 1, at 20.

[23] *Id.* at 32.

responded to Nygren by pointing out that "in turning to another person with love, man is not a 'channel' and a 'conduit.' Then if ever he is truly subject and person."[24] Loving our neighbor, to Pieper, means allowing the neighbor's existence to enter into our experience and affirming that existence. "The creative power of human love" stems from the explicit confirmation of the neighbor's existence.[25]

This confirmation expresses itself through dynamic, challenging relationships of love. Even within the black community of his own city, King showed that love is not passive. King worked to motivate the community to organize and persist in the Montgomery bus boycott, and he later wrote that the people, even though they were "exhausted by the humiliating experiences that they had constantly faced on the buses ... came to see that it was ultimately more honorable to walk the streets in dignity than to ride the buses in humiliation."[26] King put his own being into the shoes of his neighbor (painfully aware of her exhaustion and humiliation), but he pushed the neighbor to embrace a reality that may have lain beyond her view at the time (eventually she came to see that it was more honorable).

We act as subjects in willing love toward the neighbor based on our personal recognition and response to her worth and her needs. We also acknowledge the neighbor as a

[24] Josef Pieper, *Faith, Hope, Love* (1997), 220.
[25] *Id.* at 174.
[26] Martin Luther King Jr., *Strength to Love* (1981), 151.

subject, not as an object. King cited Martin Buber's "I-Thou" relationship in which one views another person as a "thou," rather than an "It," and thereby avoids relegating persons to the status of things.[27] If the object of our love is a subject in her own right, our love must not be paternalistic or infantilizing; it must reflect an authentic and respectful human encounter. In loving his neighbor – friend or foe, black or white – King was a subject, investing himself in the neighbor in order to see the world through the neighbor's eyes, but insisting that the neighbor expand her view to encompass a truer, less isolated vision of her own well-being.

II. Lawyers (and Clients) as Subjects

Many lawyers will bridle at the suggestion that they should "love" their clients. It can be challenging enough just to serve one's clients effectively, much less to set up unrealistic and unhelpful expectations about the quality of the personal relationship that should blossom in a strictly professional context. Much of this discomfort is based on a misconception of what type of love King was talking about. As noted, agape is not about affection or emotional attachment; it is a selfless commitment to another's well-being. In this sense, the problem is not that lawyers resist such a commitment; the problem is that they are prone to make presumptions about the client's well-being that are in tension with the client's nature.

[27] Martin Buber, *I and Thou* (1923).

Admittedly, expecting agape to gain real-world traction within the legal profession faces significant obstacles. Agape's lessons for lawyers will go nowhere unless lawyers actually conceive of themselves as subjects, a task that is easier said than done. They are not empty vessels or mere extensions of the client's autonomy. Lawyers are moral subjects retained to counsel and, as necessary, to advocate on another subject's behalf. In the United States, unlike the United Kingdom, lawyers are not common carriers, required to represent clients despite moral objection to the cause being pursued. American lawyers are accountable for the clients they decide to take on, as recent controversies reflect.[28] As subjects, they are also accountable for the advice they give, or fail to give.[29]

Lawyers must also acknowledge their clients as subjects. Replacing the "lawyer as mouthpiece" paradigm by elevating the lawyer's own moral convictions as a trump card over the client's own commitments and priorities does

[28] *See* Sacha Pfeiffer, "Harvard Law Group Hits Ropes & Gray," *Boston Globe*, March 15, 2006, at E1 (reporting on Lambda organizing boycott of law firm that represented Catholic Church in effort to circumvent ban on discrimination against same-sex couples in adoption services); Ronald Goldfarb, "Should Lawyers Be Judged by Who Their Clients Are? You Bet," *Contra Costa Times*, April 13, 1997, at F9 (reporting that lawyers at Cravath, Swaine & Moore protested their employer's decision to represent Credit Suisse in dispute with families of Holocaust victims).

[29] *See, e.g.*, Russell Pearce, *Model Rule 1.0: Lawyers Are Morally Accountable*, 70 FORDHAM L. REV. 1805, 1807 (2002).

not further agape. Lawyers must guard against overreaching and remain cognizant of the power disparity in many attorney-client relationships, especially when clients are not sophisticated in legal analysis or experienced with the intricacies of the legal system. If the lawyer and client are both subjects, they will act as partners in a moral dialogue, remaining open to the possibility that their partner in the endeavor may actually teach them something.

Tom Shaffer observes that "in moral discourse, as in political and legal discourse, we don't talk about good people, we talk about rights," and we assume "that what citizens want for one another, or lawyers for their clients, is not goodness but isolation and independence."[30] Shaffer offers a prophetic (and relatively lonely) voice in this regard, objecting to the profession's assumption that "the client and the lawyer, while they may talk to one another, are not likely to influence one another."[31] In particular,

> When the conversation is resolved by the moral asser-
> tion of the client, the profession is likely to talk about the
> lawyer as representing the interests of his client and to
> defend itself by references to the adversary system. When
> the conversation is resolved by the moral assertion of the
> lawyer, the profession is likely to talk about the lawyer as
> representing the interests of society and to defend itself

[30] Thomas L. Shaffer, *Legal Ethics after Babel*, 19 Cap. Univ. L. Rev. 989, 990 (1990).

[31] Thomas L. Shaffer, *On Being a Christian and a Lawyer* (1981), 133.

by talking about the social responsibility of lawyers. The assumption in either case is that the lawyer and client both operate in moral worlds but that their worlds are isolated from one another.[32]

Even when lawyers emerge from the same social world as their clients, they tend not to engage each other on the moral dimension of the representation. Especially in cases involving large and sophisticated clients, more often than not the lawyer abdicates her moral agency in favor of the client's moral assertion – even when, as is usually the case, those assertions are never made explicit. This is a primary dynamic underlying the "lawyer as mouthpiece" paradigm. The lawyer pursues the client's objectives to the brink of illegality, never bothering to unpack the moral implications of the chosen course or to give the client reason to reflect on those implications as part of the decision-making process. The catastrophic results are reflected in several corporate scandals over the past decade, perhaps most clearly in the collapse of Enron.

In the simplest terms, Enron's downfall stemmed from the use of off–balance sheet partnerships to enter into transactions deemed too risky for ordinary commercial entities.[33] The resulting losses and debts were kept hidden from the public because the partnerships were not consolidated with

[32] *Id.*

[33] Deborah L. Rhode & Paul D. Paton, *Lawyers, Ethics, and Enron*, 8 STAN. J. L. BUS. & FIN. 9, 13 (2002).

Enron's other activities on its financial statements.[34] As the partnerships experienced credit problems and had trouble making payments, the system unraveled quickly in 2001, and Enron became the largest bankruptcy filing (at that time) in American history.[35]

Lawyers are by no means solely responsible for Enron's demise, but they do not easily escape culpability. They utterly failed to check Enron's management: reassuring executives that dubious accounting strategies were legal,[36] certifying loan transactions as "true sales,"[37] providing nonsensical justifications for the CFO who wished to avoid disclosure of his compensation,[38] complying with the CEO's request that they not explore the accountants' treatment of transactions before certifying the transactions' validity,[39] and repeatedly facilitating Enron's strategy "of structuring dubious transactions so that nobody could understand them, by using language to describe them in proxy and financial statements that, although literally and technically correct, was in practice completely opaque."[40]

David Westbrook frames Enron's collapse in terms that resonate even more directly with our focus on lawyers'

---

[34] *Id.*

[35] *Id.*

[36] *Id.* at 98.

[37] Robert W. Gordon, *A New Role for Lawyers? The Corporate Counselor After Enron*, 35 CONN. L. REV. 1186 (2003).

[38] *Id.* at 1187.

[39] *Id.*

[40] *Id.* at 1186.

willingness to act as subjects in their relationships with clients. He argues that the collapse stemmed not from a conflict of interest between managers and shareholders,[41] but from an alignment of their interests, for with the rise of equity-based executive compensation,[42] managers and shareholders are equally devoted to raising share prices.[43] To the extent lawyers take on the priorities of their clients, the lawyers will necessarily become interested in the maintenance of share price.[44] Given the degree to which the investing public's perception of the company's financial

---

[41] "[T]he corporation has been understood by the legal academy in terms of the separation of ownership and management functions, in the persons of shareholders on the one hand and managers and directors on the other. This separation has given rise to what has been understood to be the central problem of corporate governance – the perennial possibility that managers would have interests that conflicted with owners. The task of corporation law, then, has been to devise ways to keep managers from abusing their position and taking advantage of the absentee owners of the corporation, the shareholders." David A. Westbrook, *Corporation Law after Enron: The Possibility of a Capitalist Reimagination*, 92 GEO. L.J. 61, 100–1 (2003).

[42] See John C. Coffee, Jr., *What Caused Enron? A Capsule Social and Economic History of the 1990s*, 89 CORNELL L. REV. 269 (2004) ("As of 1990, equity-based compensation for chief executive officers of public corporations in the United States constituted approximately five percent of their total annual compensation; by 1999, this percentage had risen to an estimated sixty percent").

[43] Westbrook, *supra* note 41, at 97.

[44] *Id.* ("Insofar as they sympathize with their clients (one way to keep one's job), accountants and lawyers are indirectly interested in the maintenance of a corporation's share price").

status drives share price, the lawyers can be swept along in the ongoing effort to manipulate that perception. This helps explain why Enron's lawyers appear to have offered little resistance to, or even reflection on, the path charted by Enron's managers.

Or consider the case of Joseph Collins, a well-credentialed, big-firm attorney representing Refco, a financial services company that collapsed in 2005. Collins ended up in jail for helping Refco executives conceal millions of dollars in debt. Collins and his colleagues at Mayer Brown prepared loan documents "whereby one Refco entity loaned money to third parties, who in turn loaned the money to another Refco entity, so that it could pay off a debt it owed (but could not repay) to the first Refco entity." This resulted in the temporary removal of "hundreds of millions of dollars in uncollectable related-party debt from the company's books," replacing it "with what appeared to be a collectable debt from an unrelated party." In reality, the only money "that actually changed hands in these transactions was the money paid as 'interest' to the unrelated third parties who facilitated the bad debt being temporarily removed from the books."[45] Collins and Mayer Brown handled all the transactions, including the sale of a majority interest in Refco, a bond issue by Refco, an $800 million loan to Refco from

[45] Paula Schaefer, *Harming Business Clients With Zealous Advocacy: Rethinking the Attorney Advisor's Touchstone*, 12 (available at http://ssrn.com/abstract=1567657). *See In re Refco Securities Litig.*, 503 F. Supp. 2d 611 (2007).

banks, and a subsequent $670 million initial public offering. When the related-party loan transactions came to light, the company collapsed. At his trial, Collins testified that he did not knowingly violate the law, and he offered technical reasons to defend nondisclosure of these transactions; he also maintained that, in terms of both the nondisclosure decision and the round-trip loan transactions, he was acting at the company's direction.[46] All this time, Refco executives were selling their stock and pocketing millions.[47]

Dubious financial transactions are also at the center of some of the more recent travails experienced by financial services companies, including the collapse of Lehman Brothers. One such type of transaction is referred to as "Repo 105" deals. Repurchase transactions are "collateralized loans involving a sale of a security for cash in which the seller commits to buy back the security at a specified price on a designated future date."[48] These are common sources of short-term financing for many companies. Olufunmilayo Arewa explains that the Repo 105 transactions "essentially enabled Lehman Brothers to shift assets off its balance sheet at the end of each quarter in exchange for cash, making it appear as if Lehman had sold the assets when it in fact had not," thus making "Lehman's balance sheet appear to be healthier and less leveraged than was actually

---

[46] Schaefer, *supra* note 45, at 28.

[47] *Id.* at 25.

[48] Olufunmilayo B. Arewa, *Risky Business: The Credit Crisis and Failure (Part II)*, 104 Nw. U.L. Rev. Colloquy 421, 427 (2010).

the case." Though "the assets were returned to Lehman's balance sheet just days after issuing the financial reports reflecting the Repo 105 transactions," Lehman did not disclose the transactions in its financial statement filings.[49] Though the role of lawyers in these deals is not yet entirely clear, it would hardly be surprising to learn that lawyers made the transactions possible and failed to raise red flags along the way.

While many critics would accuse the attorneys for Enron, Refco, or (possibly) Lehman Brothers of being "too loyal" to their clients, in reality they were not loyal enough – they acted as conduits for the client's stated objectives, not as moral subjects calling the clients to reflect critically on the wisdom and implications of those objectives. Paula Schaefer explains:

> While lawyers defend [a] technical approach to legal compliance in the wake of a scandal, their clients are often the casualty that lies in the background. The argument seems to be that this is what the client wanted, so it is too bad the client was harmed in the process. What the argument misses is that perhaps the client did not make an informed choice to engage in the liability-creating behavior because the lawyer never provided that advice. Rather, the lawyer zealously pursued the client's stated agenda in a manner that technically complied with some aspect of the law, but nonetheless created liability that a knowledgeable client may have chosen to avoid.[50]

[49] *Id.*
[50] Schaefer, *supra* note 45, at 12.

In very practical terms, "ignoring moral intuitions about a business client's plan often means ignoring the basis for liability, such as a lack of good faith or fraudulent intent."[51]

Lawyers who fail to heed agape's admonition to act as subjects in their relationships with clients will be unable to serve as a needed reality check. In Enron's case, in particular, this meant that the managers' narrowly defined vision of the corporation's best interests went unchallenged. Much of the debacle might have been averted, in Deborah Rhode's view, if the lawyers had "brought a stronger, more objective and more critical voice to the disclosure process."[52] If we expect lawyers to help their clients steer clear of debacles such as the Enron, Refco, and Lehman Brothers collapses (as we should), we are looking to lawyers for more than technical expertise. To the extent that these companies' lawyers acted as empty vessels by which their clients could achieve their own perceived interests, the lawyers served neither the clients' actual interests nor the interests of the nonshareholder constituents with whom the client's interests are invariably linked. These companies needed a relationship with a moral subject possessing legal expertise, not simply a series of transactions with a technician possessing legal expertise.

[51] *Id.* at 18–19.

[52] Rhode, *supra* note 33, at 19. I examine the lawyers' role in the Enron collapse more closely in chapter 10 of *Conscience and the Common Good: Reclaiming the Space Between Person and State.*

Admittedly, agape may still appear to be an uneasy fit for the corporate lawyer. Most of the human beings whose interests were marginalized in these episodes – shareholders, rank-and-file employees, community members who depend on the company's continued viability – are not in direct relationship with the lawyer. They are far from the action and out of sight. Practicing agape in the context of a face-to-face relationship with a real human being is challenging enough; practicing agape in the context of representing a corporate entity made up of far-flung and often anonymous stakeholders seems more difficult by an order of magnitude.

So how does agape apply to distant and impersonal relationships? This is not a question that was foreign to Martin Luther King Jr. From the outset of his ministry, he preached agape to congregants whose oppressors included distant legislators and judges. In such contexts, agape aims less at the particular needs of the distant individual and more at what we cannot help but know about human well-being. Indeed, the conditions necessary for the flourishing of distant individuals will often be the same conditions necessary for the flourishing of those who stand before us. Racist views harmed the well-being of both the whites who jeered participants in the Montgomery bus boycott and the government officials who erected the legal framework that made the boycott necessary. The nonviolence that marked the behavior of King's congregants toward the jeerers in their immediate path had positive effects that spilled over into city councils and state legislatures across the region. Conversely, by elevating the short-term interests of the company's executives over the long-term interests of the company's shareholders and other stakeholders, Enron's lawyers did neither group any favor. Witness the fates of Ken Lay and Jeffrey Skilling.[53] One clue about what it means to practice agape in a distant and impersonal relationship may be to remember what it means to practice agape in the relationship that lies before us.

King did not always tell his audience what they wanted to hear. Nor did he limit himself to implementing predetermined courses of action. That approach would have been the easy thing to do, but it would not have been consistent with his commitment to his community's well-being, or with the premise of agape. A lawyer who aims to serve her client cannot reflexively prioritize her client's comfort, or her own.

III. Lawyers' Trust Problem

Lawyers who seek to practice agape by acting as moral subjects in their client relationships do not face an easy road. Indeed, the road is getting more difficult by the day. Competitive pressures are pushing law firms to greater efficiencies, but those efficiencies can make the attorney-client

---

[53] Alexei Barrionuevo, "Enron Chiefs Guilty of Fraud and Conspiracy," *N.Y. Times*, May 25, 2006, at A1 (reporting on guilty verdicts in trial of Skilling and Lay).

relationship more difficult to distinguish from any other provider-consumer transaction. Clients understandably have become more aggressive about reducing costs, and our globalized economy provides an array of avenues by which to do so. It remains to be seen how these changes will alter the nature of the attorney-client relationship, and whether they will contribute to marginalizing the attorney's role as trusted personal adviser and normalizing a conception of the attorney as technician.[54] There is reason to believe that trust may lose its place as a constitutive element of the attorney-client relationship as the relationship itself becomes less personal, more distant, and more fungible. As the relationship becomes more tenuous, it may lack the resources to support any function beyond the strictly technical, and the lawyer may not have the requisite knowledge or standing to act as anything more than a mouthpiece. The lawyer as subject may recede even further from view.

Exploring the professional relevance of agape thus requires us to explore the professional relevance of trust. "Trust" is a ubiquitous term, but usually left undefined, functioning as a presumptively shared but unspecified touchstone of social virtue and cooperation. What we mean precisely when we talk about trust matters a great deal,

---

[54] I don't mean "technician" as a pejorative, for an attorney who is not technically competent cannot even aspire to be a trusted adviser; my concern is that technical competence will expand from being one dimension of the lawyer's role to being the entirety of the lawyer's role.

both for our understanding of the concept itself, for our understanding of each other, and for our understanding of the lawyer's work, of which trust is such a key component. Some definitions are broad enough to avoid much controversy; they tend to center around the concept of willful vulnerability. Claire Hill and Erin O'Hara capture the expert consensus that "trust is a state of mind that enables its possessor to be willing to make herself vulnerable to another – that is, to rely on another despite a positive risk that the other will act in a way that can harm the truster."[55]

Different professional contexts may require different degrees and manifestations of trust. I may trust a baker enough to purchase my bread from him even though we know next to nothing about each other. The physical appearance of the bread and the bakery, coupled with my awareness of periodic inspections by the state health department, are usually sufficient reassurances. When I seek the help of an attorney, by contrast, the specific tasks to be performed

---

[55] Claire A. Hill & Erin Ann O'Hara, *A Cognitive Theory of Trust*, 84 WASH. U. L. REV. 1717, 1724 (2006); *see also, e.g.*, Margaret M. Blair & Lynn A. Stout, *Trust, Trustworthiness, and the Behavioral Foundations of Corporate Law*, 149 U. PA. L. REV. 1735, 1739–40 (2001) (defining trust as a "willingness to make oneself vulnerable to another, based on the belief that the trusted person will choose not to exploit one's vulnerability"); Frank B. Cross, *Law and Trust*, 93 GEO. L.J. 1457, 1461 (2005) (defining trust as "the voluntary ceding of control over something valuable to another person or entity, based upon one's faith in the ability and willingness of that person or entity to care for the valuable thing").

are not always foreseeable; my needs often implicate a range of issues and areas of expertise; the quality of the services may – depending on my level of sophistication and expertise – be inscrutable; and effective service may turn on my willingness to share information about myself (or my company) that is far more personal and private than anything I share with the baker. I need to trust my attorney in a way that is both deeper and broader than the way in which I trust the baker.[56]

Research shows that trust arises from – and is a product of – our assessment of the relationships in which we are participating, not just a knowledge-based cost-benefit analysis. Claire Hill and Lynn Stout recount that "individuals in social dilemmas decide to cooperate or defect not primarily by calculating their individual payoffs but instead by looking at and trying to decipher others' beliefs, likely behaviors, and social relationships with themselves." Trust is enhanced dramatically when researchers hint that players ought to cooperate, when players share a sense of group identity, and when players expect each other to cooperate. The power of these social variables is especially noteworthy given that they "do not change the economic structure of the game."[57]

---

[56] Some of this difference is captured in the distinction between cognitive trust – i.e., based on rational assessments of potential costs and benefits flowing from the decision to trust – and affective trust – i.e., grounded more in emotions and feelings of security arising out of the relationship.

[57] Blair & Stout, *supra* note 55, at 1742.

The social nature of trust is underscored in the context of ongoing relationships. Even if I lack the knowledge sufficient to create clear expectations about what a person will do in a given situation, I will be more likely to believe that it will facilitate my well-being when we are involved in an ongoing relationship. Tom Tyler explains that "in the context of groups with which people have social connections, people's trust judgments become more strongly linked to identity concerns, and less strongly linked to resource exchange."[58] In other words, it becomes less about predicting what I stand to gain or lose from the transaction in which I am vulnerable, and more about creating and defending my social identity. For example, the trust I have in my wife is not primarily a function of what I stand to gain or lose from any particular transaction with her, but rather of the degree to which our relationship helps ground my own identity, my belief that our relationship also helps ground her identity, and my corresponding belief that we are both favorably moved by our mutual vulnerabilities. The same considerations animate my trust in old friends, and even, to a much lower degree, my trust in faculty colleagues. When I betray the trust of a longtime friend, the resulting disruption I experience is not just a function of jeopardizing future benefits that I would have realized from the relationship;

[58] Tom R. Tyler, "Why Do People Rely on Others? Social Identity and Social Aspects of Trust," in *Trust in Society,* ed. Karen Cook (2001), 285, 289.

the betrayal is a jolt to my self-understanding and sense of personal coherence.

A cost-benefit reliance on market discipline or regulatory codes can only go so far. A trust that is grounded in the personal relationship between the attorney and client allows for a broader and deeper vulnerability than what is afforded by calculation. If my trust in my friend is based only on my calculation that my friendship is too valuable for him to risk alienating me, or I know that his reputation as a friend will suffer if he betrays me, we would hardly call that a friendship. I trust my friend because I believe that mutual trust is a central attribute of friendship – it comes with the territory.

King's relationships of trust allowed him to challenge others to embrace their better angels. He did not just explain to the African American community of Montgomery that a boycott of the bus system was in their long-term best interests, for example. He established a trust relationship through acts of solidarity and shared vulnerability. Throughout his ministry, he did not just preach at his audience; he walked with them, both figuratively and literally.

Trust in the fullest sense requires more than the awareness that legal remedies are available in the event that the trust is breached. Trust, as a willingness to make one's self vulnerable to another, is relational. An arms-length transaction between two interest-maximizing individuals may often require a certain degree of trust, but that is not the quality of trust that has made possible the attorney's roles as counselor, advocate, and public citizen. Trust as rational calculation may work fine in my relationship with "a" car dealer, but how will it work in my relationship with "my" attorney?

A. Trust under Pressure

It is this sort of relational trust – by which I mean a client's trust in the relationship itself, as opposed to the client's trust in the market or regulatory safeguards in which the relationship is embedded – that is essential to a lawyer's practice of agape, but that is under increasing pressure today. The boundaries between the provision of legal services and the provision of other business-related services are quickly blurring,[59] and lawyers need to come to grips with the fact that one's status as a "professional" is of decreasing relevance to one's success meeting the demands of customers.[60] The blurring of these boundaries can be best captured by several overlapping trends, all of which will shape the long-term viability of relational trust – and with it, the capacity to practice agape.

1. **Globalization.** Today's corporate lawyers not only face intense competition from the law firm across town; because of our

---

[59] For a helpful overview of the regulatory developments driving this trend, see Laurel Terry, *The Future Regulation of the Legal Profession: The Impact of Treating the Legal Profession as "Service Providers,"* 2008 PROF. LAW. 189.

[60] *See* Thomas D. Morgan, *The Vanishing American Lawyer* (2010).

globalized economy, they now face competition from firms across the ocean, and firms in some foreign jurisdictions have competitive advantages due to recent regulatory reforms. British and Australian firms, for example, may have easier access to capital because nonlawyer investors can take ownership stakes in the firm. In England especially, there has been a major push to make legal services more accessible by cutting traditional professional safeguards that are now viewed as drags on competition and artificial inflators of price. Lay governance of legal services is on the rise in England. As John Leubsdorf puts it, in the United States "we are witnessing the decline of the ideal of professional self-regulation at the same time that the ideal has been almost entirely demolished in England."[61]

Even more problematic is the fact that the global provision of legal services stretches the attorney-client relationship over greater distances and (often) through subcontractors, tending to involve less personal connections between provider and client. Similar dynamics hold true when a firm's operations are divided up into different locations, even within the United States.[62] The connections are stretched further,

---

[61] John Leubsdorf, *Legal Ethics Falls Apart*, 57 BUFF. L. REV. 959, 961 (2009).

[62] *See, e.g.*, "Law Firm Bringing 187 Jobs to Southwest Ohio," Associated Press, April 26, 2010 (reporting that Wilmer Hale, headquartered in Boston and Washington D.C., is establishing a business services center in Kettering, Ohio to house "current and new staff in finance, human resources, information technology and other areas to support the company's offices worldwide").

though, when work is sent outside the firm and across the ocean. There has been a dramatic rise in the number of third-party "legal process outsourcing" vendors both in the United States[63] and overseas.[64] In India, there is a booming industry of companies serving as "intermediaries between the American corporation or American law firm looking to outsource and Indians eager to do the work."[65] It is not just document review and information management. Lawyers employed by vendors in India are doing legal research, patent work, and brief writing.[66] The lack of face-to-face interaction is not conducive to trust. Researchers have found that visual contact significantly increases cooperation rates in social dilemmas even though the ability to see the other participants does not change the payoffs.[67] Further, the global provision of legal services often occurs without the shared

---

[63] *See, e.g.*, Barbara Rattle, "Legal Outsourcing Firm to Open 100-Employee Center in Provo," *Salt Lake City Enterprise*, March 12, 2012 ("Mindcrest, a Chicago-based firm that provides legal process outsourcing services in the areas of litigation, corporate legal services and legal content and publishing, is in the process of setting up a Utah office that will employ 100 people.").

[64] *See, e.g.*, Heather Timmons, "Outsourcing to India Draws Western Lawyers," *N.Y. Times*, August 4, 2010, at B1 ("Revenue at India's legal outsourcing firms is expected to grow to $440 million this year, up 38 percent from 2008, and should surpass $1 billion by 2014 ....").

[65] Jayanth K. Krishnan, *Outsourcing and the Globalizing Legal Profession*, 48 WM. & MARY L. REV. 2189, 2203 (2007).

[66] *Id.* at 2193.

[67] Blair & Stout, *supra* note 55, at 1769.

background of cultural norms and values in which trust is rooted. Trust relationships develop from a sense that we are responsible for each other.[68] Studies have also shown that trust diminishes as social distance increases.[69]

We know that trust and distrust are contagious, and one reason why trust is so fragile is that the "erosion of trust in one context reverberates throughout society in unpredictable and disruptive ways."[70] Even while stretching and "thinning" the attorney-client relationships, globalization ratchets up the level of interconnectedness dramatically. If the procompetition reforms in other countries make trust less of a hallmark of the attorney-client relationship by making the relationship just like any other provider-consumer relationship in the marketplace, the effects will not be kept off American shores easily.[71]

When an Indian legal service provider does work for a London firm who is representing a Chicago company,

---

[68] See Misztal, *infra* note 98, at 202 ("We can only learn to feel responsible for others and construct trust relationships by sharing with others a common fate, culture, rights and duties").

[69] Raymond H. Brescia, *Trust in the Shadows: Law, Behavior, and Financial Re-Regulation*, 57 BUFF. L. REV. 1361, 1395 (2009) ("Research shows consistently that where there is greater social distance between individuals, they are both less trusting, and each is more willing to take advantage of the other person.").

[70] Rebecca M. Bratspies, *Regulatory Trust*, 51 ARIZ. L. REV. 575, 605–6 (2009).

[71] *See, e.g.*, Laurel Terry, *The Legal World is Flat: Globalization and Its Effect on Lawyers Practicing in Non-Global Law Firms*, 28 Nw. J. INT'L L. & BUS. 527 (2008).

relational trust may be in short supply. At the same time, participants in the relationship "are more dependent on trust (and less on familiarity) to supplement those interstitial points where system confidence is not sufficient."[72] Parties depend on contractual safeguards, assuming that the means of enforcement are stable and predictable. More fundamentally, though, can contract maintain the sort of trust that has traditionally been thought to set attorneys apart from other providers? By outpacing personal familiarity and the reach of law, the global economy tests the boundaries of attorney-client trust. A lack of trust may contribute to the tendency to use lawyers for their technical competence on discrete tasks, rather than relying on them for a wider-ranging advisory role.

2. **The Disaggregation of Legal Services.** Much of the discussion on outsourcing focuses on the fact that an overseas third party is being brought into the attorney-client relationship, but there is another element to the outsourcing phenomenon that is just as important from the standpoint of relational trust: outsourcing is based on the disaggregation of legal services. If legal services, like manufacturing, can be stripped down to their component parts and tasked to the lowest-cost provider, is relational trust still part of the equation? Are attorneys selling a product, or are they selling, in a very real sense, a relationship? Put simply, can relationships be disaggregated?

[72] Adam B. Seligman, *The Problem of Trust* (1997), 160.

The mining company Rio Tinto recently announced that it had contracted with CPA Global, a legal process outsourcing company, to have a team of CPA lawyers in India take on a significant part of Rio Tinto's work, including "more sophisticated and strategic work," not just information management. Rio Tinto's managing attorney explained the company's standard for using CPA lawyers: "If you had a junior associate sitting next to you, would you hand the assignment to that junior associate? If the answer is 'yes,' it can probably go to India."[73]

Rio Tinto's move is a harbinger of the world to come, according to Mitt Regan and Palmer Heeton. They argue that

> to compete in this world, law firms will have to consider how they might engage in the same disaggregation process as their clients. That is, they will need to break work down into discrete units and determine who is the most cost-efficient provider of each component. In some cases, that provider may be outside the firm, and the firm will need to engage in outsourcing.[74]

---

[73] Interview by Richard Susskind with Leah Cooper, Managing Attorney, Rio Tinto (October 9, 2009), http://www.legalweek. com/legal-week/analysis/1556450/legal-process-outsourcing-r ichard-susskind-leah-cooper (quoted in Milton C. Regan, Jr. & Palmer T. Heenan, *Supply Chains and Porous Boundaries: The Disaggregation of Legal Services*, 78 FORD. L. REV. 2137, 2139 [2010]).

[74] Regan & Heenan, *supra* note 73, at 2139.

Firms may need to cultivate more capability to serve as project managers, "with the goal of selecting the optimal mix of personnel and technology to provide service on various matters."[75] Technology is a driving force here, for dramatic advances in information technology have, according to Tom Morgan, transformed "lawyer work that used to be seen as complex, unique and worthy of substantial fees into a set of 'commodities' – simple, repetitive operations that will be provided to clients by the lowest bidder."[76]

But it is not all about technology, and it is not all about routine tasks. It is also about increasing specialization among lawyers that allows the divvying up even of tasks that require technical expertise. More fundamentally, though, it is about how we view legal services. Trust in a relationship – as opposed to trust that a discrete task will be performed competently – presumes a relationship of sufficient breadth and depth to provide a baseline of mutual knowledge, familiarity, and confidence. The disaggregation of legal services makes that baseline more elusive. As Regan and Heeton point out, firms have been engaged in disaggregation for quite some time, dividing the various components of a single matter among paralegals, contract attorneys, junior associates, senior associates, income partners, and

---

[75] *Id.* at 2190.

[76] Thomas D. Morgan, *The Vanishing American Lawyer* (2010), 94; *see also* Terry, *Legal World Is Flat, supra* note 71, at 542 (arguing that lawyers will need to develop stronger skills in managing supply chains).

equity partners.[77] Intrafirm disaggregation – in which tasks are usually divided up hierarchically – can still support a meaningful relationship of trust, usually between the responsible partner and the client. To the extent that a matter is divided up horizontally between a firm and outside providers, not just vertically within the firm, will those relationships of trust suffer?

3. The Rise of In-House Counsel. The move to disaggregate is, in some ways, an extension of what corporate clients have been doing for a while now. On the client side, the focus has not been so much on splitting up particular legal matters, but on splitting up the company's legal needs into separate matters, rather than investing in an overarching relationship with a particular firm. This has corresponded to the rising power of in-house counsel vis-à-vis outside attorneys, which is another trend making lawyers less distinct from other business service providers.[78] As Morgan puts it, today "private law firms can best be understood as inside counsel's version of contract lawyers."[79] In an effort to control

---

[77] Regan & Heenan, *supra* note 73, at 2148.

[78] *See* Marc Galanter & Thomas Palay, "The Transformation of the Big Law Firm," in *Lawyers' Ideals/Lawyers' Practices: Transformations in the American Legal Profession,* ed. Robert Nelson et al. (1992), 48; Ronald Gilson, *The Devolution of the Legal Profession: A Demand Side Perspective,* 49 MD. L. REV. 869, 900–3 (1990).

[79] Morgan, *supra* note 60, at 119.

costs and provide more immediate response to management needs, general counsel report that they are more willing to handle matters internally and to turn to nonlawyers. As one general counsel remarked, "Sometimes you don't need a paralegal or lawyer to do certain things, as long as there is proper supervision."[80]

Even when outside counsel are used, they are more likely to be used intermittently on discrete projects. Rather than maintaining decades-long relationships with a primary firm tasked with all of the corporation's legal needs, the growth of in-house legal departments has allowed companies to unbundle their needs and distribute the work among many firms. This has been assumed to give companies more control over quality and price, and the ability to seek out specific expertise for specific matters. Under the old model of using a single firm for all of the company's needs over many years, the company found itself vulnerable, for the costs of exiting that relationship and educating a new law firm were significant. The flight from vulnerability, of course, might also be the flight from opportunities for trust. As an attorney's knowledge of, and experience with, the client narrows, she lacks the foundation to be anything more than a technician working on isolated projects, rather than a partner engaged in the stewardship of the client's well-being.

[80] Rachel M. Zahorsky, *Changing Demands Have In-House Counsel Gaining over Outside Firms*, ABA JOURNAL, March 15, 2010, at http://www.abajournal.com/weekly/article/changing_demands_have_in-house_counsel_gaining_over_outside_firms_gcs_say.

Recent empirical research has shown that current relationships between corporate clients and their preferred legal providers may be "stickier" than this narrative suggests,[81] but at least in comparison to the middle of the twentieth century, clients are less likely to invest in a long-term, comprehensive relationship with one law firm and are more likely to farm legal work out to multiple firms, limiting some representations to a single matter. This development may (or may not) have been good for the bottom line, but it is not good for optimizing trust between law firms and their corporate clients. Researchers have observed that participants in social dilemmas "were more likely to cooperate when they believed that their contribution was important to the group's welfare," for "as the size of the loss to the group from an individual's defection increased, the likelihood of defection decreased." In other words, "the more vulnerable one becomes, the greater the likelihood that a trusted person will in fact prove trustworthy."[82]

One-shot deals do not provide a robust grounding for trust. The result is part of a broader, societywide move (not just in law, but in medicine and securities, for example) from trust to verification – providing information to consumers, leaving it to them to engage in independent verification of the quality and veracity of the services in question. It is

---

[81] *See* David B. Wilkins, *Team of Rivals? Toward a New Model of the Corporate Attorney/Client Relationship* (ssrn.com/abstract=1517342).

[82] Blair & Stout, *supra* note 55, at 1769.

premised on a functioning market of information, rather than a set of relationships with trusted providers. Tamar Frankel sees this shift as ideological, reflecting a belief that "human nature is self-centered, selfish, and prone to dishonesty and that the markets will protect people from each other's harm by helping them to protect themselves."[83]

4. The Decline of Self-Regulation. One obvious reminder that attorneys must live up to a different set of normative standards than other market providers is that attorneys determine their own standards, or at least they have in the past. The state bar operates under the authority of the judiciary, but the courts have tended to be deferential toward the bar's recommendations. Self-regulation has been a hallmark of the profession, and its many defenders insist that lawyers understand the uniqueness of their role, and thus will carve out more appropriate – usually more demanding – ethical expectations than nonlawyers will. If trust is an important attribute of the lawyer-client relationship, lawyers can take steps to help make sure that it stays at the center of that relationship.

But what if lawyers no longer hold their regulatory future in their own hands? And what if corporate lawyers end up subject to the same set of obligations that every other business provider is? Self-regulation is in full retreat in Europe, and though the idea remains viable in the

---

[83] Tamar Frankel, *Trust and Honesty: America's Business Culture at a Crossroads* (2006), 58.

United States, legislatures have been increasingly willing to ignore it when the public interest demands. After the savings & loan crisis in the 1980s, Congress enacted the Financial Institutions Reform, Recovery, and Enforcement Act of 1989 (FIRREA), a statute that was a "get tough measure" affecting financial institutions and their directors, officers, employees, controlling stockholders, consultants, appraisers, accountants, and lawyers. As John Leubsdorf observes, "unlike the bar and bench, Congress did not think that lawyers are special."[84]

The trend came into relief in the wake of Enron and the other corporate scandals of 2001 and 2002, as Congress (and the American Bar Association in an attempt to head off Congress) placed new obligations on corporate attorneys. The Sarbanes-Oxley Act and American Bar Association (ABA) Rule 1.13 now require the attorney to go "up the ladder" when she is aware that a corporate employee is violating the law or a legal obligation to the corporation, and the violation is likely to result in substantial injury to the corporation. The attorney must report the conduct to the highest authority in the corporation if lower authorities fail to address the problem. If the highest authority fails to come through, the attorney may disclose to third parties information necessary to prevent the injury, including information normally protected from disclosure by confidentiality rules. Congress has also included lawyers in its regulation of "debt

[84] Leubsdorf, supra note 61, at II(A).

relief agencies,"[85] and on the international front, an inter-governmental body designed to combat money laundering and financing for terrorists has recommended that lawyers be required to report their clients' suspicious transactions.[86] As the delegate Lawrence Fox complained during the debate about Rule 1.13 in the ABA's House of Delegates, "Our profession is under attack."[87]

Proponents of self-regulation insist that it is necessary to maintain attorneys' independence from the state and loyalty to their clients. Recent encroachments on self-regulation have served to buttress these arguments. Some of these measures have effectively deputized attorneys to monitor and possibly report on their clients. As discussed later, these measures can threaten both client well-being and the public interest unless the attorney's duties are exercised against a robust back-ground of relational trust.[88] At the same time, the expanding range of legal compliance mechanisms applied to corporations have had the effect of diluting the attorney's distinctive

---

[85] See Bankruptcy Abuse Prevention and Consumer Protection Act of 2005, 11 U.S.C. § 101(12A).

[86] See Financial Action Task Force Recommendations 12, 16 (http://www.fatf-gafi.org/document/28/0,3343,en_32250379_322 36920_33658140_1_1_1_1,00.html); *see also* Laurel Terry et al., *Transnational Legal Practice*, 43 INT'L LAW. 943 (2009); Nicole M. Healy et al., *U.S. and International Anti-Money Laundering Developments*, 43 INT'L LAW. 795, 799 (2009).

[87] Fred Rodgers, *Actions of the ABA House of Delegates at Its Annual Meeting in San Francisco, CA, Aug. 11–12, 2003*, COLO. LAW. (October 2003).

[88] See discussion, *infra*.

role in corporate counseling. Compliance obligations generally are framed in a way that warrants their distribution
among a variety of corporate constituents. As Tanina Rostain
observes, "rather than define compliance mandates in broad
legal terms and leave to counsel their application to corporate
operations, [a compliance-based regime] calls for the participation of different types of knowledge professionals."[89] Indeed,
a compliance consulting industry "has emerged emphasizing the capacity to provide multidisciplinary services," and
nonlawyers play a significant role.[90] In-house counsel may
maintain control "over certain key functions," but nonlawyer specialists will be responsible for other functions. It is
not yet clear how the lines will be drawn, nor "what their
implications are for lawyers' power inside the corporation."[91]
If lawyers are pushed out of a broader counseling role toward
more narrowly defined technical tasks, will the capacity for
practicing agape similarly narrow?

5. **Multidisciplinary Practice.** The move toward multidisciplinary
practice (MDP) exacerbates these trends.[92] Premised on the

---

[89] Tanina Rostain, *General Counsel in the Age of Compliance:
Preliminary Findings and New Research Questions*, 21 GEO. J.
LEGAL ETHICS 465, 468 (2008).

[90] *Id.* at 481.

[91] *Id.*

[92] For a helpful overview of the debate surrounding MDP proposals,
see Paul Paton, *Multidisciplinary Practice Redux: Globalization,
Core Values, and Reviving the MDP Debate in America*, 78 FORD. L.
REV. 2193 (2010).

belief that corporate clients would prefer "one-stop shopping" for their service needs, calls for permitting MDP insist that the bar's traditional prohibition on lawyers partnering with nonlawyers is inefficient, unnecessary, and archaic. Clients' needs do not observe neat categorical boundaries; thus neither should lawyers' services. Tom Morgan forecasts that "ours will not become a society with no persons specially trained to deal with legal issues, but people we today call lawyers seem destined primarily to provide a form of business consulting service rather than traditional legal advice and litigation."[93] Clients, it seems, already view legal services providers as another category of third-party suppliers, as legal departments need to be "as metrics-driven as manufacturing, HR, or sales."[94] Fifty-nine percent of chief legal officers "had fired, or were considering firing, at least one of their outside law firms during the current calendar year, with 'cost management issues' topping their list of grievances."[95] Why should lawyers place themselves in a separate category, beyond the influence of, and synergies made available by, nonlawyer business providers?

From the perspective of trust, the relevant question is whether blurring the organizational lines between law

---

[93] Morgan, *supra* note 60, at 9.

[94] Interview with Cisco General Counsel, Quoted in William Henderson, *Are We Selling Results or Resumes? The Underexplored Linkage between Human Resource Strategies and Firm-Specific Capital*, at 5 (ssrn.com/abstract=1121238).

[95] *Id.* at 6.

firms and other providers blurs the distinctiveness of the attorney-client relationship as well. David Luban sees MDP as making lawyers "indistinguishable from accountants, investment bankers, financial advisors, or business consultants."[96] Morgan hopes that the overlap extends to the virtues traditionally associated with lawyers. He argues:

> While many of the characteristics attributed to professionals – integrity, loyalty, keeping confidences, and a commitment to serve the client effectively – represent highly praiseworthy traits to which any moral person should aspire, those characteristics are ultimately those of individuals, not groups. It is individual lawyers – and non-lawyers acting both alongside and in competition with lawyers – that we hope will act in ways traditionally called "professional."[97]

From the perspective of agapic love, my concern about MDP is not premised on a belief that individual attorneys are more virtuous than other professionals. A quick scan of attorney disciplinary matters quickly puts that fable to rest. Like anyone else, attorneys are flawed creatures, prone to self-dealing and ethical shortcuts. But has the profession's traditional narrative about the attorney's role – including relational trust as a constitutive element of that role – served as at least a partial check on the attorneys' pursuit

---

[96] David Luban, *Asking the Right Questions*, 72 TEMP. L. REV. 839, 839 (1999).

[97] Morgan, *supra* note 60, at 26–7.

of their own interests? As competitive pressures and the by-products of regulatory initiatives combine to make lawyers less distinct from other market providers, there may be a decreasing amount of definitional content built into the lawyer's role.

Notwithstanding the hollowing out of the definitional attributes of "lawyer," lawyers and clients are free to choose whatever particular level of "trust" they would like via contract. The problem is that, once we start treating trust as an off-the-rack term open for negotiation – for example, through contractual provisions covering confidentiality or conflicts of interest – we are talking about a very different sort of trust. Tocqueville insisted that social life was not based on contract, where one could withdraw from one's obligations, but "rather on a theory of community, assuming that the pursuit of their own interest by free individuals brings them into contact with others, which stimulates concern for those others."[98] Or as Stout and Blair put it, "describing a relationship as a contract both assumes and legitimates the adoption of a purely self-interested preference function by both parties."[99] Is the trust embodied by a twenty-first-century corporate lawyer defined by self-transcending relationships, rather than by self-dominated contracts, in any meaningful sense?

6. Law Firm Culture. As a by-product of social dynamics, trust obviously is shaped by the culture of the organizations in

[98] Barbara A. Misztal, *Trust in Modern Societies* (1996), 28.
[99] Blair & Stout *supra* note 53, at 1784.

which people work. Deference to organizational leaders is influenced by the perception that the leaders share the organization's values, for example.[100] More broadly, understanding trust requires us to examine "institutions as repositories of a legacy of values" and to realize the extent to which "human beings' concepts of duties and obligations are influenced by the societal institutions which organize ways in which people are bound together."[101] Dan Kahan's work has shown how, in collective action scenarios, "individuals adopt not a materially calculating posture but rather a richer, more emotionally nuanced reciprocal one." In particular, when "they perceive that others are behaving cooperatively, individuals are moved by honor, altruism, and like dispositions to contribute to public goods even without the inducement of material incentives," but when "they perceive that others are shirking or otherwise taking advantage of them, individuals are moved by resentment and pride to withhold their own cooperation and even to engage in personally costly forms of retaliation."[102]

---

[100] *See* Tom R. Tyler, "Why Do People Rely on Others? Social Identity and Social Aspects of Trust," in *Trust in Society*, ed. Karen Cook (2001), 285, 294 ("[P]eople care more about the quality of their treatment by authorities if they feel that they share the organization's values. When people share the organization's values, how they are treated by authorities has a stronger influence on their willingness to defer to those authorities.").

[101] Misztal, *supra* note 98, at 25.

[102] Dan M. Kahan, *The Logic of Reciprocity: Trust, Collective Action, and the Law*, 102 MICH. L. REV. 71, 71 (2002).

In other words, fostering trust in social settings is not all about creating external incentives in the form of rules and regulations – there is a significant affective component that is contingent on the interpersonal signals that are sent on a day-to-day basis. And trust is contagious. Kahan notes that trust breeds trust "as individuals observe others contributing to public goods and are moved to reciprocate." Distrust is also contagious, however, as "individuals who lack faith in their peers can be expected to resist contributing to public goods, thereby inducing still others to withhold their cooperation as a means of retaliating."[103] It is a good thing that not everyone trusts as rational wealth maximizers, who tend to "reward cooperation with cooperation and defection with defection in a 'tit for tat' pattern." The problem arises when trust is needed in relationships that are not long term; in that context, individuals who are "emotional and moral reciprocators" are essential because they will "condition their contribution to collective goods on the contribution of others even in fleeting transactions with multiple actors whose behavior they cannot keep track of and whose identities they can't even discern."[104]

Putting attorney-client trust to the side (for the moment), it is apparent why even building trust *within* a large law firm is so difficult. Research has consistently shown that individuals' willingness to sacrifice for common goods is

[103] *Id.* at 71–2.
[104] *Id.* at 73.

conditional on their belief that others are also willing to sacrifice.[105] External penalties can have effects opposite from the one intended. For example, when the government publicizes an increase in penalties for tax evasion, one effect is to convince individuals that their neighbors are cheating. As Kahan puts it, the resulting distrust "triggers a reciprocal motive to evade, which dominates the greater material incentive to comply associated with the higher-than-expected penalty."[106]

Levels of trust within a firm are thus contingent, in significant part, on the culture, by which I mean the priorities and values embodied in, and reflected by, the day-to-day interactions of the firm's constituents. As firms have grown exponentially in terms of both numerical size and geographical scope, building a culture that incorporates values beyond the lowest common denominator of market performance becomes increasingly difficult. As moral claims become more contested in the hurly-burly of America's pluralist public square, making one's claim is dependent on putting the claim in terms that are accessible to a wildly diverse citizenry. Large law firms are microcosms of the American experience, and the most obviously "accessible" language

---

[105] *Id.* at 74 ("[L]aboratory constructs designed to simulate collective-action problems ... have consistently shown that the willingness of individuals to make costly contributions to collective goods is highly conditional on their perception that others are willing to do so.").

[106] *Id.* at 83.

is profits per partner. A greater emphasis on lateral hiring exacerbates the trust-diminishing effects of rapid growth, as attorneys are less likely to have been enculturated in the firm's noneconomic values, even assuming that such values exist.[107] An increasing reliance on contract attorneys may also depress levels of trust within the firm.[108]

The result of these trends, according to Marc Galanter and William Henderson, is a "highly atomized environment" in which "individual lawyers within large firms are likely to find it harder to adhere to professional and ethical principles that are at odds with the client's objectives."[109] The firm itself "has remarkably little autonomy to pursue noneconomic objectives," and "the lack of credible risk sharing reduces the willingness of individual lawyers to invest in firm-wide initiatives that do not simultaneously optimize their own practice."[110] In this regard, firms are much more likely to have a "climate of insecurity" than a "culture of

---

[107] *See* Larry E. Ribstein, *The Death of Big Law*, WIS. L. REV. 749, 775 (2010); Marc Galanter & William Henderson, *The Elastic Tournament: A Second Transformation of the Big Law Firm*, 60 STAN. L. REV. 1867 (2008) ("[T]he sheer size and geographic dispersion of present-day large law firms makes it more difficult to create and sustain firm-wide cultural norms, such as collegiality, cooperation, and risk sharing, that may have moderated intra-firm competition under the original 'classic' tournament.").

[108] *See* Regan & Heenan, *supra* note 73, at 2184 (citing study of aerospace engineers finding that presence of contract engineers lowered employee trust in the company).

[109] Galanter & Henderson, *supra* note 78, at 1867–8.

[110] *Id.*

trust." The insecurity is fomented by several factors beyond the firm's sheer size, including the move away from lock-step compensation to embrace competition over partnership shares (with the accompanying specter of deequitization). With these competitive pressures – exacerbated by the current economic downturn[111] – there is less attention paid to mentoring new attorneys, resulting in the next generation's reduced sense of loyalty to the firm.[112] All in all, changes to the modern law firm have conferred "disproportionate power on the most single-minded pursuers of the bottom line."[113]

If law firm culture has become an atomized pursuit of the bottom line, we have a trust problem. As Tamar Frankel explains, "self-interest, without compassion and self-control, is bound to raise a culture devoid of empathy for others; a culture destructive of trust."[114] Further, the reluctance to

---

[111] *See, e.g.,* John Flood, *From Ethics to Regulation: The Re-Organization and Re-Professionalization of Large Law Firms in the 21st Century*, at 16–17 (http://ssrn.com/abstract=1592324) ("Equity partnerships have shrunk, largely in order to bolster declining revenues; salaried partners found they were no longer on a track to the equity; and associates found that they were welcome for a shorter number of years than before and only if they were prepared to abandon the partner track. The resemblance between the 21st century law firm and that of the 19th century is striking. Power and wealth accrue to a small number of people while the ranks of employees grow in inverse proportion to the shrinking partnerships.").

[112] *Id.* at 1910–11.

[113] *Id.* at 1906.

[114] Tamar Frankel, *Trust and Honesty: America's Business Culture at a Crossroads* (2006), 202.

trust can become a vicious circle, as the "unwillingness of distrusters ... to engage in social interactions deters distrusters from correcting their depressed level of trust."[115] By contrast, a high level of background trust increases the likelihood of cooperation, and cooperation contributes to new trust relationships.[116]

Back in 1995, Judge Richard Posner compared the trend in the market for legal services to "the evolution of the textile industry from guild production to mass production, and the concomitant decline of artisanality."[117] The movement has become more pronounced since then, with important consequences for both the nature of the lawyer's work and the lawyer's place in civil society. I am focused specifically on how the move from guild production to mass production impacts trust and, correspondingly, lawyers' capacity to practice agape. Does the emerging twenty-first-century global law firm maintain space for relationships of trust? If trust relationships build gradually, only after a person "develops a sense of the trustworthiness of another across specific contexts, and these specific trust assessments appear to cumulate over time to inform a sense of residual

---

[115] Toshio Yamagishi, "Trust as a Form of Social Intelligence," in *Trust in Society*, ed. Karen Cook (2001), 121, 122.

[116] Barbara A. Misztal, *Trust in Modern Societies* (1996), 199 ("The greater the level of trust within a society, the greater the likelihood of cooperation, which in turn contributes to the establishment of trust relationships.").

[117] Richard Posner, *Overcoming Law* (1996), 47 (Quoted in Frankel, *supra* note 83, at 139).

trust that guides the general relationship,"[118] does a lawyer still traffic in relationships of trust?

The weakening of trust within the firm cannot help but impact an attorney's stance toward clients. When a partner's standing within the firm is solely a function of revenue, that priority will shape her client relationships. When high attorney turnover within the firm, coupled with an intensely competitive environment, hinders the development of collegial relationships, the attorney's sense of isolation and distrust will be felt by the client. Perhaps the "eat what you kill" law firm model has bred a lawyer culture that values self-reliance over cooperation, competition over collegiality, short-term profit over the client's long-term good, and the avoidance of vulnerability over the espousal of trust. Trust is contagious in a sense that should be troubling to clients, even large corporate clients: studies have shown that "the extent to which one says one trusts others may, in fact, be a reflection of that person's trustworthiness," for the results suggest that "the best way to determine whether or not a person is trustworthy is to ask him whether or not he trusts others."[119] A lawyer whose workplace is devoid of relational trust will not be well equipped or inclined to practice law as a moral subject in a professional relationship marked by agape.

[118] Claire A. Hill & Erin Ann O'Hara, *A Cognitive Theory of Trust* (2006), 84 WASH. U. L. REV. 1717, 1749.

[119] Raymond H. Brescia, *Trust in the Shadows: Law, Behavior, and Financial Re-Regulation*, 57 BUFF. L. REV. 1361, 1380 (2009).

B. Why Trust Matters

Given these trends, it may be more accurate to say that the legal profession is moving from a paradigm of "trusting in" to "trusting that." In other words, perhaps lawyers' distinctive service was providing business with a "thickness" of relationship that allowed clients to trust "in" the lawyer. And now as lawyers' services have grown less distinctive and their firms have marginalized noneconomic values, perhaps clients are asked only to trust "that" a lawyer will not act contrary to the client's interests in a specific scenario. Hill and O'Hara refer to "trust that" as "trust as prediction," versus "trust in a person." They observe that, if a person "can earn a livelihood based merely on the fact that we 'trust that' he will perform, he may have little incentive to invest in the more costly set of attributes that ensure that we can 'trust in' him."[120] O'Hara explains that "something akin to 'trust that' trust could exist in the absence of any information about the target's trustworthiness."[121] If the legal profession is now resigned to using ethics rules, contract, or other market incentives to ensure that corporate clients can accurately predict how their lawyers will behave in a given situation,[122] rather than cultivating a more gen-

[120] Hill & O'Hara, *supra* note 55, at 1725–6.
[121] Erin Ann O'Hara, "Trustworthiness and Contract," in *Moral Markets: The Critical Role of Values in the Economy* (2008), 173, 177.
[122] Hill & O'Hara, *supra* note 55, at 1744.

eral trust that the lawyer, because she is a lawyer, is worthy of the client's trust, what have we lost?

Embracing a role as subject is only possible for an attorney if trust finds fertile ground in her relationship with clients. The client must trust that the attorney has the client's best interests at heart, and that widening the conversation to encompass considerations beyond the narrowly technical need not invariably function as an entryway for the attorney's own self-interest. The attorney must trust the client enough to listen authentically, to step beyond her own assumptions long enough to encounter the client as a moral subject, and to question whether her own perspective accurately reflects the client's best interests. A "thick" attorney-client relationship requires mutual trust because approaching the other as a subject requires mutual vulnerability.

If the emerging model of trust for the legal profession is best expressed as trust "that" an attorney will perform the discrete task for which she is hired, much as we trust a photocopier technician to get the machine running again,[123] then contract and market incentives should be more than sufficient. But if lawyers are more

---

[123] Stephen L. Pepper, *The Lawyer's Amoral Ethical Role: A Defense, a Problem, and Some Possibilities*, 1986 AM. B. FOUND. RES. J. 613, 624. (comparing a lawyer's client to "someone who stands frustrated before a photocopier that won't copy," and who needs "a technician ... to make it go," and noting that the technician is ordinarily not concerned with "whether the content of what is about to be copied is morally good or bad").

than technicians, then clients are losing something when the thinning of trust contributes to the thinning of the attorney-client relationship. And, of course, attorneys are losing something too, not just in the loss of their distinctiveness among market providers, but also in the loss of a sense that they are involved in a vocation that entails more than technical competence.

Absent trust, the attorney's ability to introduce into the representation considerations beyond those articulated (or even discerned) by the client is compromised. To the extent that the attorney is a technician hired to handle a single transaction, the attorney is not realistically in a position to vindicate any interests other than those raised by the client in that particular transaction. If the client lacks trust in the attorney sufficient to include her in the business's ongoing conversation in any sustained way, the attorney will not be in a position to counsel the client about the business's overall direction and how that direction implicates the interests of other constituents, including the interests of the surrounding community. Even if the attorney somehow gained sufficient knowledge, a client who does not trust the attorney enough to include her in the conversation is hardly likely to trust the attorney enough to heed her (unsolicited) advice. Economic considerations already give attorneys the incentive to defer to management,[124] and the limitations inherent

[124] David Wessel, "Venal Sins: Why the Bad Guys of the Boardroom Emerged en Masse," *Wall St. Journal*, June 20, 2002 (quoted in Frankel, *supra* note 83, at 141) ("The professional gatekeepers

in their piecemeal, episodic knowledge of the company give them ample justification for doing so.

It is not entirely clear whether laws such as Sarbanes-Oxley will contribute to the problem. Such laws reinforce the attorney's duty to challenge the client to look beyond short-term gain and consider the broader, longer-range interests of the organization. The reinforcement is particularly important given the market and intrafirm competitive pressures not to make waves. The discretion to disclose the information outside the organization is a closer call. It is important that this aspect of the rule is discretionary, not mandatory. If we are concerned about the attorney's potential role as healer[125] – a role that encompasses the interaction of trust and the vindication of public norms – the client has to be treated as a subject capable of reflection and reform, not as an object to be threatened with disclosure as the price for intransigence. Trust is relational, and our regulatory regime must reflect that.

Further, the dynamic could become a self-perpetuating cycle, for as the diminution of trust diminishes the attorney's ability and inclination to introduce public values into the representation, the trust-enhancing regulatory framework may erode as well. Attorneys enjoy a range of legal privileges – most notably, for this purpose, protection against the compelled disclosure of confidential information – based,

were greatly compromised by finding they could make tremendous profits by deferring to management").

[125] *See* Chapter 3.

at least in part, on the belief that the privileges promote the public good. If the privileges are perceived to do nothing other than enhance the market profitability of lawyers, their long-term political sustainability is open to question.[126] If the public decides that it is pointless to give attorneys the opportunity to persuade clients to do the right thing, our regime will make more of these duties mandatory and reduce attorney discretion. It is not clear why the public should value the work of attorneys if that work is simply a series of self-interest-maximizing market transactions, removed from the relationships of trust in which a more fulsome understanding of the client's well-being and the public interest can be productively explored.[127] As Russ Pearce

[126] David B. Wilkins, *Team of Rivals? Toward a New Model of the Corporate Attorney/Client Relationship* at 745 (ssrn.com/abstract=1517342) ("In order to maintain this privileged status [re access to law] ... corporate law firms must not be seen as consistently undermining the public purposes of the law. Corporations, therefore, have a stake in ensuring that law firms do not squander this valuable resource by placing the firm's short-term economic gain above its long-term interest in its own legitimacy."); Luban, *supra* note 96, at 854 ("We must ask realistically whether the new forms of practice are variations on the traditional lawyer's role as public citizen. If the answer is 'yes,' then we can proceed to address the bar's question about how best to protect core lawyer values in new settings. But if the answer is 'no,' so that what we confront is not a lawyer but a schmayer, then there is no reason to grant any of the unique privileges of lawyers to them").

[127] *See, e.g.*, Bruce A. Green & Russell G. Pearce, *"Public Service Must Begin at Home": The Lawyer as Civics Teacher in Everyday Practice*, 50 WM. & MARY L. REV. 1207, 1237–8 (2009) (arguing

observes, King encourages us "to recognize personal moral responsibility as the most powerful source of commitment to the public good."[128]

As noted previously, globalization puts pressure on trust by stretching attorney-client relationships over greater distances, across less frequent and less personal contacts, and beyond the reach of regulatory frameworks. At the same time, however, the opportunity for attorneys to meet client needs by building relationships of trust is unmistakable. International business practice is complicated by uncertainty about legal jurisdiction and conflict resolution, and many businesses overestimate these complications. As a result, clients engaged in cross-border transactions tend to rely on "the assumption that the lawyer who can make use of the international structures of his law firm will be able to provide adequate legal or non-legal solutions for any type of conflict that can arise out of the transaction."[129] In other words, "the stabilization of expectations can occur only at the level of the role of the lawyer and not at the level of the

> that "[t]hinking about professional relationships as an expression of one's civic understandings" can undergird a lawyer' preference "for developing relationships of trust, for treating others fairly, for complying with the spirit of the law, and for negotiation and compromise").

[128] Russell Pearce, *Professional Responsibility for the Age of Obama*, 22 GEO. J. LEGAL ETHICS 1595, 1597 (2009).

[129] John Flood & Fabian Sosa, *Lawyers, Law Firms, and the Stabilization of Transnational Business*, 28 Nw. J. INT'L L. & BUS. 489, 494 (2008).

legal system."[130] Because, in the cross-border context, there is insufficient confidence in the legal system, trust in the lawyer is essential.

Even beyond confidence in the legal system, there is a more general lack of "system trust" in the international arena because actors are often operating outside their normal social systems, and thus background cultural norms and practices may provide limited guidance for their interactions. Rebecca Bratspies explains that individuals are "embedded in social systems, with rules and resources that powerfully constrain or enable individual interactions," and "system trust" can be much more important than interpersonal trust relationships.[131] If system trust is lacking due to the lack of a coherent "system," interpersonal trust relationships may be even more essential to facilitating cooperation.

Changes to the profession make trust more important, but not simply because of the increased economic pressure that those changes have produced.[132] Trust becomes more

---

[130] *Id.*

[131] Rebecca M. Bratspies, *Regulatory Trust*, 51 ARIZ. L. REV. 575, 603 (2009); *see id.* at 605 ("Because these safeguards function independently of the personal motivations of any of the participants at any given time, one can repose trust in the system itself, instead of being forced to depend wholly on the thick trust based on individual relationships.").

[132] For example, the Association of Corporate Counsel's "Value Challenge" includes a "Covenant with Counsel" reminding lawyers that clients "understand our relationship is built on mutual trust; unless we tell you otherwise, we don't need or want a 'no

important because of the changes themselves – in particular, as the role expectations of attorneys become more fluid and uncertain, the background assumptions that shape the attorney-client relationship become fewer in number and weaker in strength. There is a void to be filled, but only if interpersonal trust is available. Trust is needed given the unpredictability of social life and the indeterminacy of social interaction.[133] Given the trends discussed previously, it would not be surprising to find that indeterminacy in the provision of legal services is rising. As role negotiability increases in a system, opportunities for trust correspondingly increase.[134]

The connection between trust and role negotiability makes sense if we can see that we do not need to trust a person whose behavior is totally dictated by her role. Trust plays a minimal role in my interaction with a cashier because, unless the cashier breaks out of role, she will simply take my money, give me change, and let me walk out with my purchase. When I give my money to the cashier, I am simply expressing my confidence in the normative behavioral patterns embedded in the system[135] – patterns reinforced by criminal law. I do not need to form any opinion

stones unturned' approach." ACC Value Challenge, Covenant with Counsel (http://www.acc.com/valuechallenge/upload/Value-Challenge-Brief_022510.pdf).

[133] Adam B. Seligman, *The Problem of Trust* (1997), 13.

[134] *Id.* at 41.

[135] *Id.* at 63.

on the trustworthiness of this particular cashier, much less of cashiers in general. Adam Seligman describes trust as "a recognition of alter's agency, an agency which ... only appears when the 'fit' between the person and the role is loose, when the role does not – indeed cannot – circumscribe all of alter's possible behavior."[136]

Lawyers are not cashiers. Their behavior has never been circumscribed entirely by their role; discretion has always been part of a lawyer's work, and thus a lawyer's trustworthiness, both individually and as a categorical professional attribute, has always been a significant component of her value to clients. But as the role-defined boundaries become more malleable, the need for trust increases, for "we do not have to 'trust' in [the] other's agency until that agency becomes a realizable potential."[137]

IV. Lawyers as Subjects: Future Prospects

So if the trust-driven capacity of lawyers to act as subjects is eroding, can anything be done to reverse the trend? Lawyers may reflexively reach for legal reform as an antidote, but the law is not a magic elixir for ensuring trust's centrality. The legal framework can facilitate trust, but an overreliance on law can actually marginalize trust. Lynn Stout and Margaret Blair's work in the corporate context is instructive,

---

[136] *Id.* at 62.
[137] *Id.* at 63.

as they found that "corporate participants often cooperate with each other not because of external constraints but because of internal ones," and that "internalized trust and trustworthiness play important roles in encouraging cooperation within firms."[138] As Larry Ribstein observes, "Legal constraints may increase the probability that one will perform as promised, but cannot increase one's willingness either to perform in the absence of constraints or to make oneself vulnerable to the risk of non-performance."[139]

In fact, external constraints can often communicate messages that have the effect of lowering trust. For example, as Mark Hall explains, "Elaborate provisions informing patients of their rights and regulating the behavior of managed care organizations could easily convey to patients the impression that HMOs and their doctors cannot be trusted," and correlatively "suggest to doctors and insurers that they are not in fact trusted and are not expected to act on the basis of intrinsically trustworthy motivations."[140] Regulations help set expectations of behavior – including expectations of others' behavior – not simply by discouraging certain behavior through threat of punishment, but by implicitly communicating the social prevalence of certain behavior. As noted

---

[138] Margaret M. Blair & Lynn A. Stout, *Trust, Trustworthiness, and the Behavioral Foundations of Corporate Law*, 149 U. PA. L. REV. 1735, 1735 (2001).

[139] Larry E. Ribstein, *Law v. Trust*, 81 B.U. L. REV. 553, 562 (2001).

[140] Mark A. Hall, *Law, Medicine, and Trust*, 55 STAN. L. REV. 463, 509–10 (2002).

previously, cries for stepped-up enforcement of tax laws can actually decrease compliance by signaling to taxpayers that their fellow citizens are flouting the law.[141]

Nevertheless, despite these limitations, the regulatory framework still matters. A background level of confidence can be a necessary precursor to willingly embracing vulnerability, and the law can help establish that confidence. When we embark on new regulatory initiatives or reforms, we should allow trust to help shape our understanding of the nature, scope, and prudence of the objectives underlying the law governing lawyers. For example, trust helps us understand the attorney's fiduciary obligation "because it suggests that the essence of a fiduciary relationship is the legal expectation that the fiduciary will adopt the other-regarding preference function that is the hallmark of trustworthy behavior," and "the law encourages fiduciaries to do this not only or even primarily by threatening punishment but by framing the relationship between the fiduciary and her beneficiary as one that calls for a psychological commitment to trustworthy, other-regarding behavior."[142]

Other regulatory changes might look different when viewed in relationship to trust as a professional attribute. The "appearance of impropriety" standard has fallen into disfavor as a relevant regulatory concern,[143] but has

---

[141] *See* text accompanying note 106.

[142] Blair & Stout, *supra* note 55, at 1743.

[143] *See, e.g.,* Charles W. Wolfram, *Former-Client Conflicts*, 10 GEO. L.J. 677, 686–7 (1997) ("I forego the opportunity to flail, yet again,

its disappearance made it easier for the profession to lose sight of the fact that public perception is an element of public trust? And given the ABA's recent revision of Model Rule 1.10 to permit a firm to hire a lawyer with a conflict of interest provided that the lawyer is screened from participation in the matter at issue, a lawyer could conceivably switch to the opposing firm in the middle of litigation without the affected client's consent. What does this revision tell a client about the wisdom of "trusting in" her lawyer, even if she "trusts that" her former lawyer will be screened from participation in the case? Also, while the lawyer as trusted adviser does not preclude her bearing public responsibilities – and trust is essential to the ability to carry out those public responsibilities – the whistle-blowing role contemplated in post-Enron Rule 1.13 and Sarbanes-Oxley puts stress on attorney-client trust; the whistle-blowing role cannot be expanded infinitely without diminishing background levels of trust. Even in this sense, analyzing the law against the particulars of what we know about trust can be instructive, particularly the knowledge that "'trust in' trust becomes irrelevant to people's decisions to interact as it gets swamped by very high levels of 'trust that' trust."[144]

Legal education has a role to play in emphasizing the importance of trust. Patient-physician trust is driven by

the mostly dead dog of appearance of impropriety, for it is clear that it plays only a minor, if irritating and potentially distorting, role in modern conflicts opinions.").

[144] Hill & O'Hara, *supra* note 55, at 1753.

relationship factors (how well patients know their doctor and how much choice they had in picking the doctor)
and personality traits (whether the doctor is a good lis-
tener and whether she projects confidence), not from phy-
sician demographics or professional characteristics.[145] Law
schools do not fulfill their potential on this front simply by
having students learn what Rule 1.6 says about confidentiality; they should also have students think about, talk
about, and practice the relational aspect of the lawyer's
work. Corporate clients' definition of attorney effectiveness
"moves beyond excellent technical competence toward excellent relationship skills."[146] Very little time in law school is
spent on client counseling exercises, for example, or on the
importance of empathy and perceptual clarity. Listening
skills can – and often must – be taught. (In a classroom
client counseling exercise, I have noted that many of my
first-year students who were acting as attorneys did not ask
the clients any questions before giving them advice.) Also,
as Carole Silver notes, "Lawyers working in a global context must master the art of communicating with lawyers
and law graduates who were educated and work in foreign

---

[145] Mark A. Hall, *Law, Medicine, and Trust*, 55 STAN. L. REV. 463, 474
(2002).

[146] Neil Hamilton & Verna Monson, *The Positive Empirical
Relationship of Professionalism to Effectiveness in the Practice of
Law*, 24 GEO. J. LEG. ETHICS (2011), 137, 62.

(non-US) jurisdictions."[147] An entire field is devoted to the study of professional ethical identity development – moving in stages from external definitions of self and viewing professional status as a credential, to an awareness of interdependence and the capacity for interpersonal openness and presence[148] – but the resulting insights are largely ignored within legal education.[149]

If we care about maintaining trust as a central feature of the attorney-client relationship, we have to care about the legal profession being more than the sum of its market-driven parts. It is important that attributes of trustworthiness flow, at least in part, from a lawyer's status as a lawyer, not simply from her willingness to market herself as trustworthy or to enter into contracts that limit her ability to take advantage of the client's trust. These attributes can be facilitated, though of course not guaranteed, by the expectations that are embedded in professional identity, and

---

[147] Carole Silver, *Educating Lawyers for the Global Economy: National Challenges*, at 11 (http://ssrn.com/abstract=1519387).

[148] See Muriel J. Bebeau & Philip Lewis, *Manual for Assessing and Promoting Identity Formation* (Ctr. for the Study of Ethical Dev., Draft, 2004); James Rule & Muriel J. Bebeau, *Dentists Who Care: Inspiring Stories of Professional Commitment* (2005), 162.

[149] *But see* Verna E. Monson & Neil W. Hamilton, *Entering Law Students' Conceptions of an Ethical Professional Identity and the Role of the Lawyer in Society*, 35 J. OF LEG. PROF. (2011), 385; Neil W. Hamilton, *Assessing Professionalism: Measuring Progress in the Formation of an Ethical Professional Identity*, 5 U. ST. THOMAS L.J. 510–11 (2008).

those expectations, including those held by the public and lawyers themselves, are shaped by the messages communicated by the profession.[150]

If we hope to support lawyers' ability to practice agape as moral subjects who care for their clients' well-being, not just for their autonomy, the profession's rhetoric and self-conception matter. Are we photocopier technicians or trusted advisers? With the globalization of legal practice, there has been an increased effort at formulating ethics codes that are not restricted to particular countries. American lawyers, accustomed to detailed codes of conduct backed up by disciplinary authorities, may tend to roll their eyes at the seemingly quaint and solely aspirational products of these efforts. We have to ask, though, which form of ethics code is more important to professional viability? For example, the Turin Principles of Professional Conduct, promulgated by the Union Internationale des Avocats in 2002, reminds lawyers that they "have the right and the duty to practice their profession in a manner that furthers knowledge, understanding and application of the law, whilst protecting the interests entrusted to their care."[151] This

---

[150] Henry Farrell, *The Political Economy of Trust: Institutions, Interests, and Inter-Firm Cooperation in Italy and Germany* (2009), 43.

[151] Union Internationale des Avocats, Turin Principles of Professional Conduct (2002) (http://www.abanet.org/cpr/gats/uia_ex_1.pdf).

sweeping breadth may be of little guidance to regulatory authority, but its value may lie in its premise: that we can still speak meaningfully when speaking of lawyers as a category. Indeed, the Turin Principles reflect a cognizance of the very forces that lead Tom Morgan and others to herald the death of the legal profession. Instead of excusing lawyers for viewing themselves as no different from other market providers, the Turin Principles call legal services providers to remember that "the lawyer" continues to play an essential role in defending human rights, in ensuring that the rules of law are respected and observed, in "maintaining stability in legal relationships despite and increasing trend toward self-regulation, deregulation and globalization," and in practicing "the profession in a spirit of service and humanism."[152]

For our purposes, the content of these aspirations is less important than the continued insistence that "the lawyer" still exists and still can bear the weight of a shared professional identity, even as the blurring of geographical, technological, and business model boundaries puts increasing pressure on that identity.[153] In the end, it may be the fact of this insistence that proves most valuable in maintaining

[152] *Id.*

[153] "[W]hen we talk about trust as a policy we stress the issue of solidarity not as necessarily requiring empathy and sameness with others but one based on some mutual understanding, common interest and destiny." Barbara A. Misztal, *Trust in Modern Societies* (1996), 219.

the distinctiveness of lawyers in a sea of homogenizing market forces. If lawyers only bring technical competence to the table, much of what lawyers do can be stripped down to separate tasks and distributed to other providers. But what if the bundle of tasks is more than the sum of its parts? If a "more than the sum" approach is to prove viable in the marketplace, it will be trust that makes the lawyer's role coherent and distinctive. Absent authentic relationships of trust between lawyer and client, King's vision of agape is a nonstarter within the legal profession.

Agape's contribution to the work of the attorney is to serve as a reminder that seeking the good of the client requires the lawyer to act as a moral subject, not as a mouthpiece. King's reliance on agape teaches us that the attorney's provision of legal services occurs in the context of a real human relationship with her client, whether the client is an actual person or an organization managed by, and created to serve the interests of, actual persons. The richness of the relationship will be a function, in part, of the tasks for which the attorney has been retained. The opportunities for, and appropriateness of, moral engagement will vary from a one-time routine closing on a home sale, to document-intensive discovery work, to an ongoing counseling role in a business, to a contentious child custody case. Whether or not the practice of agape manifests itself in every case, agape can shape the lawyer's self-conception and deepen her commitment to active participation in facilitating the client's well-being in a way that cannot easily be limited to certain categories of legal practice.

Agape also tells us that the attorney should see her client in the context of the client's relationships. In other words, agape helps prevent the attorney and client from being isolated from each other, but it can also avoid presuming that the client is isolated from others. King's invocation of agape was geared toward the neighbor's development of closer human relationships – breaking down walls between enemies, encouraging the shared pursuit of higher purposes among friends. To understand why, we need to account for King's belief in the interconnectedness of humanity and the unifying narrative of the universe. This, in turn, requires us to explore personalism.

3

Personalism

Lawyers as Healers

In one of the most famous lines from his "Letter from Birmingham City Jail," King proclaimed that "injustice anywhere is a threat to justice everywhere."[1] He did not just mean that injustice unchecked will eventually affect everyone; he was making the more radical claim that injustice anywhere harms the human community to which we all belong. As he explained in the same letter, "We are all caught in an inescapable network of mutuality, tied into a single garment of destiny," and thus "whatever affects one

---

[1] Martin Luther King Jr., "Letter from Birmingham City Jail" (1963), in *A Testament of Hope: The Essential Writings of Martin Luther King Jr.,* ed. James M. Washington (1986), 289, 290 (hereinafter *A Testament of Hope*).

directly, affects all indirectly."[2] This view of the world fundamentally shaped his witness, as he worked tirelessly to repair the breach in what he referred to as "the beloved community."[3] In a real sense, King was a healer.

Viewing King's work as a ministry of healing can help underscore its distinctiveness. His advocacy for the law's expansion and enforcement of individual rights was not grounded in the autonomy-maximizing rhetoric that much of today's rights advocacy seems to be; King looked to rights as tools to help repair the breach in the human community. Observing that we tend to see each other as religious, ethnic, or racial categories, he lamented our failure to "see people in their true humanness ... to think of them as fellow human beings made from the same basic stuff as we, moulded in the same divine image."[4] He did not embrace the theory-driven fiction of a rights-bearing individual who stands alone, without context or commitments. His advocacy was not just premised on the person as a social being as a

---

[2] *Id.*

[3] "The concept of beloved community has been widely known in philosophical circles at least since the appearance of Josiah Royce's The Problem of Christianity. In this book Royce outlined his understanding of the beloved community. The latter is a community of love and loyalty, the highest expression of corporate Christian faith. Due to his own idealistic, Hegelian orientation, Royce's beloved community is more of a rational construct than King's more historical and biblical conception." Ira G. Zepp, *The Social Vision of Martin Luther King Jr.* (1989), 209.

[4] Martin Luther King Jr., *Strength to Love* (1963), 29.

descriptive matter, but also as a normative proposition. As discussed in Chapter 1, King's commitment to human dignity – both as an expression of intrinsic value and as a relative quality of human action – was rooted in his belief that we are oriented by our very nature to relationship. His work to enhance the legal and political standing of the individual was inseparable – and in a real sense, indistinguishable – from his work to restore the human community.[5] As we will see in this chapter, King's conception of human existence as a process of recognizing and affirming relationships among sacred and unique beings emerged from his deep grounding in the personalist tradition.

Agape's focus on "somebodiness" teaches lawyers to treat their clients (and themselves) as subjects, not objects. Personalism broadens the relational view, challenging lawyers to recognize their potential role as healers: counselors who can help repair breaches in the human community. Personalism speaks not only to the way we relate to our

---

[5] Nicholas Wolterstorff's explanation of human rights is helpful on this point:

[W]hen we speak of human rights, we are not imagining individuals stripped of all social status and then asking what rights these naked individuals have. We take human beings as they come, in all their social embeddedness. We notice that each of them has many different statuses to which rights are attached. It occurs to us to wonder whether the status that all these beings necessarily share, namely, that of being human beings, also has rights attached to it. That is the question we ask. We do no stripping.

Nicholas Wolterstorff, *Justice: Rights and Wrongs* (2007), 313.

clients, but also to the way we would hope our clients relate to others. A client may decide to ignore the social dimension of human nature and the relational commitments that flow from that dimension, but her lawyer should not assume that those commitments are mere add-ons, or that the default function of legal representation is to maximize the client's self-interest, as defined in narrow, individualist terms.

I. King and Personalism

King consistently returned to the language of personalism in articulating his animating worldview – a belief in "the sacredness of human personality" and a conviction that "every man is an heir to a legacy of dignity and worth."[6] To treat him otherwise "is to depersonalize the potential person and desecrate what he is."[7] Further, given the interconnectedness of humanity, when we deny the dignity of a person, "the image of God is abused in him and consequently and proportionately lost by those who inflict the abuse."[8] Given the structure of the universe, "the self cannot be self without other selves," and "I cannot reach fulfillment without thou."[9] As Richard Wills puts it, King's "was a theological

[6] Martin Luther King Jr., "Ethical Demands of Integration" (1963), in *A Testament of Hope*, *supra* note 1, at 117, 118.
[7] *Id.* at 119.
[8] *Id.*
[9] *Id.* at 122.

anthropology that emerged from a struggle to be, in a climate that inferred that he did not belong."[10]

The Scriptures support King's emphasis on the importance of mutually recognizing the sacredness of personality. In Jesus's parable about the rich fool Dives, the poor Lazarus lay at Dives's gate, "covered with sores [and longing] to satisfy his hunger with what fell from the rich man's table; even the dogs would come and lick his sores."[11] According to King:

> The rich fool was condemned, not because he was not tough-minded, but rather because he was not tenderhearted. Life for him was a mirror in which he saw only himself, and not a window through which he saw other selves. Dives went to hell, not because he was wealthy, but because he was not tenderhearted enough to see Lazarus and because he made no attempt to bridge the gulf between himself and his brother.[12]

Bridging the gulf between self and brother captures the core of King's ministry. This emphasis on the need for the mutual recognition and affirmation of personality emerged from the personalist theological tradition, which held that "any pretended relation to God which is also not a relation to people is spurious religion," for personal religion must "reach out

---

[10] Richard Wayne Wills Sr., *Martin Luther King Jr. and the Image of God* (2009), 23.

[11] Luke 16:20.

[12] Martin Luther King, *Strength to Love* (1981), 14.

toward the objective unity of a God whose interest includes the whole of humanity."[13] Two fundamental tenets of personalism are "the infinite, inviolable worth of persons as such, and a personal God to whom people are of supreme value."[14]

Under the personalist view, the religious believer must take an interest in society's welfare, but not because "we are all victims of a common fate; rather, it comes from the discovery of a supreme divine value which society can neither give nor take away, but which imparts an eternal meaning to every human life and hence transforms the struggles of society into stages of a cosmic drama."[15] One key for understanding King's work – and its implications for lawyers – is the personalist belief that the point of freedom "is not to be as queer and individual and 'original' as possible, but, rather, to discover or create universal agreements on some points and so to find a program and means for social cooperation."[16] Liberation is about reconciliation, not independence; liberation is for community.[17]

Personalism's influence on King was significant. He chose Boston University for his doctoral work because

---

[13] Edgar Brightman, *Personality and Religion* (1934), 126.

[14] Rufus Burrow, Jr., *God and Human Dignity: The Personalism, Theology, and Ethics of Martin Luther King, Jr.* (2006), 6.

[15] Brightman, *supra* note 13, at 135.

[16] *Id.* at 154.

[17] *See* Paul R. Garber, "King Was a Black Theologian," in *Martin Luther King Jr.: Civil Rights Leader, Theologian, Orator* (1989), 407.

Edgar Brightman, the leading exponent of personalism, was on the faculty.[18] (King's faculty adviser at Crozer Theological Seminary, George W. Davis, was a follower of Brightman.)[19] As modern theology's attempts to mimic the scientific method amounted, in Taylor Branch's wonderful phrasing, to "more and more elaborate shrugs," Brightman and other personalists looked to "the intensely personal God of the Jewish scriptures and to early Christian theologians such as Augustine."[20] King embraced personalism's teaching "that there was rich, empirical meaning in religious experience."[21] In his own recounting, the tradition's "insistence that only personality – finite and infinite – is ultimately real strengthened me in two convictions: it gave me metaphysical and philosophical grounding for the idea of a personal God, and it gave me a metaphysical basis for the dignity and worth of all human personality."[22]

Personalism is a sweepingly broad school of thought, encompassing most theistic traditions.[23] Brightman explained that it includes any theory "that makes personality the supreme philosophical principle (that is, supreme

---

[18] Taylor Branch, *Parting the Waters* (1989), 90.

[19] *Id.* at 90.

[20] *Id.* at 90–1.

[21] *Id.* at 91.

[22] Clayborne Carson, ed., *The Autobiography of Martin Luther King Jr.* (2001), 31–2.

[23] *See* Edgar Brightman, *Nature and Values* (1945), 113 ("[P]ractically all theists are personalists, whether they be scholastics, Barthians, religious realists, or idealists.").

in the sense that the ultimate causes and reasons of all reality are found in some process of personal experience)."[24] Personalism holds "that persons and selves are the only reality, that is that the whole universe is a system or society of interacting selves and persons – one infinite person who is the creator, and many dependent created persons."[25] The social nature of personality is front and center, given the fact that "personalities develop in relationship with each other."[26]

Brightman identified three principles of personalism: first, a respect for personality: healthy self-respect, respect for others, and respect for God[27]; second, a belief in nature as "a revelation of Divine Personality"[28]; and third, a view of history as the story of the human struggle for freedom. "Freedom," in the personalist sense, was not limited to freedom of choice or political liberty; rather, it refers to "a personal freedom that allows a person to become what he was meant to be as a person, to develop his potential to the fullest as a human being, to be permitted to experience worth, dignity, and value or in religious terms to know himself as a child of God."[29] The French personalist Emmanuel Mounier fleshed this out further, explaining that "I am not free

[24] Edgar Brightman, *Introduction to Philosophy* (3d ed. revised by Robert Beck) (1964), 330.

[25] *Id.*

[26] *Id.* at 346.

[27] Zepp, *supra* note 3, at 183.

[28] *Id.*

[29] *Id.* at 184 (discussing *Nature and Values* at 163–5).

simply by the exercise of my spontaneity; I only become free in so far as this spontaneity moves toward human liberation – that is, toward the personalization of myself and of my world."[30] In this regard, my freedom's "supreme moments are not those in which I exercise most will-power; they are moments rather of giving-way, or of offering myself to a freedom newly encountered or to a value that I love."[31] Mounier saw "the first act of personal life" as "an awakening to the consciousness of this anonymous life and a revolt against the degradation that it represents."[32] The resonance of this language with King's later work is obvious. He challenged his listeners to see that freedom can only confer dignity when it is exercised in a way that reflects our accountability to and for one another.

King's exposure to personalism's view of human freedom began at Crozer under George Davis's teaching. Davis wrote that "God's intention in history is, in part, to produce free personalities," and that, whether "a tyrannical spirit is found in a father, an employer of labor, a minister of religion, or an Adolf Hitler," the tyrant fights not only "against his child, his workman, his parishioner, or humanity, he fights as well against God at work in this unquenchable tendency of the ages."[33] Humanity's historical narrative, according to

---

[30] Emmanuel Mounier, *Personalism,* 61.

[31] *Id.* at 66.

[32] *Id.* at 27.

[33] George W. Davis, "God and History," *Crozer Quarterly,* January 1943 at 25 (quoted in Zepp, *supra* note 3, at 18).

Davis, includes three important, freedom-promoting shifts: "from external rites to inner attitude, from treating people as things to treating people as persons, and from the individual to the social."[34] Whether or not Davis's description is accurate – a strong case could be made that the more pronounced shift has been from the social to the individual[35] – it nicely lays out the normative thrusts of personalism.

King's personalism helped clarify his misgivings about the ascendant approaches within the Protestant theology of his day. Paul Tillich's theology, for example, was too abstract and impersonal. As Noel Leo Erskine explains, the problem was that "in trying to prove that God transcends existence," Tillich sacrificed the idea that God is one being among other beings. In other words, King saw Tillich as giving up on the idea of a personal God. Worshipping and trusting God "presuppose[s] the personality of God," and it is difficult to "have communion with" a "creative event."[36] Especially in light of his formation in the African American church, "the central question for King was not does God exist?," but rather "does God care?"[37] A caring God is foundational to King's ministry, which is aimed at reconciliation: "Liberation becomes the motive love that empowers the community in its quest for a restored community."[38]

---

[34] Zepp, supra note 3, at 19.

[35] *See, e.g.*, Charles Taylor, *A Secular Age* (2007).

[36] Noel Leo Erskine, *King among the Theologians* (1995), 45–6.

[37] *Id.* at 46.

[38] *Id.* at 155.

Personalism also opposed naturalism and materialism, both of which "whittle experience down to its bare spatial properties."[39] While personalists and naturalists agree that "the structure of experience is social," naturalists hold that social relations "are manifestations of a nonsocial reality." By contrast, personalists hold that "social categories are ultimate," and "every personal experience includes something which the person did not invent or create, but which he received from his interaction and communication with other persons." Brightman saw a firmer foundation for democracy arising from this worldview, for "if the universe is a society of interacting persons, all partly determined and partly free, then democracy is an attempt to live politically in tune with the infinite."[40] This is why the acknowledgment of humans as created beings within the Declaration of Independence made that document so important to King and his ministry. The Declaration bridged metaphysical reality and our political community's aspirations, linking the "is" to the "ought."

To respect personality means to love the person, "not for what he is, but for what he may be, or even to love him as he is in order that he may become better."[41] The personalists demand that even God respect personality. "Faith in God means that he can be respected because he himself always will respect personality," according to Brightman, for "through all man's agonies and sins and despairs, God will

---

[39] Edgar Brightman, *Nature and Values,* 116.

[40] *Id.* at 117.

[41] *Id.* at 149.

never abandon hope for humanity and will never refuse his aid." If God "were to give us no future either in this world or in the world to come, our respect for him would change into horror."[42] Extending the personalist criterion to the divine underscores the personalist belief that the universe consists of interconnected and (on the human side) dependent personalities, and failing to honor that relational quality is to ignore reality.

It is tempting to overemphasize the academic orientation of personalism, as though it sprang from the abstract theorizing of professional theologians. In reality, the personalist teaching of King's professors resonated with him because the underlying concept had shaped King's worldview long before he could name it. King's slave forbears had embraced a view of humanity that reflected personalist premises: according to Lewis Baldwin, "From their reading of the Bible, the slaves caught the significance of the fact that every human being has dignity and worth in the sight of God." This view "found powerful expression in slave narratives, songs, sermons, and tales" and helps explain how they were "able to maintain their essential humanity despite that wall of assumptions and definitions which white society sought to impose."[43] King was a personalist all the way down.

[42] *Id.* at 152.

[43] Lewis V. Baldwin, "Martin Luther King, Jr., the Black Church, and the Black Messianic Vision," in *Martin Luther King, Jr. and the Civil Rights Movement,* vol. 1, ed. David Garrow (1989), 93, 100.

II. Lawyers as Personalists

Personalism's emphasis on the relational nature of human existence – relational as an inescapable reality, not simply as a normative aspiration – has implications for many domains of knowledge. Stefano Zamagni, for example, challenges the asocial presumptions underlying economists' reliance on "utility" as the relevant metric for decision making. He explains:

> It is rather difficult to make sense of economics as long as one sticks to an anthropology that says that human beings are asocial, that their "true" nature is something outside human relationality. Basically, the reason is that whereas utility is the property of the relation between a human being and a good (or service), happiness express the property of the relation between a person and (at least) another person. In this sense, while the economic agent can maximize utility in isolation – as the story of Robinson Crusoe reminds us – it takes (at least) two to be happy.[44]

If we truly aim for happiness, then we must account for relationships in our methodologies, for "the other is a condition of the self, since the self to appreciate its own value has structural need for 'hospitality,' that is, of being recognized."[45] "The other" must exist not just because she serves

---

[44] Stefano Zamagni, "Happiness and Individualism: A Very Difficult Union," in *Economics and Happiness: Framing the Analysis,* ed. Luigino Bruni & Pier Luigi Porta (2006).

[45] *Id.* at 2.

our instrumental ends in transactional terms, but because our existence requires her existence, as our existence is premised on recognition by others. While traditional economics looks to the other only for instrumental significance, one's identity is constituted by "the ability to recognize and to be recognized," for "identity, like trusting, is an interpersonal relation."[46] Traditional economics can speak to efficiency, but not to happiness.[47] When economists attempt to measure (and facilitate the attainment of) quality of life, they must recognize that quality of life entails a demand for more than well-made goods; "it is a demand for care, for participation – in other words, for relationality."[48]

How would a recognition of this "relationality" play out in the lawyer's work? The most obvious venue is the attorney-client relationship itself, which has tended to be portrayed within the profession's narrative as a straightforward principal-agent relationship in which the attorney is essentially an extension of the client. Besides disregarding the responsibility of both attorney and client to act as subjects (as discussed in Chapter 2), this conception minimizes the lawyer's capacity (much less responsibility) to remind the client of her own relationality.

Tom Shaffer and Bob Cochran provided one of the earliest (and only) attempts to broaden and deepen the notion of "relationship" between attorney and client. They count four

[46] *Id.* at 3.2.
[47] *See id.* at 5.
[48] *Id.* at 3.2.

possible approaches to moral issues that arise in the relationship: (1) the lawyer makes whatever decision will help the client win, ignoring the interests of others; (2) the lawyer defers to the client's decision, acting as hired gun and (purportedly) maximizing client autonomy; (3) the lawyer makes what she believes to be the right decision, acting as a sort of moral guru, and the client defers to that decision; and (4) the lawyer and client wrestle with, and resolve, the moral issue together, with the lawyer acting as a friend to the client by helping her think about the good.[49] Shaffer and Cochran believe that the fourth option is the best, as the lawyer should not only be concerned with the goodness of the result, but also with the goodness of the client. The client's goodness depends on doing right by others, for "the center of the client's life – the very stuff of it – is in relationships with other people."[50] It matters not so much "that the client does the right thing; it is that two friends are mutually concerned that both of them be and become good persons," and that they "care enough for one another to confront one another when the occasion demands the painful truth."[51]

Agape and personalism help elucidate the Shaffer/ Cochran framework. Agape can shape a lawyer's orientation toward the client, cautioning against both overreaching (which denies the client's status as subject) and passive

[49] Thomas L. Shaffer & Robert F. Cochran, *Lawyers, Clients, and Moral Responsibility,* 2d ed. (2009), 3–4, 42, 47.

[50] *Id.* at 44.

[51] *Id.* at 48.

acquiescence (which denies the lawyer's status as subject). When both the lawyer and client act as subjects, the lawyer may raise considerations that bear on the client's interests even before the client recognizes them, much less articulates them, as relevant. Personalism provides some of the substance to this aspect of the counseling relationship. The lawyer should be prepared to call to the client's attention the nexus between the matter under discussion and the well-being of those to whom the client is linked.

For example, the uncritical acquiescence of Enron's lawyers, as discussed in Chapter 2, precluded them from helping management take a broader view of the company's interests. Personalism's lessons are not that Enron's investors must sacrifice their profits for the greater good; from the personalist perspective, Enron's own interests are invariably wrapped up with (though obviously not always identical to) the interests of its investors, employees, customers, and members of the surrounding community. The fact that slavish devotion to short-term share price has proven to be a recipe for disaster would not surprise King, who insisted on the empirical reality of the human community.

Just as lawyers need to engage clients as subjects, lawyers should encourage clients to view third parties as subjects, not as objects. Atticus Finch remains the paradigmatic lawyer-hero because of the trust he inspired in his client *and* in the members of his community.[52] This speaks to the

[52] Harper Lee, *To Kill A Mockingbird. See, e.g.,* Note, *Being Atticus Finch: The Professional Role of Empathy in* To Kill A Mockingbird,

lawyer's view of the third party and to the lawyer's view of the client – that is, the lawyer should not treat the client as isolated from the rest of the human community. We are not talking about the ultimate direction of the representation, to be sure, for the lawyer owes the client deference, and if the client persists with an isolating and narrow conception of her self-interest, the lawyer's only choice is to withdraw or abide by the client's direction. The important point is for the lawyer to have the conversation with the client, not to hijack the representation. The conversation itself may look different depending on the context, for a lawyer committed to treating her client as a subject must also remain cognizant of power disparities in the relationship. The way in which a lawyer reminds a client of her relational commitments will look different in the legal aid office than in the corporate boardroom.

The tendency among legal ethicists is to assume that the attorney who introduces extralegal values into her work will be an individualist, refusing to assimilate to the values that predominate in her professional setting. Alice Woolley and Brad Wendel, for example, analyze the relationship between

117 HARV. L. REV. 1682 (2004); Cynthia L. Fountaine, *In the Shadow of Atticus Finch: Constructing a Heroic Lawyer*, 13 WIDENER L.J. 123 (2003); Steven Lubet, *Reconstructing Atticus Finch*, 97 MICH. L. REV. 1339 (1999); Monroe Freedman, *Atticus Finch – Right and Wrong*, 45 ALA. L. REV. 473 (1994); Marie A. Failinger, *Gentleman as Hero: Atticus Finch and the Lonely Path*, 10 J. L. & RELIGION 303 (1994); Thomas L. Shaffer, *The Moral Theology of Atticus Finch*, 42 U. PITT. L. REV. 181 (1981).

legal ethics theory and lawyer qualities, asking "who is the person tacitly presupposed as the ideal lawyer by these normative theories."[53] David Luban's approach, under which the lawyer remains morally responsible for the causes she represents, requires a lawyer who is, according to Wendel and Woolley, "highly – perhaps even radically – individualistic in her approach to decision-making."[54] This lawyer might be unwilling to defer to the professional values embodied in the organization in which she practices, but does that make her "individualistic in her approach to decision-making"? Operating under a moral framework that takes precedence over the legal profession's moral framework does not make the lawyer individualistic, in terms of either her substantive moral claims or the process by which the claims' implications are discerned. Perhaps, by importing (or extending) a competing moral framework to her professional role, the lawyer is finally able to live out her relational framework more fully. Lawyer individualism is not the only alternative to prevailing professional norms. Sometimes professional norms can be "radically individualistic" – in terms of both the substance and methodology of the lawyer's decision making – and the "maverick" may in fact be introducing a more robust vision of our social nature into the process. As is evident from the life and ministry of King, a willingness

---

[53] Alice Woolley & W. Bradley Wendel, *Legal Ethics and Moral Character*, 23 GEO. J. LEGAL ETHICS 1065, 1067 (2010).

[54] *Id.* at 1088.

to flout conventional norms might require courage, but it does not make one an individualist.

Individualist premises also tend to shape the hypothetical clients on whom legal ethicists construct the dilemmas designed to explicate professional norms and values. In our teaching and scholarly exploration of legal ethics, we too often trigger ethical quandaries by presuming that clients are self-interest-maximizing, asocial beings. Building on her earlier work,[55] Katherine Kruse explains that "clients whose objectives include wanting to do the right thing, maintaining their reputations, sustaining relationships with others, and treating others fairly do not create the kind of conflicts between lawyers' professional duties and the commitments of ordinary morality on which the legal ethicists want[ ] to focus."[56] Lawyers ignore the lessons of personalism to the extent that they "view clients as walking bundles of legal rights and interests rather than as whole persons whose legal issues come deeply intertwined with other concerns – relationships, loyalties, hopes, uncertainties, fears, doubts, and values – which shape the objectives they bring to legal representation."[57]

The danger is that real lawyers will make assumptions about their real clients that may have no basis in reality, but that will have significant, even life-changing, repercussions for

---

[55] *See* Chapter 1, *supra* at 223–229.

[56] Katherine R. Kruse, *Lawyers in Character and Lawyers in Role*, 10 Nev. L.J. 393, at *3 (2010).

[57] *Id.*

the clients and others. A staple of the legal ethics curriculum is *Spaulding v. Zimmerman*,[58] a case in which the defendants' lawyers withheld information about the plaintiff's potentially fatal injury out of apparent fear that it would increase their clients' liability. The plaintiff was suing defendants for injuries suffered in a car accident. The plaintiff's doctor did not notice an aortic aneurysm on the x-ray, but the doctor retained by the defendants did. The defendants' lawyers did not tell their clients or the opposing counsel, and a settlement was finalized without the plaintiff's (a twenty-year-old boy) learning about his life-threatening condition. Only by chance was his injury eventually discovered, during a medical examination for the army, and remedied through surgery. The settlement was reopened by the court, but the attorneys faced no discipline, as the ethics rules did not compel, or even permit, disclosure.[59] (Today's rules would not compel disclosure either, though they would permit it.)[60] The client could have chosen to permit disclosure, of course, but the attorneys apparently presumed, without bothering to confirm, that the client cared more about limiting his financial losses than about the life of a young man. Such dramatic examples are rare, but the

[58] 263 Minn. 346 (1962).

[59] The rule governing at the time provided:

It is the duty of a lawyer to preserve his client's confidences.... The announced intention of a client to commit a crime is not included within the confidences which he is bound to respect. He may properly make such disclosures as may be necessary to prevent the act or protect against whom it is threatened.

ABA Canons of Prof'l Ethics Canon 37 (1937).

[60] *See ABA Model Rules of Prof'l Conduct R.1.6.*

mindset that attributes to the client objectives grounded in such narrow self-interest is not.

The social nature of the human person is not equally relevant to every legal context, though. In criminal defense especially, the attorney is right to keep a narrow focus on ensuring that state power does not deprive the client of her liberty without a solid factual basis, legal justification, and observation of due process. The myriad relational interests implicated by the client's decisions in most advocacy and counseling situations narrow considerably in criminal defense to a single question: has the state proved the client guilty beyond a reasonable doubt? Criminal law orients itself toward the protection of the individual, as an individual, for good reason: it is the individual who stands accused, with her very life in the balance. This is not to suggest that the lawyer's accountability runs only to the criminal defendant. Monroe Freedman has written thoughtfully about the dilemma facing a criminal defense lawyer whose client intends to commit perjury given the attorney's duty of candor to the court,[61] and Rick Garnett has reflected on the moral, not just legal, dilemma faced by an attorney representing a inmate who tells his attorney to let the prisoner submit to execution and stop challenging the sentence.[62] In

---

[61] Monroe H. Freedman, *Professional Responsibility of the Criminal Defense Lawyer: The Three Hardest Questions*, 64 MICH. L. REV. 1469 (1966).

[62] Richard W. Garnett, *Sectarian Reflections on Lawyers' Ethics and Death Row Volunteers*, 77 NOTRE DAME L. REV. 795 (2002).

general, though, the criminal defense attorney functions primarily as a bulwark to protect the client's interests as an individual because the most basic (autonomy-driven) sense of human dignity is at stake. The ability to consider relational goods and the human flourishing they support presupposes physical freedom.

The social dimension of human existence is not foreign to law – indeed, it is the premise from which law begins – but even outside the criminal defense context, the law often appears committed to the Hobbesian view that our social existence is primarily a liability for which we must construct defenses. The law then becomes a crude (but nevertheless important) baseline for protecting individuals against the encroachments of others, rather than a more fulsome embodiment of the extent to which we derive meaning from our relationships, both intimate and more communal. By expanding the attorney-client dialogue beyond the letter of the law, attorneys can draw this more fulsome understanding of our social natures into the picture. But even when the relational accountability at issue is of a type that the law purports to embody, lawyers sometimes will need to go beyond the law's letter in conveying the stakes of a decision to the client. The law is a highly imperfect instrument, and often the law struggles mightily to capture precisely how we are accountable to each other. The lawyer may be in a position to help the client understand that struggle in a way that sheds more light on the interests implicated by the client's decision.

BENEFITS:

Savings – 180 burn deaths, 180 serious burn injuries, 2100 burned vehicles.
Unit Cost – $200,000 per death, $67,000 per injury, $700 per vehicle.
Total Benefit – 180x($200,000)+180x($67,000)+2100x($700) = $49.5 million.

COSTS:

Sales – 11 million cars, 1.5 million light trucks.
Unit Cost – $11 per car, $11 per truck.
Total Cost – 11,000,000x($11)+1,500,000x($11) = $137 million.

Figure 3.1. Cost-benefit analysis from internal Ford memo addressing "fatalities associated with crash induced fuel leakage and fires."

Take the infamous "Ford Pinto memo," for example. In the 1970s, the Ford Motor Company was aware that the gas tank in some of its models, including the popular Pinto, was susceptible to rupture from rear impacts because the tank could be pushed forward into a set of bolts. The company conducted a cost-benefit analysis to determine whether an eleven-dollar protective plate should be installed in the vehicles to remedy the problem. Figure 3.1 provides the key analysis from the memo.[63]

Accordingly, Ford's management opted to pay the wrongful death verdicts rather than install the plates. If a lawyer had been in the room when management debated this issue, what should the lawyer have said? Perhaps the lawyer

---

[63] E. S. Grush and C. S. Saunby, *Fatalities Associated with Crash Induced Fuel Leakage and Fires* (available at http://www.autosafety. org/uploads/phpq3mJ7F_FordMemo.pdf).

could have shown her technical competence by attesting to the accuracy of $200,000 as a predictable damages award for lost wages and other components of wrongful death. Predicting verdicts is an important contribution by lawyers to the client's decision making. But how much richer could the conversation have been if the lawyer explained how and why the legal system had struggled for generations to put a dollar value on life. At common law, damages resulting from death were not recoverable, and the rise of wrongful death statutes was controversial, in part, because of concerns regarding the jury's ability to arrive at a financial award that could compensate for the life lost. This sort of conversation could still be steered toward Ford's bottom line, of course, as our discomfort with the law's attempt to place a value on human life could foreseeably be shared by jurors and redirected toward Ford – since Ford not only placed a value after the fact, but utilized that value in a case where death was avoidable. (In fact, a jury ultimately expressed its discomfort by awarding significant punitive damages against Ford.)[64]

But assume that the jury would somehow be precluded from exceeding the $200,000 prediction. Even if Ford's financial analysis played out accurately, could there have

---

[64] See Grimshaw v. Ford Motor Co., 174 Cal. App. 3d 757, 813 (1981) (reducing jury's punitive damages award from $125 million to $3.5 million where evidence showed that company "decided to defer correction of the shortcoming [in the Pinto's design] by engaging in a cost-benefit analysis balancing human lives and limbs against corporate profits").

been a useful conversation between lawyer and management about the law's struggle with the broader human interests in these cases that are not readily captured by a cost-benefit analysis? As a corporation made up of relationally accountable human persons, would Ford have benefited from a conversation about the myopic premises underlying this memorandum? If we want someone to help a client navigate the tensions, human values, and unavoidable imperfections embedded in the law, the lawyer has to be ready. There is a temptation to use the law's (apparent) grant of permission as the end of the conversation. If we are committed, with King, to the social nature of the human person, the law's grant of permission is the conversation's beginning. Lawyers are in the best position to see that.

Personalism cautions against viewing the attorney-client relationship in isolation; the relationship is part of the broader community, and our accountability does not end at the boundaries of the relationship. To be sure, an attorney's role presumes a privileged place for the client; an advocate is not impartial. But an exclusive focus on the client carries real human costs, not the least of which is impairing the legal system's ability to secure the common good. This lesson has not been totally lost on the legal profession. For example, attorneys who are participating in a matter enjoy a vastly circumscribed right of free speech when their comments could prejudice the proceedings.[65] More controversial were

---

[65] *See ABA Model Rules of Prof'l Conduct* R. 3.6.

the post-Enron developments noted in Chapter 2: Congress and the ABA expanding lawyers' whistle-blowing responsibilities, requiring lawyers to report "up the chain" within an organization when they learn of misconduct by employees, and empowering lawyers to disclose confidential information when the highest authority within an organization fails to deal with the misconduct effectively.[66] Similar "gatekeeping" responsibilities have been imposed by Congress in other contexts.[67] The best option for the lawyer is to help the client recognize her own accountability to others, but the law is increasingly willing to force the lawyer to treat the accountability as real, even when the client refuses to do so.

To a certain extent, the legal profession has been dragged kicking and screaming into this expanded gatekeeping role. Some lawyers avoid broader public responsibilities by narrowing their understanding of their roles and the identity (and relevant constituents) of their corporate clients.[68] Portraying the corporation as a mere "nexus of contracts" tends to marginalize the human concerns that they are designed to serve.[69] Other lawyers operate with an

---

[66] *See ABA Model Rules of Prof'l Conduct* R. 1.13; 17 C.F.R. § 205.3(b) (2007) (implementing Sarbanes-Oxley Act).

[67] *See* Chapter 2 at pages 122–3.

[68] Sung Hui Kim, *Lawyer Exceptionalism in the Gatekeeping Wars*, 63 S.M.U. L. Rev. 73, 77 (2010) (noting "client confusion" among attorneys "in which the human manager, and not the corporation, is mistaken for the true client").

[69] *See, e.g.*, Frank H. Easterbrook & Daniel R. Fischel, *The Corporate Contract*, 89 Colum. L. Rev. 1416 (1989) ("An approach that

unduly narrow conception of their client's interests, as noted previously, and fail to take the time to verify that the client indeed is uninterested in considering the well-being of third parties. And some lawyers remain justifiably skeptical of expanded public responsibilities, fearing that such measures will erode the attorney's ability to serve as an effective advocate for clients by disrupting the trust necessary for the attorney-client relationship to flourish. Whether or not any particular measure has gone too far, a personalist could not object to the notion that the client is not the only source of an attorney's obligations. The restoration of community is premised on a broader view of interpersonal accountability, even among professionals devoted to serving their client's interests.

III. Lawyers' Partisanship Problem

This raises the more fundamental question, one that is at the crux of the personalist lawyer's dilemma: how can a lawyer reconcile her professional duties to a client with her more general moral duties to all humankind? Put differently, can a personalist favor the interests of some persons over others? If we are, as King put it, "caught in an inescapable network of mutuality," how can lawyers devote themselves to

emphasizes the contractual nature of a corporation removes from the field of interesting questions one that has plagued many writers: what is the goal of the corporation?").

zealously advocating on behalf of one person, often at the expense and in deliberate disregard of another?

The moral good made possible by the legal system provides the traditional justification for promoting the interests of the client over the interests of the opponent or third parties. The legal system is the political community's chosen mechanism for the peaceful resolution of conflicts among the citizenry. The system's effectiveness is premised on attorneys' committing to advocate on behalf of a particular party to the dispute, with other actors designated as the ultimate decision makers on the legal merits of parties' claims. The lawyer's role is morally defensible, not necessarily because the lawyer is advocating for a morally defensible client or cause, but because her advocacy makes possible a morally defensible system.

This justification has been widely challenged, with two criticisms gaining the most attention: first, the system justification only works to the extent that the system works, and the inadequacy of resources to secure effective representation, along with the corruption or incompetence of institutional actors, means that the system in practice is far from an ideal venue for the just resolution of conflicts. Second, even when the system works as intended, it only resolves the claims of those who appear as participants. Many legal disputes have implications that go far beyond the interests of whoever happens to be filling the roles of plaintiff and defendant. The narrowness of the court's vision – focused only on the guilt or innocence of an individual in criminal cases, the liability of a defendant in civil cases, or the (much rarer) possibility of injunctive relief prescribing or proscribing certain action by the defendant sued – leaves many interests on the outside looking in. As a personalist, King called us to expand the field of our moral vision; the legal system, designed for the technical and precise adjudication of disputes under the law, conveys a much narrower view of what matters.

The most recent sustained effort at buttressing the traditional justification is that of Daniel Markovits, who argues that the nature of the lawyer's work requires a role-based reorientation of the moral analysis employed by nonlawyers. Provocatively, he describes lawyers as liars and cheaters because "to deceive others by asserting a proposition that one privately (and correctly) disbelieves is to lie; and to exploit others by promoting claims or causes that one privately (and correctly) thinks undeserving is to cheat."[70] In fact, Markovits believes that lying is unavoidable for advocates "because the principles of lawyer loyalty and client control that constitute the foundations of their professional role require them to betray and disguise their beliefs, in order to mislead others as their clients command."[71] And cheating is a reality "unless our system of adjudication presented a case of pure procedural justice, in the Rawlsian sense of a process that is constitutive of the justice of its outcomes."[72] Whether

---

[70] Daniel Markovits, *A Modern Legal Ethics: Adversary Advocacy in a Democratic Age* (2009), 36.

[71] *Id.* at 77.

[72] *Id.* at 37.

or not his examples – bluffing in negotiations, undermining truthful testimony, or making legal arguments that they would reject if they were the judge – count as "lying,"[73] and whether or not suspending judgment as to the merits of a position amounts to "cheating," the salient point is that lawyers as advocates regularly engage in behavior that would be deemed objectionable if engaged in by nonlawyers.

Even assuming that the laws implemented by the legal system are just, and that access to legal services can be fairly distributed, Markovits points out that the lawyer faces an uphill struggle in using the system's moral value to justify her own behavior. The system-based justification is an impartial argument; what is missing is a first-personal argument, "which concerns a person's interest in achieving her own (suitable) ambitions and emphasizes the special relation of authorship that a person has to her own actions and life plans."[74] He uses the idea of integrity to capture the distinction, arguing that "lawyers betray their integrity when, abandoning their ordinary ambitions to honesty and fair play, they lie and cheat, including even when, as under the adversary system defense, they are impartially justified in doing so."[75] The problem is worsening, in Markovits's estimation, as the growing pressure to be "more aggressively partisan" increases the "divergence between lawyers'

[73] *Id.* at 3.
[74] *Id.* at 9.
[75] *Id.*

professional obligations and ordinary first-personal moral ambitions."[76] Lawyers have to be concerned not only about the results they produce, but also about the kind of person they will become.[77]

The gap between systemic justification and personal virtue is illustrated by Arthur Applbaum's classic commentary on professional detachment. Writing as the executioner of Paris in the wake of the Reign of Terror, Applbaum appeals to the social value of order and stability, explaining:

> My profession is the guardian of a political value that is of utmost moral importance. Although the good sought by my profession is valuable for all of society and capable of being recognized as valuable by all subjects and citizens, this good cannot be pursued except from within my professional role or roles like it.... My devotion is not to any one regime or political ideology, but to the good of social order and the stability and security it brings. By stability, I do not mean the stability of any regime or form of government, but of civilized life itself; and by security, I mean security from the random horror of murderous mobs. To realize the good of social order, my profession is committed to a simple principle: the state must maintain its monopoly over violence.[78]

[76] *Id.* at 214.

[77] *Id.* at 110.

[78] Arthur Isak Applbaum, *Professional Detachment: The Executioner of Paris*, 109 HARV. L. REV. 458, 481–2 (1995).

Applbaum leaves the reader wondering how the legal profession's role-based moral justification differs from the executioner's, and what the similarities might mean for the lawyer's own moral integrity.

By way of more explicit illustration of this point, Markovits cites the philosopher Bernard Williams's famous story about a man named Jim who visits a tribal village where government soldiers are about to execute twenty Indians because of recent political protests despite no evidence that they were involved in the protest. The soldiers' leader invites Jim to kill one of the Indians, and if he does, the soldiers offer to set the rest free in his honor. We would expect Jim to hesitate before accepting that offer even if he is convinced that the soldiers actually will proceed with the executions if he does not accept. Jim's moral analysis cannot just consider results – one innocent person dying versus twenty innocent people dying – he also has to consider the conduct "from the inside," evaluating what the act would mean in light of the type of person he aims to be.[79]

The problem with the system-based justification of lawyers' conduct, according to Markovits, is that lawyers have first-personal ambitions "in favor of honesty and fair play that, like Jim's ambition not to kill innocents, figure prominently in their ethical self-understandings."[80] Just as Jim's

---

[79] *See* Bernard Williams, "A Critique of Utilitarianism," in *Utilitarianism: For and Against* J. J. C., ed. Smart & Bernard Williams (1973).

[80] Markovits, *supra* note 70, at 115.

willingness to kill in order to reduce the amount of killing would threaten his integrity, so too does a lawyer's willingness to carry out professional obligations at the expense of her personal ethical ambitions.[81] At a certain point, impartial moral considerations override first-personal moral ambitions – for example, Jim would probably execute one to save one thousand – but this is not the same as saying that first-personal ambition is precisely bounded by impartial moral considerations.[82] Ignoring the limits of impartial moral justification is to ignore human nature, for the boundaries of lawyers' "moral personalities" are formed by the beliefs, intentions, and endeavors "that are distinctly theirs."[83]

After stating the problem so starkly, Markovits pivots and lays out the path toward a solution. Put simply, he attempts to turn lawyerly vices into lawyerly virtues by recognizing that lawyers specialize in "negative capability: that is, in the capacity to speak not in one's own voice but rather, effacing one's private judgments, faithfully and authentically to render the subjectivity of another – in the case of lawyers by giving voice to clients who would otherwise remain inarticulate."[84] By giving voice and thereby helping persons who face intractable social disagreements sustain peaceful social

---

[81] *Id.* at 115.
[82] *See id.* at 139–40.
[83] *Id.* at 150.
[84] *Id.* at 11.

coordination, lawyers function as peacemakers.[85] Lawyers' negative capability – their dedication to serve their clients without judging them – is essential to this function because it is the only way in which lawyers "can successfully invite litigants to engage the legal process."[86] These, in his account, are lawyerly virtues.

Markovits sees another problem to the lawyer's dilemma, though – one that may prove insurmountable in the current environment. Besides identifying role-based moral content that can justify the gap between lawyers' professional role and ordinary first-personal moral ambitions (which he does with the concept of negative capability), the dilemma can only be resolved if that role-based justification is "practically accessible to lawyers, who must be able to adopt the idiosyncratic ambitions it elaborates as their own and to sustain those ambitions against the insistent encroachments of ordinary first-personal ethics."[87] In other words, the justification may work as an academic theory, but will it be persuasive enough to lawyers to help shape their own moral identity in a way that can withstand the pressure of ordinary (i.e., noncheating and truth telling) first-personal moral ambitions?

Markovits says no. He does not believe that the legal profession is up to the task of redescribing the lawyer's role in a way that can turn the vices (lying, cheating) into virtues

[85] *Id.* at 208.
[86] *Id.*
[87] *Id.* at 171.

(negative capability so as to give voice to the citizenry). This stems from three features of the modern profession: first, the bar is much more diverse and "much less involved in shaping lawyers' professional attitudes."[88] Second, the bar's mechanism for regulating members has shifted from fraternal admonitions to "fixed rules backed by formal sanctions in a bureaucratic regulatory scheme."[89] There is much less of an aspirational narrative reflected in a regulatory code than in a broad articulation of professional values, even if the latter does not provide a ready framework for disciplinary proceedings. Third, the bar is no longer running the show; the state now has a significant say in controlling the conduct of lawyers.[90] The profession, including its ethical regime, has become "more cosmopolitan than insular, and therefore unable to sustain any distinctive first-personal ethical creed that might replace more ordinary ethical ambitions and protect lawyers' integrity against the pressures associated with their professional obligations."[91] In other words, the profession does not have the resources to withstand the pressure on lawyers' self-conception that results from ordinary morality. Vices will remain vices, whether one is a lawyer or not.

So while Markovits ultimately deems his solution untenable, the solution itself should give the personalist lawyer

[88] *Id.* at 228.
[89] *Id.* at 228–9.
[90] *Id.* at 229.
[91] *Id.* at 233.

pause. Markovits does not deny the relevance or importance of the attorney's moral aspirations, but his focus on negative capability essentially calls for lawyers to adopt the client's moral aspirations as their own – that is, the attorney's moral aspiration should be to erase her own views from the relationship. As Brad Wendel observes, "Rather than centering professional ethics around an ordinary moral ideal like struggling against oppression," Markovits's theory requires lawyers to "incorporate the professional ideal of fidelity to clients and self-effacement into their own personal commitments."[92] This does not hold much promise for the attorney's own integrity in the long run. Benjamin Zipursky points out that "the virtues of honesty, trustworthiness, candor, and constancy that lie at the core of integrity do not permit a lawyer to ignore the incongruities of justice or to wrap herself in the cocoon of client fidelity," for these virtues "demand judgment, moderation, sensitivity to community understandings and expectations, and ... practical engagement."[93] The problem is compounded for a lawyer who holds a personalist view of the universe: commitment to the reality of our interconnectedness does not permit us to ignore the needs and interests of others. Because the ability to live consistently with that broad sweep of vision will lie at the core of the

[92] Bradley W. Wendel, *Lawyers and Fidelity to Law* (2010), 165.
[93] Benjamin Zipursky, *Integrity and the Incongruities of Justice: A Review of Daniel Markovits's* A Modern Legal Ethics: Adversary Advocacy in a Democratic Age, 119 YALE L.J. 1948, 1991 (2010).

personalist's commitments, it will also lie at the core of any meaningful account of her integrity.

One way to avoid the difficulties associated with recasting ordinary vices as lawyerly virtues is to reduce the need for lawyers to engage in ordinary vices in the first place. Zipursky argues, for example, that "the way to deal with one's awareness of the incongruities of justice is not single-minded commitment to the virtue of client fidelity, but practical engagement with the mid-sized problems of improving our systems for realizing justice."[94] Knowing human fallibility, we also know that corruption, inadequate resources, and flawed decision making will always be part of the system. So as we work toward systemic improvement, we also need to consider ways in which lawyers can close the gap between vice and virtue in their own practices. What if, instead of pining for insularity as a shield from moral accountability, lawyers open themselves to moral claims by considering the possibility that clients might be open to those moral claims? As Katherine Kruse noted,[95] the professional narrative tends to assume that clients are motivated by individual self-interest with little care or concern for, or sense of accountability to, the communities through which much of their identities are formed and lived out. Maybe the problem is not so much a lawyer's behavior as

[94] *Id.* at 1955.
[95] Kruse, *supra* note 56.

the presumptions about human nature underlying the law-yer's behavior.

Still, Markovits is correct to point out the importance of loyalty. If a client insists on rejecting the underlying tenets of personalism – that is, if the client affirmatively chooses to act in disregard of any relational accountability – then the attorney faces decisions about whether she can continue the representation. My point is simply that the starting place for the conversation with the client matters, and per-sonalism pushes back against the presumptions that have defined that starting place to be the maximization of the client's individual self-interest.

With this starting place in mind, privileging a relation-ship with a particular client by giving voice to her interests and perspective is fully consistent with personalism. Just as it is morally permissible to care for my own family before I care for needs outside my family, it is morally permissible to include my clients in my immediate circle of care in a way that recognizes a special duty to them that I do not have to humanity more broadly. In all of life, we are equipped to build up from more particular allegiances to become more broadly inclusive. Practicing empathy, giving voice, and standing in the shoes of a client can help lawyers learn how to recognize and internalize the interests of others. Gilbert Meilander writes in this regard that when we are "moved by particular loyalties to detect worth even when it is not always in evidence, we may become able to see it also in those to whom we have no special attachment."[96] Perhaps the attorney-client relationship can be a training ground for an ever-widening circle of empathy, moral agency, and action. When we learn to adopt someone else's gaze, our field of vision need not end there.

IV. Lawyers as Healers: Why Clients Should Care

Acting as a healer is not necessarily inconsistent with the client's interests; in some contexts, lawyers acting pursuant to their presumed adversarial commitments do real harm to their clients. Though lawyers might be prepared to wage war against the entire world on behalf of their clients, few clients find it plausible, much less desirable, to stand apart from the world that is their home. This reality is not always reflected in professional rhetoric, whether in the Model Code's instruction that clients are "entitled to ... seek any lawful objective through legally permissible means"[97] or in Lord Brougham's centuries-old description of the advocate as one who

> in the discharge of his duty, knows but one person in the world, and that person is his client. To save that client by all means and expedients, and at all hazards and costs

---

[96] Gilbert Meilander, *Neither Beast nor God: The Dignity of the Human Person* (2009), 64.

[97] *See ABA Model Code of Prof'l Resp.* EC 7–1.

to other persons, and, among them, to himself, is his first and only duty; and in performing this duty he must not regard the alarm, the torments, the destruction which he may bring upon others. Separating the duty of a patriot from that of an advocate, he must go on reckless of consequences, though it should be his unhappy fate to involve his country in confusion.[98]

A seeming reflexive reliance on the profession's adversarial, rights-focused values is evidenced in a range of cases,[99] perhaps most notably in one of the most wrenching public scandals in recent years: the Catholic Church's response to the sexual abuse of children by priests. Though we may never know what the church's lawyers told the bishops in confidence, the evidence suggests that the lawyers approached their client as a bundle of legal interests to be maximized, rather than as a community with a broad set of constituents who had suffered a serious breach of trust.

---

[98] Geoffrey C. Hazard, *The Future of Legal Ethics*, 100 YALE L.J. 1239, 1244 (1991) (quoting 2 Trial of Queen Caroline 3, ed. Joseph Nightingale, [1821]); *see generally* Monroe H. Freedman, *Henry Lord Brougham and Zeal*, 34 HOFSTRA L. REV. 1319 (2006) (contextualizing Lord Brougham's statement); *see also* James W. Jones, *Future Structure and Regulation of Law Practice: An Iconoclast's Perspective*, 44 ARIZ. L. REV. 537, 541 (2002) (noting that profession's paradigm forces "our clients to define every problem in legal terms, and then we impose on ourselves the ethical obligation to maximize every legal advantage").

[99] *See, e.g.*, Robert A. Kagan, *Adversarial Legalism: The American Way of Law* (2001).

The lay review board commissioned by the United States Conference of Catholic Bishops faulted the bishops for adopting the presumptions and prejudices of their legal counsel in their effort to minimize the impact of the allegations.[100] The board found that the church's lawyers raised "inappropriate defenses that could be construed as blaming the victim, such as assumption of risk or contributory negligence," and disclaimed "responsibility for ... priests by claiming that they were 'independent contractors.'"[101] In other cases, they forced plaintiffs who wished to remain anonymous to reveal their identities publicly in bringing litigation;[102] sought to depose the therapist the church had hired to help abuse victims, notwithstanding the therapist's insistence that she was hired with the understanding that her communications with the victims would remain confidential;[103] demanded that a victim present himself without an attorney for questioning by church officials if he wished to have his request that a priest be defrocked considered (a demand quickly disavowed

---

[100] The National Review Board for the Protection of Children and Young People, *A Report on the Crisis in the Catholic Church in the United States* 1 (February 27, 2004) (available at http://www.bishop-accountability.org/usccb/causesandcontext/2004–02–27-CC-Report.pdf) (accessed September 30, 2011) ["Review Board"].

[101] *Id.* at 120.

[102] Michael Paulson and Michael Rezendes, "Openness of Bishops Still at Issue," *Boston Globe*, June 17, 2003, A1.

[103] Ralph Ranalli, "Clergy Abuse Settlement Seen Unlikely," *Boston Globe*, May 19, 2003, A1.

by church officials themselves);[104] and filed countersuits accusing victims' parents of negligence for entrusting their children to priests.[105] Many of the church's attorneys "counseled Church leaders not to meet with, or apologize to, victims even when the allegations had been substantiated, on grounds that apologies could be used against the Church in court."[106] In the words of one bishop:

> We made terrible mistakes. Because the attorneys said over and over "Don't talk to the victims, don't go near them," and here they were victims. I heard victims say "We would not have taken it to [plaintiffs' attorneys] had someone just come to us and said 'I'm sorry.'" But we listened to the attorneys.[107]

These problems were exacerbated by the lawyers' frequent recommendation that the victims sign confidentiality agreements as a prerequisite to settlement. In the review board's estimation, these agreements stifled victims' "ability to discuss their experience openly and thwarted awareness by the laity of the problem."[108]

None of the lawyers' mistakes excuse the bishops from their underlying failure to respond appropriately to evidence

---

[104] *Id.*

[105] Michael Powell and Lois Romano, "Roman Catholic Church Shifts Legal Strategy," *Washington Post*, May 13, 2002, A1.

[106] Review Board, *supra* note 100, at 121.

[107] *Id.*

[108] *Id.* at 120.

of sexual abuse by priests. But in crafting the legal strategy to defend the church's "interests," did the lawyers do a disservice by construing the interests in such narrow terms, as though the bishops exist separate and apart from the victims (who were and, in many cases are, members of the church)? A lawyer needs to recognize that her client's social accountability is not always coextensive with her legal accountability, though they are often intertwined. Further, a lawyer needs to recognize that respecting the relationships that are part of the client's identity must be included in any fulsome conception of the client's interests. When lawyers do not help the clients discern how the legal representation might impact – or be impacted by – those relationships, lawyers are not authentically serving their client's best interests.

Compared to a church, not every client will bring such an obvious moral interdependence as part of her deliberately and explicitly cultivated raison d'etre. But even for more routine clients and causes, the representation may present opportunities to affirm or deny the impact that the client's decisions have on other members of the human community. When a lawyer has to advise a client about "loopholes" in an environmental regulatory regime, or advise a company whether to close a plant in a small town that is economically dependent on the company for jobs, or draft a will for a client who is estranged from her children, or engage in plea bargain negotiations, or help navigate a custody dispute, or interpret a litigation opponent's request for sensitive documents, there is an opportunity for moral engagement regarding the existence and implications of a belief in the human community. To be clear, these considerations are not *created* by personalism; they are simply *acknowledged* by personalism. Further, as will be discussed in Chapter 5, acknowledgment is not imposition: introducing a personalist reality into the conversation cannot, in a client-directed endeavor, dictate a particular outcome.

Personalism asks us to begin the process of moral reflection and deliberation from the premise that we are social by nature and thus that a true account of human flourishing has to make space for human relationship. This premise is not especially controversial in most circles, but its impact on our day-to-day decision making is often hard to find. King urged us close the gap between believing in our social nature and living as though we believe in our social nature. Lawyers must be mindful to avoid such a gap in their own lives, but also to avoid presuming that a client either 1) rejects the premise that relational accountability is a key component of human flourishing or 2) prefers to live with a disconnect between her core beliefs and her morally laden decision making. Economic liability can be one measure of our relational accountability, though few of us would identify the human interests that arise from our social natures solely with the maximization of our economic positions, whether individually or in a corporate venture. Lawyers can and should devote themselves to a particular client's interests, but they should remain open to a broader conception of those interests in light of personalism's insights. Clients may reject the personalist premise, but lawyers should not begin their representation by presuming that rejection.

Personalism's contribution to the work of the attorney, in a sense, is to expand our view in a way that aligns our work more closely with human nature. In criticizing materialism, Brightman argues that "moral obligation extends beyond what the eye can see into the field of all that the mind can see," and it is "the task of religion to prevent the moral man from any artificial narrowing of his range to the needs of his body and his bank account, and to expand his vision so that the spiritual possibilities of life will be real and vivid to him."[109] An individual's intuition is not a sufficient moral guide, for it cannot "be trusted as leading to truth about conduct or fact until it has been criticized and tested by the way in which it fits into the rest of our experience." After all, even "deep-rooted convictions may be no more than the predominant social practice of the age," and thus "the appeal to intuition [may be] simply a disguised form of the appeal to social authority."[110]

Given its emphasis on the need to awaken personality to the social nature of reality, it is no surprise that personalism viewed religion as a source of creative tension with the status quo. Brightman counted "the passionate revolt against

[109] Edgar Brightman, *Religious Values* (1925), 62.
[110] Edgar Brightman, *Moral Laws* (1933), 83.

the status quo" as "one of the credentials" of true religion's "divine origin."[111] Coming to grips with reality inescapably shapes the personality's stance toward those who wield power within that reality. The worldview provided by personalism helped produce King the prophet.

[111] Edgar Brightman, *Personality and Religion* (1934), 123.

4

Justice

Lawyers as Prophets

Martin Luther King Jr. was, as James Cone puts it, "a theologian of action," and his thinking "emerged from his efforts to establish a just society."[1] In his sermons, he railed against Christians who "worship Christ emotionally and not morally."[2] Even though personalism resists rigid moralizing, its espousal of a personality-centered universe as objective reality carries strong claims of moral truth. For

[1] James H. Cone, "The Theology of Martin Luther King, Jr.," in *Martin Luther King, Jr. and the Civil Rights Movement,* vol. 1, ed. David Garrow (1989), 21, 21.

[2] Martin Luther King Jr., "Pride versus Humility: The Parable of the Pharisee and the Publican," sermon at Dexter Avenue Baptist Church (September 25, 1955), in *The Papers of Martin Luther King Jr.*: Volume VI: Advocate of the Social Gospel (2007), 230, 232.

his part, King developed a robust vision of the moral law as the impetus for legal and social reform, particularly in his critique of segregation:

> Any law that uplifts human personality is just. Any law that degrades human personality is unjust. All segregation statutes are unjust because segregation distorts the soul and damages the personality. It gives the segregator a false sense of superiority, and the segregated a false sense of inferiority. To use the words of Martin Buber, the great Jewish philosopher, segregation substitutes an "I-it" relationship for the "I-thou" relationship, and ends up relegating persons to the status of things. So segregation is not only politically, economically, and sociologically unsound, but it is morally wrong and sinful. Paul Tillich has said that sin is separation. Isn't segregation an existential expression of man's tragic separation, an expression of his awful estrangement, his terrible sinfulness?[3]

As such, King "can urge men to disobey segregation ordinances because they are morally wrong."[4] Moreover, a person "who breaks a law that conscience tells him is unjust, and willingly accepts the penalty by staying in jail to arouse the conscience of the community over its injustice, is in reality expressing the very highest respect for law."[5]

[3] Martin Luther King Jr., "Letter From Birmingham City Jail" (1963), in *A Testament of Hope: The Essential Writings and Speeches of Martin Luther King Jr.* (1986), 289, 294.

[4] *Id.*

[5] *Id.*

In that single letter, we see how different themes in King's worldview coalesced into a prophetic stance. Respect for the human person serves as the benchmark for justice. A lack of respect not only denies the dignity of the person disrespected, but also of the person who failed to show respect, by preying upon human vulnerability instead of affirming relationship in the face of that vulnerability. The call to justice is about more than lifting up the marginalized and oppressed; it is about restoring the relationships that are breached by marginalization and oppression, connecting us all with our true natures as created, mutually dependent beings. King the prophet calls for justice by calling to restore community.

This brings into relief a key dimension of King's practice of love: it did not derive from other-worldly sentimentality or an individualized feeling of affection. It was intensely personal, but with implications that were inescapably social. It was thus cognizant of the necessary relationship between love and justice, and, correspondingly, between love and power. The foundational role of love in the just wielding of power was captured in a story recounted by King:

> I learned a lesson many years ago from a report of two men who flew to Atlanta to confer with a Negro civil rights leader at the airport. Before they could begin to talk, the porter sweeping the floor drew the local leader aside to talk about a matter that troubled him. After fifteen minutes had passed, one of the visitors said bitterly to his companion, "I am just too busy for this kind of nonsense. I haven't

come a thousand miles to sit and wait while he talks to a porter." The other replied, "When the day comes that he stops having time to talk to a porter, on that day I will not have the time to come one mile to see him."[6]

King explained that "power without love is reckless and abusive," but "love without power is sentimental and anemic." And while "power at its best is love implementing the demands of justice," "justice at its best is love correcting everything which stands against love."[7] Love must satisfy justice, or else it "is no love at all."[8]

King viewed love in real-world terms, describing love as "justice concretized."[9] This required him to take an unvarnished look at the social conditions surrounding him; his love was prophetic to the extent that he was able to discern the real from the unreal. For example, as Ira Zepp relates, the Montgomery bus boycott that King led "uncovered the uneasy peace existing beneath a surface of order and tranquility."[10] Critics attacked him for upending the peace, but he knew that the status quo was no peace at all. King invoked Christ on this point:

---

[6] Martin Luther King Jr., "Black Power Defined" (1967), in *A Testament of Hope, supra* note 3, at 303, 308.

[7] Martin Luther King Jr., *Where Do We Go From Here: Chaos or Community?* (1968), 37.

[8] *Id.* at 89–90.

[9] *Id.* at 90.

[10] Ira G. Zepp, *The Social Vision of Martin Luther King Jr.* (1989), 47.

"I have not come to bring peace, but a sword." Certainly Jesus did not mean that he came to bring a physical sword. He seems to have been saying in substance: "I have not come to bring this old negative peace with its deadening passivity. I have come to lash out against such a peace. Whenever I come, a conflict is precipitated between the old and the new. Whenever I come, a division sets in between justice and injustice. I have come to bring a positive peace which is the presence of justice, love, yea, even the Kingdom of God."[11]

As did the biblical prophets, King did not mistake true peace for the superficial avoidance of conflict. His mission was in part to bring conflict to the surface in order to pave the way for a more lasting peace grounded in the restoration of relationship. In responding to the white ministers who criticized his direct action campaign in Birmingham, he pointed out that "we who engage in nonviolent direct action are not the creators of tension," but "merely bring to the surface the hidden tension that is already alive," so that the underlying injustice can be exposed.[12]

Restoring relationships not only defined the objectives of King's efforts, but also constrained the means by which he could get there. His belief in nonviolent resistance was grounded in the conviction that "the means must be as

---

[11] *Id.* (quoting Martin Luther King Jr., *Stride toward Freedom* 25).
[12] Martin Luther King Jr., "Letter from Birmingham City Jail," in *A Testament of Hope, supra* note 3.

pure as the end, that in the long run of history, immoral destructive means cannot bring about moral and constructive ends."[13] For King, constructive means and ends could be identified by their propensity to heal the wounds in the human community.

Lawyers hardly shrink from conflict. In fact, one frequent criticism of lawyers is their tendency to exacerbate conflict by pushing their client's interests to the exclusion of others' interests. Another line of criticism goes further, insisting that lawyers, either by nature or as a consequence of socialization within the profession, tend to make conflicts more personal and deeply entrenched with a "no holds barred" approach to zealous advocacy. Lawyers are essential for bringing conflict into the light of our legal system, but do they create more conflict along the way than is necessary for carrying out this function? The problem may lie, at least in part, in the profession's failure to provide meaningful content to the concept of justice or, more specifically, in its failure to connect justice to either the means or the ends of lawyering. King's own advocacy for justice has something to teach us about both.

I. King and Justice

King's prophetic stance was shaped significantly by his formation in the African American church, where the Hebrew

[13] Zepp, *supra* note 10, at 116 (quoting Martin Luther King Jr., "Love, Law, and Civil Disobedience," *The New South*, December 1961, 5).

prophets were important spiritual models of how faith in God should be socially transformative, not just personally transformative. King also found sustenance for these commitments in the work of Walter Rauschenbusch, whose book *Christianity and the Social Crisis* had, as King later recollected, "left an indelible impression on my thinking by giving me a theological basis for the social concern which had already grown up in me as a result of earlier experiences."[14]

Rauschenbusch looked to the prophets as part of a broader effort to reclaim the social nature of Christian faith. He pointed out that the Old Testament prophets "were not religious individualists," for "they conceived of their people as a gigantic personality which sinned as one and ought to repent as one."[15] The subsequent development of personal religious consciousness, through which "the individual realized that he personally was dear to God and could work out his salvation not as a member of his nation, but as a man by virtue of his humanity" was liberating, but, Rauschenbusch cautioned, we should not assume "that this change in religion was pure gain."[16]

Just as personalists defined individual well-being against the background of a healthy social fabric, Rauschenbusch's call for justice derived from his reorientation of religious

---

[14] Martin Luther King Jr., *Stride toward Freedom: The Montgomery Story* (1987), 73.
[15] Walter Rauschenbusch, *Christianity and the Social Crisis*, ed. Robert Cross (1964) (1907), 8–9.
[16] *Id.* at 28.

value beyond its individualist emphasis to encompass the community. The Old Testament prophets, when they insisted on personal holiness during the Exile, did so "because it was the condition and guarantee of all national restoration," not "because that was the end of all religion."[17] In Rauschenbusch's view, "personal religion was chiefly a means to an end; the end was social."[18]

The social theme did not end with the coming of Christ. Rauschenbusch saw significance in the fact that Jesus "was not a Greek philosopher or Hindu pundit teaching the individual the way of emancipation from the world and its passions, but a Hebrew prophet preparing men for the righteous social order."[19] Jesus sought to "create in men ... the goodness that would enable them to live rightly with their fellow-men and to constitute a true social life."[20] Jesus's teachings were not codes of personal holiness, but expressions of love's centrality to human goodness. For example, Rauschenbusch explained that if another "smites us in the face, we must turn the other cheek instead of doubling the barrier by returning the blow." Such lessons "are not hard and fast laws or detached rules of conduct," which would "become unworkable and ridiculous." Instead, they are "the most emphatic expressions of the determination that the fraternal relation which binds men together must not be

17 *Id.* at 29.
18 *Id.*
19 *Id.* at 67.
20 *Id.*

ruptured."[21] He extrapolated to pronounce that "all human goodness must be social goodness,"[22] and that "salvation is the voluntary socializing of the soul."[23] The Christian mission to bring about the Kingdom of God "is not a matter of saving human atoms, but of saving the social organism."[24] As Rufus Burrow puts it, Rauschenbusch "maintained that Jesus essentially worked through the individual person, but his aim was for the social ends of the kingdom."[25]

As the living embodiment of this mission, the early Christian churches "were not communities for the performance of a common worship, so much as communities with a common life."[26] Further, Christianity "must have had a strong social impetus to evoke such stirrings of social unrest and discontent."[27] Still today, "the State is the representative of things as they are; the Church is the representative of things as they ought to be." As such, the church "must be in perpetual but friendly conflict with the State, pushing it on to ever higher lines of duty."[28] This prophetic tension, in Rauschenbusch's view, is inexorably part of the Christian

---

[21] *Id.* at 68.

[22] *Id.* at 67.

[23] Walter Rauschenbusch, *A Theology for the Social Gospel* (1917), 99.

[24] Rauschenbusch, *Christianity and the Social Crisis, supra* note 15, at 650.

[25] Rufus Burrow, Jr., *God and Human Dignity: The Personalism, Theology, and Ethics of Martin Luther King, Jr.* (2006), 67.

[26] Rauschenbusch, *Christianity and the Social Crisis, supra* note 15, at 119.

[27] *Id.* at 140.

[28] *Id.* at 186–7.

experience. He asserted, "Unless a man finds his judgment at least on some fundamental questions in opposition to the current ideas of the age, he is still a child of this world and has not 'tasted the powers of the coming age.'"[29]

The "ideas of the age" are not limited to those emanating from the state, of course, and Rauschenbusch's prophetic stance was not directed solely to those operating the levers of state power. Indeed, he noted the limits of law in producing social harmony. In language that would later be echoed directly by King, Rauschenbusch wrote:

> The law can compel a man to support his wife, but it cannot compel him to love her, and what are ten dollars a week to a woman whose love lies in broken shards at her feet? The law can compel a father to provide for his children and can interfere if he maltreats them, but it cannot compel him to give them that loving fatherly intercourse which puts backbone into a child forever. The law can keep neighbors from trespassing, but it cannot put neighborly courtesy and good-will into their relations.[30]

The more fundamental changes require changes in personality: repenting "of the sins of existing society, cast[ing] off the spell of the lies protecting our social wrongs, hav[ing] faith in a higher social order, and realiz[ing] in ourselves a new type of Christian manhood which seeks to overcome the evil in the present world, not by withdrawing from the

[29] *Id.* at 349.
[30] *Id.* at 373.

world, but by revolutionizing it."[31] So while the responsibility for a just social order rests with each personality, the modern prophet can help a person face that responsibility:

> The greatest contribution which any man can make to the social movement is the contribution of a regenerated personality, of a will which sets justice above policy and profit, and of an intellect emancipated from falsehood. Such a man will in some measure incarnate the principles of a higher social order in his attitude to all questions and in all his relations to men.... If he speaks, his judgment will be a corrective force. If he listens, he will encourage the truthteller and discourage the peddler of adulterated facts and maxims. If others lose heart, he will stay with them with his inspired patience. If any new principle is to gain power in human history, it must take shape and life in individuals who have faith in it.[32]

The prophet is a checking force on the excesses of those around them, be they attitudes of despair or false optimism. Rauschenbusch noted that the Old Testament prophets changed their tone as soon as disaster occurred, for as long as "the people were falsely optimistic, the prophets persisted in destroying their illusions," but "when the people were despairing, the prophets opposed their false hopelessness."[33]

---

[31] *Id.* at 412.
[32] *Id.* at 351–2.
[33] *Id.* at 39.

As did many other critics, King faulted Rauschenbusch for displaying false optimism himself, for falling victim to the "cult of inevitable progress." Further, according to King, Rauschenbusch "came perilously close to identifying the Kingdom of God with a particular social and economic system – a tendency which should never befall the Church."[34] Nevertheless, King credited Rauschenbusch for "insisting that the gospel deals with the whole man, not only his soul but his body; not only his spiritual well-being but his material well-being."[35] Even though Rauschenbusch did not discuss racism, "King felt his horizons broaden precisely because of Rauschenbusch's analysis of class and poverty."[36] Rauschenbusch convicted King that "any religion which professes to be concerned about the souls of men and is not concerned about the social and economic conditions that scar the soul is a spiritually moribund religion only waiting for the day to be buried."[37]

Both King and Rauschenbusch practiced prophetic ethics by speaking the truth to a religious order that too often tried to escape responsibility for reality by retreating into a world-to-come piety, or, especially in King's case, through a don't-rock-the-boat conception of responsible Christian citizenship. The social gospel cut through the carefully

[34] Martin Luther King Jr., *supra* note 14, at 73.

[35] *Id.*

[36] Thomas F. Jackson, *From Civil Rights to Human Rights: Martin Luther King, Jr., and the Struggle for Economic Justice* (2006), 350.

[37] Martin Luther King Jr., *Supra* note 14, at 73.

constructed delusions of the governing order. As the theologian Walter Brueggemann puts it, "prophecy is an assault on public imagination, aimed at showing that the present presumed world is not absolute, but that a thinkable alternative can be imagined, characterized, and lived in."[38] King's prophetic advocacy helped the public imagine the beloved community and join him in taking one key step toward its realization: the end of a racially segregated society.

II. Lawyers and the Means of Justice

There are no limits to the scope of justice's call – as King famously stated, "Injustice anywhere is a threat to justice everywhere."[39] As his ministry evolved, King became more and more aware of his duty to call attention to injustice beyond the question of race. When he expanded his advocacy to express opposition to the Vietnam War and to urge new initiatives against poverty, he was heavily criticized for purportedly diluting his impact on race and overreaching his level of expertise. For King, though, remaining silent in the face of injustice was not an option, notwithstanding our eagerness to categorize injustice by labeling and limiting certain "causes."

[38] Walter Brueggemann, *A Social Reading of the Old Testament,* ed. Patrick D. Miller (1994), 224 (quoted in Thomas L. Shaffer, *Lawyers as Prophets*, 15 St. Thom. L. Rev. 469, 469 (2003)).

[39] Martin Luther King Jr., "Letter from Birmingham City Jail," in *A Testament of Hope, supra* note 3.

Though King would resist any attempt to construct boundaries that would limit the breadth of our recognition of, and responsibility for responding to, injustice, he firmly believed in the necessity of boundaries to govern the means by which we battle injustice. On the eve of the Montgomery bus boycott – the dawn of his civil rights activism – King was already clear about those limits, reminding his audience that "we are not advocating violence," and "the only weapon we have in our hands this evening is the weapon of protest."[40] Though he never advocated violence, David Garrow points out that King was not always fully committed to nonviolence;[41] he grew into it, in significant part through the influence of Mahatma Gandhi, the legendary Indian pacifist who helped usher in the end of British rule through widespread campaigns of civil disobedience.

As far back as 1936 – nearly two decades before the Montgomery bus boycott – Gandhi had remarked that "it may be through the Negroes that the unadulterated message of non-violence will be delivered to the world."[42] King began to explore Gandhi's work when others encouraged him to look to it as a resource for the nonviolent campaigns

[40] Taylor Branch, *Parting the Waters: America in the King Years 1954–1963* (1989), 140 (quoting King's address on eve of Montgomery bus boycott).

[41] David J. Garrow, "The Intellectual Development of Martin Luther King, Jr: Influences and Commentaries," in *Martin Luther King Jr. and the Civil Rights Movement,* ed. John A. Kirk (2007), 39, 46.

[42] Mahatma Gandhi: An Anthology of His Writings on His Life, Work, and Ideas (2012), 280.

that had become the centerpiece of the civil rights movement. King connected Gandhi's nonviolence with the suffering of Jesus,[43] and by the time he traveled to India,[44] his level of admiration was such that he commented, "To other countries I may go as a tourist, but to India I come as a pilgrim."[45]

As a weapon against British rule in India, Gandhi had developed the practice of satyagraha – *satya* meaning "truth" and *agraha* meaning "firmness in." There were four elements: first, one has a duty to respond to unjust laws through civil disobedience; second, the disobedience must be carried out with nonviolence and love; third, protesters practicing satyagraha should look upon their disobedience "as an offering of their bodies, souls, and lives to God"; and fourth, because it is more important to change hearts and minds than to change laws, "only when those who had previously supported and defended the unjust law had been turned around, only then could one say that satyagraha had been successful."[46] In a theme we have seen throughout our survey of King's thought, satyagraha emphasized that "even the oppressor can be a member of the community."[47]

[43] James H. Cone, "The Theology of Martin Luther King, Jr.," in *Martin Luther King, Jr. and the Civil Rights Movement,* vol. 1, ed. David J. Garrow (1989), 215, 218.

[44] King never met Gandhi, who was assassinated in 1948.

[45] Quoted in Stanley Wolpert, *Gandhi's Passion: The Life and Legacy of Mahatma Gandhi* (2001), 264.

[46] A. L. Herman, *Community, Violence, & Peace* (1999), 80–1.

[47] *Id.* at 81.

For our purposes, Gandhi's influence on King is particularly noteworthy because Gandhi was a practicing lawyer for much of his public life. When Gandhi urged noncooperation with unjust laws, he was speaking as an insider, as a professional whose business it was to make the legal system run by providing access to its rights and privileges. So when King borrowed Gandhi's framework for nonviolent resistance to injustice, he was operating implicitly from a lawyer's perspective. Indeed, Gandhi believed that lawyers had a unique responsibility to resist unjust laws. As he explained it, "Lawyers are the persons most able to appreciate the dangers of bad legislation and it must be with them a sacred duty by committing civil breach to prevent a criminal breach." Lawyers, in Gandhi's estimation, must be "guardians of the law and liberty" and must accordingly keep the country's statutes "pure and undefiled."[48]

Admittedly, few American lawyers would applaud every aspect of Gandhi's understanding of legal practice. As John Leubsdorf explains, Gandhi "assumed far more responsibility for the merits of his cases than United States professional standards require."[49] He had been known to withdraw from a case in the middle of a hearing if he realized that his client had deceived him.[50] Gandhi complained that "lawyers are consciously or unconsciously led into untruth for the sake of

[48] M. K. Gandhi, *The Law and the Lawyers* (1962), 144.

[49] John Leubsdorf, *Gandhi's Legal Ethics*, 51 RUTGERS L. REV. 923, 926 (1999).

[50] M. K. Gandhi, *see id.* at 925–6

their clients," lamenting the fact that "an eminent English lawyer has gone so far as to say that it may even be the duty of a lawyer to defend a client whom he knows to be guilty."[51] Such views misperceive the lawyer's duty, in Gandhi's view, which is "always to place before the judges, and to help them to arrive at, the truth, never to prove the guilty as innocent."[52] Most lawyers would (sensibly) point out the wisdom of requiring the state to meet its burden of proof, and the crucial role that lawyers play in making that burden meaningful. While a lawyer's role cannot exhaust her moral obligations, it can shape them. It is one thing to say that a lawyer cannot ignore blatant injustice; it is another to ignore the presumption of innocence in defining injustice so as to preclude the representation of the guilty.

Gandhi was not focused only on facilitating truth in a specific case; he was also concerned about the lawyer's role in supporting an unjust system. As part of the noncooperation campaign aimed at undermining British rule in India, he "urged all Indian lawyers to cease practicing."[53] During his years living and practicing in South Africa, he "urged lawyers to desert the legal system and to establish a new one."[54] He also repeatedly broke the law in both South Africa and India. However, Gandhi never gave in to cynicism about the law. As Leubsdorf points out, he "never treated the existing

---

[51] *Id.* xi.

[52] *Id.* xi–xii.

[53] Leubsdorf, *supra* note 49, at 923.

[54] *Id.* at 936.

system as a mere power structure that lacked any legitimacy, so that revolutionaries should manipulate or disregard it at will."[55] That attitude, in Gandhi's view, would have been "fatal to the moral growth of both the manipulators and the manipulated."[56] As with King, Gandhi never sought to make a mockery of the system,[57] and he always implored the judge to give him the maximum sentence under the law in order to draw attention to the injustice while encouraging the system to enforce the law to the letter.

Even as he violated laws and urged lawyers to abandon the system, Gandhi was motivated by a vision of the lawyer's role in supporting the rule of law. The rule of law was not simply about giving power to the positive law, but about reclaiming the true nature of law: norms that reflect our shared humanity and relational nature. In his own practice, he recalled realizing that "the true function of a lawyer was to unite parties riven asunder."[58] The need to restore relationships sometimes required lawyers to disrupt a profession that too easily became complicit in separation and

[55] *Id.* at 937.

[56] *Id.*

[57] Compare Gandhi's and King's attitudes toward the legal system with other noteworthy trials of political protestors, such as the "Chicago 7," who, with the assistance of their lawyers, turned their trial into a no-holds-barred media circus. *See* Milner S. Ball, *The Play's the Thing: An Unscientific Reflection on Courts under the Rubric of Theater*, 28 STAN. L. REV. 81, 97 (1975) (describing Chicago conspiracy trial as "theater of the absurd" due to frequent disruptions).

[58] Gandhi, *The Law and the Lawyers*, 71.

marginalization. King was equally assertive in disrupting the comfort and trite rationalizations of the clergy, whom he saw as formidable obstacles to progress (and who provided the impetus for his "Letter from Birmingham City Jail").

Gandhi's influence on King is well known, as King developed similar points to Gandhi's approach in his own model of nonviolent resistance,[59] even explaining that "Christ furnished the spirit and motivation while Gandhi furnished the method."[60] Using the term "soul force" to connote the idea behind satyagraha, King urged African Americans to get to the point where they

> can say to their white brothers, paraphrasing Gandhi: "We will match your capacity to inflict suffering with our capacity to endure suffering. We will meet your physical force with soul force. We will not hate you, but we cannot in good conscience obey your unjust laws. Do to us what you will and we will still love you.... We will soon wear you down by our capacity to suffer. And in winning our freedom we will so appeal to your heart and conscience that we will win you in the process."[61]

Nonviolence did not reject just physical violence, but also what King called the "internal violence of spirit," the

---

[59] Martin Luther King Jr., "Nonviolence and Racial Justice," in *A Testament of Hope, supra* note 3, at 7–8.

[60] Martin Luther King Jr., "Stride toward Freedom", in *A Testament of Hope, supra* note 3, at 447.

[61] *Id.*

rejection of which connects back to the principle of love, or "understanding goodwill."[62]

His embrace of nonviolence also fit well with King's fondness for the Hegelian dialectic, which refers to the method of addressing an issue through the steps of thesis, antithesis, and synthesis. As his teacher Harold DeWolf observed, "Regardless of subject matter, King never tired of moving from a one-sided thesis to a corrective, but also one-sided antithesis and finally to a more coherent synthesis beyond both."[63] King himself wrote that "the principle of nonviolent resistance seeks to reconcile the truths of two opposites – acquiescence and violence – while avoiding the extremes and immoralities of both."[64] Or as Garrow put it, King saw Gandhian nonviolence as "an active path of resistance that avoided the sins of passivity and despair in the face of injustice, but a form of resistance that avoided the multiplication of evil."[65] It is perhaps not surprising, given the compatibility between nonviolent resistance and the Hegelian dialectic, that both Gandhi and King were often criticized for being too quick to compromise with their oppressors. (The middle

---

[62] Martin Luther King Jr., "The Christian Way of Life in Human Relations," Address Delivered at the General Assembly of the National Council of Churches (December 4, 1957), in *The Papers of Martin Luther King Jr.,* vol. VI (1992), 322, 324.

[63] David J. Garrow, "The Intellectual Development of Martin Luther King, Jr: Influences and Commentaries," in *Martin Luther King Jr. and the Civil Rights Movement*, ed. John A. Kirk (2007), 39, 48.

[64] *Id.* at 49 (quoting Martin Luther King Jr., *Stride Toward Freedom,* 213–14).

[65] *Id.* at 49.

ground was a familiar end point for Gandhi as a lawyer as well, as he prided himself on settling most of his cases.)[66]

At one level, the relevance to lawyers of King's chosen means by which to pursue justice is obvious, for King relied on the persuasive power of words. As he reminded an audience in Memphis, "We don't need any bricks and bottles, we don't need any Molotov cocktails, we just need to go around to these stores and to these massive industries in our country and say, God sent us here, to say to you that you're not treating his children right."[67] Lawyers also rely on the power of words. They are advocates who, given the frequent indeterminacy of legal directives, must target the hearts and minds of the relevant decision makers in order to be effective at their work. Further, lawyers must, like King and Gandhi, decide when injustice has reached the point at which they are morally obligated to oppose a particular law or, in extreme cases, the entire legal system.

King's commitment to nonviolence also speaks powerfully, though perhaps not as obviously, to lawyers. In King's ministry, justice was not just about ends; the means chosen were a central component of justice because they bore powerful witness to the advocate's view of the human person who

[66] "[A] a large part of my time during the twenty years of my practice as a lawyer was occupied in bringing about private compromises of hundreds of cases. I lost nothing thereby – not even money, certainly not my soul." M. K. Gandhi, *The Law and the Lawyers* (1962), 236.

[67] Quoted in Richard Wayne Wills Sr., *Martin Luther King and the Image of God* (2009), 122.

was at the center of the very concept of justice. The discipline of nonviolence carries a twofold implication for attorneys: first, it fends off the extremes of advocacy and their potential to injure the advocate. As King recognized, "non-violence saves [discontent] from degenerating into morbid bitterness and hatred. Hate is always tragic. It is as injurious to the hater as it is to the hated. It distorts the personality and scars the soul."[68] Second, nonviolence opens one's horizon to the humanity of one's adversary and the deeper need for individual and relational healing. Can lawyers effectively advocate for their clients without falling prey to the "internal violence of spirit" that King warned about?

The legal profession tends to lionize those who epitomize the equation of zealous advocacy with a violence of spirit. Take one of the most celebrated and successful trial lawyers in American history, Joe Jamail. A generation of law students has watched YouTube clips of Jamail's depositions, where he seeks to maximize his clients' bargaining positions, at least in part, by demeaning litigants, intimidating witnesses, and even threatening to fight other lawyers. Consider the following exchange between Jamail and opposing counsel during one deposition:

> **MR. JAMAIL:** He's not going to answer that. Certify it. I'm going to shut it down if you don't go to your next question.

[68] Martin Luther King Jr., "An Address before the National Press Club" (1962), in *A Testament of Hope, supra* note 3, at 102.

MR. JOHNSTON: No. Joe, Joe –

MR. JAMAIL: Don't "Joe" me, asshole. You can ask some questions, but get off of that. I'm tired of you. You could gag a maggot off a meat wagon. Now, we've helped you every way we can.

MR. JOHNSTON: Let's just take it easy.

MR. JAMAIL: No, we're not going to take it easy. Get done with this.

. . .

MR. JOHNSTON: Are you finished?

MR. JAMAIL: I may be and you may be. Now, you want to sit here and talk to me, fine. This deposition is going to be over with. You don't know what you're doing. Obviously someone wrote out a long outline of stuff for you to ask. You have no concept of what you're doing. Now, I've tolerated you for three hours. If you've got another question, get on with it. This is going to stop one hour from now, period. Go.[69]

After being reprimanded by the Delaware court for his behavior, he responded that "I would rather have a nose on my ass than go to Delaware for any reason."[70] Jamail wins trials, though. According to a profile in the *American Bar Association Journal*, he has tried more than five hundred cases, recovering more than $13 billion in judgments for his clients. He is worth an estimated $1.5 billion,[71] and his

---

[69] *Paramount Comm'ns Inc. v. QVC Network Inc.*, 637 A.2d 34, 52 (Del. 1994).

[70] Mark Curriden, *Joe Jamail*, ABA JOURNAL (March 2, 2009).

[71] *Id.*

name graces the University of Texas football field, law school building, and endowed professorship of law and advocacy. Judging by the trophies he has accumulated along the way, he is not an obvious object lesson of the dangers of ignoring King's insights.

But King's lessons do not aim at worldly success; they aim at moral truth, at living authentically and consistently with our created natures, and at being open to the possibility that clients have an interest in doing the same. Jamail's bullying may have helped particular clients maximize their recoveries in particular cases – though we have no way of knowing whether he could have recovered as much absent the bullying – but his legacy in terms of affirming and restoring human relationships is decidedly more mixed. To the extent that we complain about lawyers' willingness to sacrifice the long-term well-being of a client's community and constituents in order to maximize the client's short-term interests (e.g., Enron), we should not excuse a lawyer's willingness to employ degrading and demeaning methods of advocacy in pursuing their client's interests. Unless we are willing to conclude that justice is irrelevant to the means employed by lawyers, we have to be willing to condemn the relationship-crushing tactics of Jamail (and many others), no matter how "successful" they have been.

Some of this sentiment is captured in the profession's recurring focus on the need for renewed civility among lawyers. These efforts are often dismissed as a sign of the bar's misplaced priorities, as though emphasizing manners and social graces is at odds with the lawyer's adversarial responsibilities. Tom Shaffer notes that the modern legal ethics enterprise emerged from the aftermath of Watergate, "born in outrage at the abuse of legal power,"[72] but the enterprise may have been compromised by its preoccupation with lawyer civility. Shaffer believes that the Hebrew prophets "would say that the trouble with us [lawyers] is not that we tend to be uncivil to one another." Rather, "they might say that we are too civil, civil to the wrong people, civil in the wrong direction."[73] Our real problem might be that "we are not angry enough."[74] Shaffer is correct that civility should never be interpreted as precluding righteous anger; otherwise the civility project would be directly opposed to prophetic ethics. Further, if the profession's efforts aim only to moderate the surface tensions among lawyers that routinely blow up into public spectacles, we risk making civility the ultimate objective. Civility, more properly situated, is *evidence* of social interactions grounded in mutual respect and affirmations of our shared dignity.[75] Commitment

---

[72] Thomas L. Shaffer, *Lawyers as Prophets*, 15 St. Thom. L. Rev. 469, 469 (2003).

[73] *Id.* at 470.

[74] *Id.*

[75] Deborah Cantrell has noted how King's emphasis on love of neighbor can shape even seemingly mundane aspects of legal practice such as seating arrangements at the initial meeting with a client. Deborah Cantrell, *What's Love Got to Do with It? Contemporary Lessons on Lawyerly Advocacy from the Preacher Martin Luther King, Jr.*, 22 St. Thom. L. Rev. 296, 329 (2010).

to nonviolence in one's pursuit of justice is more than the display of manners. King's nonviolent resistance requires lawyers to recognize those who hire them and those who oppose them – lawyer and nonlawyer alike – as persons with whom they are called to relationship. From that basic recognition, civility is a natural outgrowth.

Nonviolence should also shape the lawyer's stance toward the legal system, in particular the means by which the lawyer will seek to vindicate her client's interests. In pushing back against violence as a means by which to combat injustice, King was also pushing back against cynicism. Noble ends do not justify violent means, and the means chosen must reflect the same respect for personhood to which the ends aspire. For lawyers, seeking the beloved community requires us to respect the legal institutions through which disagreements among members of that community are heard and resolved. In other words, the project of restoring relationships requires us to respect the institutions by which our relationships are honored. A failure to show such respect is depressingly common, ranging from the abuse of power displayed by lawyers holding elected office to the manipulation of the judicial system by lawyers looking for every possible advantage on behalf of a client.[76]

---

[76] *See, e.g.*, Randall Samborm, *Chicago Judge Sanctions Firm*, NAT'L L.J., April 18, 1994, at A4 (reporting on lawyers who filed five identical suits within fourteen minutes on behalf of their client, hoping to land one of them with a preferred judge and then voluntarily dismiss the rest).

The beloved community could not be founded via tactics – the degradation of human personality through violence – that defied the very premise of the beloved community. For the same reason, lawyers cannot restore relationships, notwithstanding the relational goods they may achieve in a given case, by subverting or manipulating the institutions established by the political community. Our chosen means must reflect the requirements of justice, not only because it is difficult to predict what the achieved ends actually will be (as Hannah Arendt argued),[77] but also because the means and ends were, to a significant extent, one and the same for King.

III. Lawyers and the Ends of Justice

With all the focus on the means (nonviolent resistance), it is tempting to underemphasize the ends, especially the extent to which the ends require deliberate choices among contested conceptions of the good. King never fell to that temptation, as he believed that justice requires a telos. The civil rights struggle was part of a greater narrative that aimed at a distinct telos: the beloved community. King's work was not just about establishing justice in our tactics or process; the justice also lay in the end goal.

---

[77] Hannah Arendt, *On Violence* 4 (1970) ("Since the end of human action ... can never be reliably predicted, the means used to achieve political goals are more often than not of greater relevance to the future world than the intended goals.").

As a telos-driven narrative, King's advocacy invoked history at every turn. In his "Letter from Birmingham City Jail," King says very little about the details of the protest for which he was arrested or about the surrounding local events. Instead, as David Luban points out, he "devotes most of his attention to the political narrative that will confer legitimacy on the Birmingham campaign," because he needs to persuade the reader "that the marches and sit-ins are indeed mere husks of a more profound story."[78] In this regard, King's arguments for civil rights displayed the key trait of persuasive legal argument, which "works in a medium of historical time that is backward-looking and redemptive in structure."[79] Luban argues, based in part on the example of King's advocacy, that legal narrative gives us "a past that makes us comprehensible."[80] John Rathbun makes a related point about King's use of historical imagery to support the portrayal of the civil rights struggle as part of a bigger narrative: King's "sharpened awareness of the prophetic role in history combines with an equally strong sense of the significance of history."[81]

And history builds toward the realization of the beloved community, arising from the recognition of "the dignity

---

[78] David Luban, *Difference Made Legal: The Court and Dr. King*, 87 MICH. L. REV. 2152, 2193 (1989).

[79] *Id.* at 2221.

[80] *Id.* at 2222.

[81] John W. Rathbun, "Martin Luther King: The Theology of Social Action," in *Martin Luther King Jr. and the Civil Rights Movement*, vol. 3, ed. David J. Garrow (1989), 743, 747.

and worth of human personality" – a founding principle of personalism, which "in King's hands ... becomes a moral telos for American society."[82] Nonviolent resistance aimed at reconciliation all along. King wrote that the nonviolent resister must acknowledge that "non-cooperation and boycotts are not ends within themselves; they are merely means to awaken the sense of moral shame within the opponent." The ends, though, are redemption and reconciliation.[83] As a Christian minister espousing a "theology of community," King's telos pointed to the fact that "persons not only were made in the image of God but also, and of equal importance, were made for relationship."[84]

King's legal/political narrative emerged from his theological narrative, and both were premised on the notion never to mistake what is given for what could be. This theme is exemplified by his explication of Jesus's parable about the wealthy Dives and the poor Lazarus[85]:

There are certain gulfs in life which originate in the accident of circumstance. So in the parable Lazarus was poor,

[82] Garth Baker-Fletcher, *Somebodyness: Martin Luther King, Jr. and the Theory of Dignity* (1993), 50.

[83] Martin Luther King Jr., "The Christian Way of Life in Human Relations," Address Delivered at the General Assembly of the National Council of Churches (December 4, 1957), in *The Papers of Martin Luther King Jr.,* vol. VI, at 322, 324 (1992).

[84] John H. Cartwright, "The Social Eschatology of Martin Luther King, Jr.," in *Martin Luther King, Jr. and the Civil Rights Movement,* vol. 1, ed. David Garrow (1989), 161, 166.

[85] For another example of King's use of this parable, see Chapter 3, *supra*, text accompanying notes 11 and 12.

not because he wanted to be, but because tragic circumstances had made him so. There is a circumstantial gulf
between Lazarus and Dives. Now Dives' sin was not that
he made this gulf between him and Lazarus; this gulf had
come into being through the accidents of circumstance.
The sin of Dives was that he felt that the gulf which existed
between him and Lazarus was a proper condition of life.
Dives felt that this was the way things were to be. He took
the "isness" of circumstantial accidents and transformed
them into the "oughtness" of a universal structure.[86]

Justice requires the resistance of the status quo, not for the
sake of resistance, but because the status quo can obstruct
our view of the beloved community. Contrary to the assertions of his more militant detractors who became prominent
as the 1960s unfolded, King's resistance to the status quo
was anything but passive; it was a radical commitment to
mending relationships – a commitment that, as he stated at
an antiwar rally late in his life, required us to "demonstrate,
teach and preach, until the very foundations of our nation
are shaken."[87]

This resistance requires a capacity and willingness to
distinguish between the "given" of our social nature and the

---

[86] Martin Luther King Jr., The "Impassable Gulf (The Parable of
Dives and Lazarus)," sermon at Dexter Avenue Baptist Church
(October 2, 1955), in *The Papers of Martin Luther King Jr.*, vol. VI
(1992), 235, 237.

[87] Stephen B. Oates, *Let the Trumpet Sound: A Life of Martin Luther
King Jr.* (1994), 431.

contingent dimension of social life. As noted in Chapter 1, the observable truths of the human condition that transcend a particular time and place – such as our shared vulnerability – serve as a needed anchor to the advocate's commitment to human dignity. But living out that commitment requires openness to the possibility that dignity's implications for our life together have not yet been realized, or even imagined. The prophet who loses sight of first principles slides easily into cynicism, then apathy. The ability to practice resistance while staying rooted was thus integral to King's ministry.

A lawyer who embraces King's prophetic ethics will, put simply, speak truth to power. This is difficult to capture in regulatory reforms or concrete action items. The implications are broader and deeper. Prophetic lawyers will call the client to confront reality, including the reality of the human community, as torn and frayed as it might be. The community is not static, and its vitality is shaped by countless day-to-day decisions by human beings affecting other human beings. The client has a role to play, and a prophetic lawyer can – with due deference toward the client as ultimate decision maker – remind the client of that role. Lawyers too often facilitate their clients' stated objectives by pushing third parties to the margins of the human community, or at least to the margins of the client's cognizance of the human community.

When the system works as intended, lawyers can serve both justice and the law simply by playing their part. By the same token, King could have tended to his own congregation in Montgomery if the religious leaders in Birmingham had addressed the pervasive injustice in their city. Role-based morality becomes less tenable when the system breaks down. The prospect of unjust legal proceedings makes this tension acute, but even then, the lawyer has a range of alternatives. Alexandra Lahav outlines five methods by which lawyers can express resistance to unjust proceedings: first, engaging in collective boycott (as Gandhi did); second, individually refusing to participate in the proceeding; third, using legal argument within the tribunal in an effort to overcome the injustice; fourth, making a record for a higher tribunal in hopes that the injustice will be remedied on appeal; and fifth, appealing to public opinion.[88]

King himself faced similar questions in plotting legal strategy during his campaigns. Significantly, King pushed back against his advisers, who told him not to bother opposing the government's requests for the courts to enjoin the proposed marches. King would respond, "Not every judge will issue an injunction; we can't assume that."[89] When Fred Shuttlesworth, a top aide, asked, "Where are those converted judges? Where did niggers ever move and law was not used to beat our heads, with judges helping?"[90] King

---

[88] Alexandra Lahav, *Portraits of Resistance: Lawyer Responses to Unjust Proceedings*, 57 UCLA L. Rev. 725, 730 (2010).

[89] Alan F. Westin & Barry Mahoney, *The Trial of Martin Luther King* (1974), 94 (quoting Bayard Rustin).

[90] *Id.*

would respond, "We can't take that for granted."[91] Even unjust laws were the products of a democratic system that deserved a measure of respect – though not necessarily obedience.[92] Respect for the law meant giving the legal system the chance to work as it was supposed to work, though King obviously did not believe that giving the system that chance fulfilled his moral responsibility to remedy injustice.

In some cases, though, participation in the proceeding may actually render the lawyer culpable to the extent that participation lends the appearance of credibility to the unjust proceeding.[93] In the military trials conducted for suspected terrorists detained at the U.S. naval base at Guantanamo Bay, Cuba, this was a real concern for the defense lawyers. Participants noted that "the most compelling argument against Guantanamo was that it was lawless," but "the presence of lawyers, the filing of motions, and the appearances before judges all suggested that there was both law and justice at Guantanamo."[94] Indeed, the

---

[91] *Id.*

[92] *See* Timothy P. Jackson, "Martin Luther King Jr.," in *The Teachings of Modern Christianity: On Law, Politics, and Human Nature* (2006), vol. I, 437, 447 ("For King ... especially within a society that aspires to be democratic, the social processes by which laws are passed, as well as the political actors who interpret and enforce these laws, are due a measure of respect.... What he objected to was these laws being given undue force or authority, their 'lawness' alone being taken as a compelling reason for obedience").

[93] *See* Lahav, *supra* note 88, at 745.

[94] Muneer I. Ahmad, *Resisting Guantanamo: Rights at the Brink of Dehumanization*, 103 Nw. U. L. Rev. 1683, 1755 (2009).

National Association of Criminal Defense Lawyers issued an advisory ethics opinion in August 2003 concluding that "it is unethical for a criminal defense lawyer to represent a person accused before these military commissions because the conditions imposed upon defense counsel before these commissions make it impossible for counsel to provide adequate or ethical representation."[95] These conditions included government monitoring of attorney-client communications, prohibiting requests for adjournments, limiting access to information, prohibiting the sharing with experts of even unclassified information, and waiving counsel's rights to protest closed proceedings.[96]

Guantanamo presents a challenging case for working out the implications of both the means (nonviolent resistance) and ends (restoring relationship) of King's justice-driven advocacy. The political community, in the wake of the 9/11 attacks, sought to secure its own safety by pushing certain individuals outside the law's reach. As suspected terrorists, prisoners at Guantanamo were deemed undeserving of the legal protections that we have grown to associate, in societies committed to the rule of law, with one's status as a human being. As Muneer Ahmad, one of the Guantanamo defense lawyers, puts it, we have imposed "the inverse of citizenship" on the prisoners there: "no right to have rights, a rights vacuum

---

[95] Lahav, *supra* note 88, at 738.
[96] *Id.*

that enables extreme violence, so as to place Guantanamo at the center of a struggle not merely for rights, but for humanity – that state of being that distinguishes human life from mere biological existence."[97]

Lawyers have been essential in making the case for the prisoners' humanity. Even though rights discourse is frequently (and understandably) criticized for presenting an overly narrow conception of what it means to be human, a claim of right is, at its core, a claim to be recognized as a member of the community.[98] Even when resistance does not succeed in the recognition of legal rights or political equality, the mere fact of resistance, "the assertion of the self against the violence of the state," is "a way of staying human."[99] The challenge at Guantanamo is that the relevant political community "did not admit of the prisoners' membership," casting "the prisoners both physically and metaphysically as far away as possible."[100]

In working to reclaim the prisoners' humanity against the wishes of the political community, the lawyers were labeled as somehow being beyond the pale of professional norms, especially early on in the effort. Cully Stimson, the deputy assistant secretary of defense for detainee affairs, identified some of the major law firms that were representing

[97] Ahmad, *supra* note 94, at 1687.
[98] *See* Martha Minow, *Interpreting Rights: An Essay for Robert Cover*, 96 Yale L.J. 1860, 1880 (1987).
[99] Ahmad, *supra* note 94, at 1688.
[100] *Id.* at 1749.

detainees and predicted in an interview that "when corporate CEOs see that those firms are representing the very terrorists who hit their bottom line back in 2001, those CEOs are going to make those law firms choose between representing terrorists or representing reputable firms," adding that "it's going to be fun to watch that play out."[101] David Luban finds significance in the fact that Stimson "was not sandbagged or ambushed by reporters, nor was he the victim of a document leak."[102] Evidently he planned to raise the idea "that corporate CEOs pressure lawyers into abandoning their clients, and he clearly brought the list of law firms [into the interview] with him."[103]

If we understand law as serving justice by bringing the "beloved community" envisioned by King closer to reality, we have to admit that lawyers are on both sides of such efforts. Sometimes the state's own lawyers facilitate injustice by using the tools of legal interpretation and advocacy to legitimize the marginalization of those who are disfavored by those wielding power. In the post-9/11 context, this was most obvious in the legal advice provided by the Department of Justice's Office of Legal Counsel (OLC) to President Bush regarding the definition of "torture" under statutes prohibiting the practice. In the most infamous of the "torture memoranda," the OLC interpreted a statute

---

[101]   David Luban, *Lawfare and Legal Ethics in Guantanamo*, 60 STAN. L. REV. 1981, 1981 (2008).

[102]   *Id.* at 1983.

[103]   *Id.*

requiring pain or suffering to be "severe" to constitute torture.[104] On the basis of the dictionary definition, the OLC attorneys concluded that "the adjective 'severe' conveys that the pain or suffering must be of such a high level of intensity that the pain is difficult for the subject to endure."[105] Linking torture with the ability to endure encompasses any interrogation technique premised on physical pain, so the OLC effectively narrowed the prohibition by looking to the use of the term "severe pain" in statutes "defining an emergency medical condition for the purposes of providing health benefits."[106] The language relied on defines an emergency condition as one

> manifesting itself by acute symptoms of sufficient severity (including *severe pain*) such that a prudent lay person, who possesses an average knowledge of health and medicine, could reasonably expect the absence of immediate medical attention to result in – placing the health of the individual ... (i) in serious jeopardy, (ii) serious impairment to bodily functions, or (iii) serious dysfunction of any bodily organ or part.[107]

[104] Memorandum from Jay S. Bybee, Assistant Attorney General, to White House Counsel Alberto Gonzales, August 1, 2002, at 5 (available at http://fl1.findlaw.com/news.findlaw.com/wp/docs/doj/bybee80102mem.pdf) (accessed October 4, 2011). *See also* Michael Hirsch, et al., "A Tortured Debate," *Newsweek,* June 21, 2004 (reporting that John Yoo drafted the Bybee memorandum).

[105] Memorandum, *supra* note 104.

[106] *Id.*

[107] *Id.* at 6 (quoting 18 U.S.C. § 1395w-22(d)(3)(B)).

The statute simply provides that severe pain is one type of symptom that *might* lead a person to believe that her health was in serious jeopardy, her bodily functions would be seriously impaired, or an organ would suffer serious dysfunction. Other symptoms, the language implies, might also lead a person to such a belief. Nevertheless, the OLC's memo *equates* severe pain with the three conditions, extracting from the quoted language the conclusion that "severe pain," as used in the entirely unrelated torture statute, must rise to "the level that would ordinarily be associated with a sufficiently serious physical condition or injury such as death, organ failure, or serious impairment of bodily functions – in order to constitute torture."[108]

Later in the memo, the OLC offers additional protection for the Bush administration's authority to engage in interrogation techniques that normally would be legally prohibited as torture. Noting that the necessity defense "can justify the intentional killing of one person to save two others,"[109] the OLC asserts that "any harm that might occur during an interrogation would pale to *insignificance* compared to the harm avoided by preventing [a terrorist] attack, which could take hundreds or thousands of lives."[110] The OLC's implausible interpretation of the governing statutes reflects a willingness to manipulate the law in order to secure the ends desired by those in power, obscuring the reality of the

[108] *Id.*
[109] *Id.* at 40.
[110] *Id.* at 41 (emphasis added).

human community in the process. Labeling any harm that could be inflicted on another human being during an interrogation as "insignificant" reflects a willingness essentially to dehumanize those who are suspected of being involved in terrorism. The confluence of legal and moral malleability in the content of the lawyer's advice makes her a potentially powerful weapon in the service of injustice.

This is hardly a new phenomenon, of course. In Vichy France, the legal profession was an essential element of the aggressive interpretation and enforcement of the anti-Jewish laws enacted by the Nazi collaborationist government. Richard Weisberg, the leading expert on the subject, concludes that the French legal profession "behaved pervasively to make the Jewish statutes live," and they did so, at least in part, for a reason that is also present in the legal profession in other Western countries such as the United States, the United Kingdom, Canada, and Australia. It comes down, in Weisberg's analysis, to the profession's engrained approach to reading legal texts. He explains:

> The French, at one and the same time read their constitutional text flexibly so as to accommodate the noble values of the 1790s and still exclude from their protections a selected group of "others." They also read their statutory texts narrowly to identify only a single low-level generalization issue as consistently important and to rule out immediately other legal issues that might have led to a very different set of outcomes for the population persecuted by the statutes. This two-headed coin is emblematic

of risks always tangible in liberal constitutional regimes. The story of embedded values may at any time be distorted to exclude people and groups from the otherwise still egalitarian tale; and the work of statute reading may always fall prey to an ingrained professional sense that almost delights in limiting legal discourse to the narrowest range of issues possible under the statute.[111]

Put differently, the legal profession often displays interpretive flexibility at the level of foundational normative documents – documents that are not supposed to change along with the political winds – thereby justifying selective exclusion based on the prevailing political will. At the same time, the legal profession tends to stick close to the text of the particular statutes and regulations by which the political will is implemented. In Vichy France, the anti-Jewish statutes "could have provoked the legal community to focus on much higher levels of generalization that would have tended to protect substantially greater numbers of Jews."[112] Weisberg does not think that this failure to generalize resulted from

---

[111] Richard H. Weisberg, *Vichy Law and the Holocaust in France* (1996), 4; *see also id.*, 389 ("The Vichy hermeneutic ran as follows: French lawyers managed to interpret the still extant constitutional principles of their training flexibly, i.e., in a manner permitting relatively open-ended understandings of once-ensconced concepts such as 'equality'; at the same time, they brought to the new statutory texts a rigorous, low-level technical precision that inhibited them from making liberal legal arguments extending protection to thousands of additional people.").

[112] *Id.* at 4.

anti-Semitism (at least as it is traditionally understood), but rather from "the narrowness that always risks appearing when lawyers do their technical work."[113] He laments "the ability of decent people to use their professional skills narrowly and perversely, to avoid myopically the central issues of their legal workday, and to employ low levels of generalization to produce high levels of grotesque and aberrational French legal rhetoric."[114]

The disparate degrees of flexibility displayed by lawyers are understandable. When it comes to a society's constitutional narrative, lawyers are more inclined to defer to the political realm's efforts to shape the narrative, whether toward more or less inclusivity. Lawyers tend not to perceive of themselves as having any unique role in what largely amounts to a question of a political community's self-conception. On the other hand, when it comes to the day-to-day work by which the positive enactments of society's unfolding self-conception are implemented, the lawyers are experts without peer, and that level of expertise is central to the profession's self-conception. But crucially, that expertise is widely perceived as being strictly technical in nature.

For lawyers following in King's footsteps, it seems that a more resolute commitment to the system's foundational norms in articulating boundaries on the means and ends

---

[113] *Id.*
[114] *Id.* at 11.

of lawyering, rather than greater interpretive flexibility at the point of implementation, is the more promising course. The "torture memo" reflects badly on the profession, not just because of the underlying dehumanization that seems to have motivated the interpretive gymnastics that drove the OLC's analysis, but because those interpretive gymnastics depart from the level of technical proficiency that the profession expects of itself. Bad legal interpretation is a problem whether it is put to just or unjust ends. The profession is better served by being forthright about the ideals at stake in the matter, rather than attempting to avoid the injustice by engaging in willful manipulation of the relevant legal directives. "Letter from Birmingham City Jail" can be read along these lines, with King advocating the fulfillment of the equal protection promised in the Constitution through the end of a segregationist legal order. As David Luban observes, "King's is an authoritative unofficial reading of the Constitution that overthrows Southern officials' readings."[115] King was not in the business of looking for loopholes. He resisted injustice by holding the powerful accountable to the animating ideals of the legal order.

That said, even at the point of implementation, lawyers must be careful not to pretend that the interpretation of legal directives is always automatic or perfectly objective. With indeterminacy comes discretion, and with discretion, the lawyer's own extralegal commitments are implicated

[115] David Luban, *Difference Made Legal: The Court and Dr. King*, 87 MICH. L. REV. 2152, 2199 (1989).

by the interpretive project. The aura of objectivity can be dangerously misleading. Consider some of the scholarly treatments of the Vichy anti-Jewish laws from that time. E. H. Perreau instructed lawyers that, in interpreting the laws, "one must avoid oneself, noting about all what is concrete, objective, and generally abstaining from judgment."[116] Another commentator praised the statutes' formal style as being "designed not only to reveal the lawyer's duty, but still more to underscore that he is erasing himself totally from the laws and regulations in order to derive from them an objective significance."[117] Others cautioned against giving in to "the hurrahs or to the boos," rather than "to analyze with serenity and probity the numerous texts promulgated since the new regime has come into being."[118] The danger in casting these inquiries as technical is not only that the relationship between the narrowly technical (statute) and the broadly normative (constitutional narrative) is deemed irrelevant, but also that statutory interpretation is portrayed as *exclusively* technical, as though there are no moral considerations to talk about, or reflect upon, in filling the gaps of indeterminacy that arise in many cases requiring the application of statutory or regulatory directives. For example,

[116] E. H. Perreau, *The New Jewish Law in France* (1941) (cited in Weisberg, *supra* note 111, at 394–6).

[117] Duverger, "La perversion du droit," in *Religion, Societe et Politique: Melanges en Hommage a Jacques Ellul* 707 (1983) (cited in Weisberg, *supra* note 111, at 394–6).

[118] Baudry and Ambre, *La Condition publicque et privee du Juif en France* 16 (1942) (cited in Weisberg, *supra*).

one book published in France in 1943 set out to address two questions: "that of the definition of the Jew, in a country where nothing distinguishes him legally from others, and, subsequently, the attribution of Jewishness to economic entities or corporate structures in which Jews participate." This inquiry, the author confidently asserted, is "of a legally technical nature."[119]

In Vichy France, the lawyers faced a system that had departed so far from basic norms of justice that they may have been obliged to follow justice's call by, as Gandhi advocated in his response to the injustice of British rule, abandoning the system itself. At a minimum, Vichy lawyers had a moral duty to acknowledge the gap between France's egalitarian constitutional narrative and the premises of the anti-Jewish statutes. American lawyers today do not face a system that presents such stark choices. The rule of law, as reflected in the American legal system, is morally justified, and working to make its framework of rights and privileges accessible is itself morally justified. But that itself is a conclusion resulting from a moral inquiry, and that inquiry should not be deemed as falling outside the scope of one's professional role. Otherwise, the gap between the promise of America's constitutional narrative and the on-the-ground legal treatment of individuals may escape the profession's notice, as some undoubtedly hoped would happen in the

[119] Andre Broc, *La Qualification juive* 6 (1943) (cited in Weisberg, *supra*).

Guantanamo cases. Moral assessment must always be part of the conversation.

But assume that the conversation does not bring the client around to a view that is consistent with justice. Since the client makes the ultimate call on whether to proceed with a course of conduct that may be legally permissible but runs counter to the social demands of justice, to what extent is a lawyer morally culpable for her client's choices? And if justice's relevance to the representation is not exhausted by the letter of the law, is a lawyer morally culpable for agreeing to represent a client whose very cause runs counter to justice's demands? At least in the United States, where the lawyer has considerable latitude to decline cases that she finds morally objectionable (or for virtually any other reason), and to withdraw from the representation where the client persists in conduct that the lawyer deems morally objectionable,[120] the lawyer cannot shirk moral accountability.

Consider a recent flap over the lawyers involved in defending the Defense of Marriage Act (DOMA), the statute defining marriage to include one man and one woman for purposes of federal law, and permitting states to deny recognition of valid same-sex marriages performed in other jurisdictions. In 2011, the Obama administration announced that the Justice Department would no longer defend the statute's

---

[120] *See ABA Model Rules of Prof'l Conduct* R. 1.16 (b)(4) (permitting withdrawal when "the client insists upon taking action that the lawyer considers repugnant or with which the lawyer has a fundamental disagreement").

constitutionality. The U.S. House of Representatives inter-
vened in litigation to defend the statute and retained
Paul Clement, a well-known appellate litigator at King &
Spalding, to handle the case. Gay rights groups protested
the firm's decision, and there was apparently some pressure
from the firm's biggest client, Coca-Cola, to extricate itself
from the situation. Shortly thereafter, the firm withdrew
from the case, and Paul Clement resigned from the firm in
protest.[121]

A similar dynamic had played out a few years earlier
in Boston, where the law firm Ropes & Gray had agreed
to represent Catholic Charities in its effort to avoid a state
requirement that adoption agencies not discriminate against
same-sex couples in placing children.[122] The Harvard Law
School's student chapter of Lambda protested the firm's
involvement in the case and threatened to picket future
on-campus interviewing by the firm. The firm subsequently
announced that it would no longer work on the case.[123]

If we believe that the lawyer is a moral subject (as
argued in Chapter 1) and that justice has a substance that
is not categorically coextensive with law (as argued here),
then lawyers are accountable for the cases they accept, and

---

[121] *See* Steve Visser, "Lawyers Question Firm's Withdrawal," *Atlanta
Journal-Constitution*, April 27, 2011, A3.
[122] *See* Patricia Wen, "Catholic Charities Stuns State, Ends
Adoptions," *Boston Globe*, March 11, 2006.
[123] *See* Sacha Pfeiffer, "Harvard Law Group Hits Ropes and Gray,"
Boston Globe, March 15, 2006.

for the conduct they facilitate by virtue of their representation. That does not mean, however, that a lawyer's moral accountability fits neatly with the moral status of the client or cause on whose behalf she labors. There is a second-order moral justification in play. There is a moral value to providing access to our legal system, especially in cases where the unpopularity of the client jeopardizes access. This line of reasoning was prominent in the aftermath of King & Spalding's withdrawal. No matter their views on DOMA itself, the upper echelons of the legal profession – including Supreme Court Justice Elena Kagan and Attorney General Eric Holder – rallied to Clement's side, lauding the fact that he was upholding a noble tradition of the profession by providing representation to an unpopular cause.

The unhealthy precedent set by Ropes & Gray and King & Spalding should not define the debate over a lawyer's accountability for justice, though. Neither firm was a model of moral accountability; more accurately, they were examples of firms caving in to pressure out of fear for their own economic interests – in the case of Ropes & Gray, it was concern that the firm would suffer in its efforts to recruit new attorneys, and in the case of King & Spalding, it (apparently) was concern that clients might take their business elsewhere. Moreover, both firms "discovered" their misgivings about the cases only after agreeing to take on the cases, potentially leaving the clients high and dry. The morally engaged lawyer may need to withdraw when changing circumstances make it apparent that the course of conduct chosen by the client is fundamentally incompatible with the lawyer's commitment to justice, but not on the basis of circumstances in which all that has changed is the lawyer's perception of increased pressure to abandon a politically unpopular client.

I do not purport to offer a ready blueprint for discerning the point at which a representation is sufficiently contrary to justice so as to warrant the lawyer declining the case or withdrawing from an ongoing case. My point is a more basic one: these considerations have to be part of the lawyer's decision making if she is truly committed to her own moral agency and to a conception of justice that is not fully reflected in the positive law. It is not enough to point out discrepancies between the client's position and the relational ends of justice – there is something to be said for facilitating access to the legal system, even for unjust causes. At the same time, a lawyer cannot dismiss the controversy over the clients she chooses by insisting that such choices are somehow immune from moral reproach. Of course, a lawyer's decisions to accept or continue with a case have a moral dimension, and a lawyer committed to justice should be ready and willing to account for how her work contributes to its achievement. Lawyers may want to reach for a categorical justification by identifying justice with legal merit,[124] but King will not let them off the hook so easily. Justice may be

---

[124] *See, e.g.,* William H. Simon, *The Practice of Justice: A Theory of Lawyers' Ethics* (1998), 138.

(and ideally is) reflected in part by law, but it is bigger than that. However she ultimately resolves a quandary about a particular client or case, a lawyer committed to justice must be cognizant of the extent to which her accountability is not defined fully by law.

King's conception of justice contributes to the work of the attorney by providing a substantive end of justice (the restoration of relationships) to help orient the attorney's counsel in the myriad instances when the positive law is indeterminate or silent about a proposed course of conduct, and by cautioning against the violence of spirit that afflicts the profession when "by any means necessary" becomes the touchstone of zealous advocacy on the client's behalf. If justice is not exhausted by the positive law, then a lawyer committed to justice cannot permit her counsel to be exhausted by the positive law. It warrants repeating, though, that this is not a license to hijack the representation or to turn its client-directed nature upside down. King was committed to truth telling, not to coercion. Lawyers are often well positioned to help their clients see the full ramifications of a proposed course of conduct. Their counsel should begin from a baseline of technical competence – including a good-faith interpretation of the law, not an interpretation shaded by extralegal moral considerations. It is within the gaps and ambiguities of the law where the lawyer should introduce other considerations to help flesh out a fuller conception of justice, but the lawyer's failure to identify clearly what is a settled legal directive and what is not disserves the client by potentially pushing for a morally justified decision under the guise of legal authority. Because King's commitment to justice has to be read in conjunction with his agapic treatment of the client as subject, co-opting an unknowing client, even in the service of justice, is impermissible.

Lawyers' willingness to tell the truth to their clients – particularly hard truths – is at the core of lawyers' traditional dual roles as client-centered advocates and public-regarding citizens. King reminds lawyers that truth telling in the service of justice requires the awareness of ultimate ends and limits on the means by which those ends are brought to fruition. Using the power of ideas to resist the pull of passivity and the temptation toward violence, King modeled an advocacy that avoided the degradation of self and others. And his power was not pointless: it aimed toward the restoration of relationship, the incremental building up of the beloved community.

Most lawyers do not work on cases that present the cause of justice as starkly or dramatically as King's ministry did. But his lessons regarding the means and ends of justice can still operate in the background of cases that will never see the headlines, guiding the lawyer's day-to-day decisions toward a broader acknowledgment of the relationships that are at stake in any representation. As detailed in Chapter 2, the marginalization of relational trust makes this process more difficult, especially in the corporate context, as it is less likely that an attorney will be in a position to counsel the client about the business's overall direction and how that direction implicates the interests of other constituents, including the interests of the surrounding community. Maintaining that trust – or, for many lawyers, discovering it for the first time – will be a central challenge in the future for lawyers who aspire to King's model of prophetic ethics.

Truth telling is not just a duty that runs from the lawyer to the client, though. Prophetic lawyers will also call the legal profession to confront reality, and to imagine its own role in repairing breaches in the human community. Occasionally this may require the lawyer to adopt a confrontational stance toward the profession. What if the profession's relaxation of conflict-of-interest rules was grounded in a concern for the real human relationships between lawyer and client, rather than the technical efficacy of screening procedures?[125] What if the profession stepped back from its relentless quest to prevent nonlawyers from providing any service that could remotely be construed as "practicing law,"[126] put economic protectionism firmly to the side, and instead focused on customer well-being, balancing the need for affordable services against the need for the protections embedded in the attorney-client relationship? On these and other issues, a prophetic lawyer must recognize that

[125] See discussion of the amendment of ABA Model Rules of Professional Conduct 1.10 in chapter 2, *supra*, at text accompanying note 144, and in chapter 5, *infra*, at text accompanying notes 107 and 108.

[126] *See, e.g., Florida Bar v. Brumbaugh*, 355 So.2d 1186 (Fla. 1978).

associations can be every bit as self-absorbed as individuals and even more socially corrosive. Recognizing the corrupting potential of associations flows from the one strand in King's worldview that remains to be addressed.[127] King's stance toward social power was more nuanced, in some ways, than that of the Hebrew prophets, or at least more nuanced than Rauschenbush's interpretation of the Hebrew prophets. King was a Christian realist.

---

[127] *See generally* Reinhold Niebuhr, *Moral Man and Immoral Society* (1932).

5

Realism

Lawyers as Fallen

Lawyers tend to be skeptical about their own ability to be neutral and objective arbiters of moral considerations, and so they feel justified in keeping morality out of the professional mix. This skepticism results in a less-than-inspiring vision of the lawyer's role.[1] Law is a complicated machine, and lawyers need to make sure it runs, but what it is used for is none of the lawyer's business.

Many lawyers would defend this limitation as a necessary concession to their own fallibility, and they may even seek support on that point from King, who was influenced

---

[1] See Stephen L. Pepper, *The Lawyer's Amoral Ethical Role: A Defense, a Problem, and Some Possibilities*, 1986 AM. B. FOUND. RES. J. 613, 624 (analogizing lawyers to photocopier technicians).

by the Christian realism of Reinhold Niebuhr. Within the profession, there is a widespread fear that encouraging lawyers to include moral considerations in their representation of clients will allow lawyers to steer the representation to the lawyer's preferred ends, failing to extend to the client the full measure of autonomy contemplated by law. When lawyers look to the law as the only relevant boundary on their pursuit of the client's interests, they are understood to be checking the temptation to substitute their own interests for the client's.

Invoking King or Niebuhr for support of the amoral lawyering paradigm is only possible by caricaturing Christian realism as nothing more than skepticism about the exercise of power by deeply flawed human beings. A bit of skepticism can be a good thing, especially among a group of professionals empowered with a state monopoly on access to the law. The problem is that, for many lawyers, unchecked skepticism spirals into unfettered cynicism. Both King and Niebuhr avoided that fate because their realism was much more than skepticism; their realism included affirmative claims about the nature of the human person and the responsibilities that flow from that nature. Those claims about reality can help us understand why lawyers who take their client's interests seriously may need to reconsider their reluctance to raise moral considerations.

Further, we need not rely solely on the claims in the abstract – we can see Christian realism lived out, particularly in King's work. As a public advocate in the prophetic tradition,

King displayed an unwavering commitment to the common good. Though he was under no professional compulsion to place a particular client's interests above those of the broader community, his practice of advocacy reflected a view of reality that has implications for the assumptions we make about an individual's best interests, and those assumptions are especially important within the attorney-client relationship.

Christian realism is premised on a pair of anthropological claims: (1) humans are sinful and therefore fallible, but (2) humans are social and therefore accountable. Lawyers tend to focus on the first while ignoring the second. Our own fallibility cautions lawyers against denying the client's moral agency or delegating their own moral agency to the profession as a whole. Our social nature reminds lawyers that the maximization of a client's legal rights may not always be in keeping with the client's best interests.

There are broader lessons here: to the extent that our political and legal discourse marginalizes moral considerations or reflects a conception of the human person as an isolated bundle of rights and interests, we are not only jeopardizing the common good – we are defying reality. Niebuhr and King may be able to help lawyers dispel the apparent conflict between individual autonomy and social accountability.

I. King and Christian Realism

Niebuhr's work aimed at recapturing the reality and relevance of original sin. He lamented modern society's failure

to recognize that, no matter how impressive its achievements, "there is no level of human moral or social achievement in which there is not some corruption of inordinate
self-love."[2] We all have "a darkly unconscious sense" of our
"insignificance in the total scheme of things," and we perpet-
ually strive to compensate for that insignificance. Ira Zepp
explains that, in Niebuhr's work, the Christian conception
of the human person is unique because, first, "it indicates
man's capacity for self-transcendence in the doctrine of
the Imago Dei"; second, "it insists on man's finiteness and
dependence, since he is a part of the natural order"; and
third, "the evil in man is a consequence of his 'inevitable
though not necessary' unwillingness to accept his dependence."[3] Human conflicts are thus not simply about survival;
they are, according to Niebuhr, "conflicts in which each man
or group seeks to guard its power and prestige against the
peril of competing expressions of power and pride."[4] Because
individual self-love is magnified at the group level, group
relations must be "predominantly political rather than ethical, that is, they will be determined by the proportion of
power which each group possesses at least as much as by

[2] Reinhold Niebuhr, "The Children of Light and the Children of
Darkness," in *The Essential Reinhold Niebuhr: Selected Essays and
Addresses* (1986), 160, 169.

[3] Ira Zepp & Kenneth L. Smith, *Search for the Beloved Community:
The Thinking of Martin Luther King Jr.* (1974), 132.

[4] Niebuhr, "The Children of Light and the Children of Darkness," in
The Essential Reinhold Niebuhr, supra note 2, at 171.

any rational and moral appraisal of the comparative needs and claims of each group."[5]

As a realist, Niebuhr emphasized the importance of grounding our worldview on an accurate understanding of the human person, including the social and transcendent dimensions of human nature. This shaped his efforts to navigate between individualist and collectivist poles of the midtwentieth century. To those who embraced the preeminence of the community uncritically, he cautioned that "no historical community deserves the final devotion of man, since his stature and structure is such that only God can be the end of his life."[6] At the same time, he reminded individualists that "freedom without community is not love, but leads to man making himself his own end." A person is "bound to seek the realization of his true nature; and to his true nature belongs his fulfillment in the lives of others."[7] In light of human nature, the will to live is also the will to self-realization, which must involve "self-giving in relations to others."[8]

As did King, Niebuhr explored the relationship between love and justice. For Niebuhr, "The norm that continues to call humans to further achievement is the law of agape:

[5] Reinhold Niebuhr, *Moral Man and Immoral Society* (2002) (1932), xxxi.

[6] Reinhold Niebuhr, "The Christian Witness in the Social and National Order," in *The Essential Reinhold Niebuhr, supra* note 2, at 93, 99.

[7] Niebuhr, "The Children of Light and the Children of Darkness," in *The Essential Reinhold Niebuhr, supra* note 2, at 170.

[8] *Id.*

the demand to express sacrificial love for all humans, even when they do not reciprocate."[9] He observed that "love is the law of life, even when people do not live by the law of love,"[10] and that justice can "prove to men and nations that there are limits beyond which their rebellion cannot go."[11] At the same time, justice will not bring repentance "if love does not shine through the justice," which does not happen unless and until the punished behold "the executor of judgment suffering with and for" them.[12] Those who strive for perfection learn that "perfection is love and not justice," and thereby "obtain mercy while they learn to be merciful." Those who "imagine themselves righteous," by contrast, "are consistently condemned."[13]

The elusiveness of justice does not excuse Christians from seeking it, however. Niebuhr never used his realism to excuse hopelessness or inaction. He urged Christians, despite their knowledge of human sinfulness, to overcome the temptation "to disavow their own responsibility for a tolerable justice in the world's affairs."[14] Justice can be an

---

[9] Thomas C. Berg, *Church-State Relations and the Social Ethics of Reinhold Niebuhr*, 73 N.C. L. REV. 1567 (1995).

[10] Reinhold Niebuhr, "Optimism, Pessimism, and Religious Faith," in *The Essential Reinhold Niebuhr, supra* note 2, at 3, 14.

[11] Reinhold Niebuhr, "The Power and Weakness of God," in *The Essential Reinhold Niebuhr, supra* note 2, at 21, 29.

[12] *Id.*

[13] Reinhold Niebuhr, "The Assurance of Grace," in *The Essential Reinhold Niebuhr, supra* note 2, at 61, 63.

[14] Reinhold Niebuhr, "The Christian Church in a Secular Age," in *The Essential Reinhold Niebuhr, supra* note 2, at 79, 86.

imperfect approximation of the law of love; as such, justice can be a more authentic measure of love than the "insufferable sentimentality" that has afflicted the church through the years, as though the world's problems would be solved "if only men would love one another."[15] While "love may be the motive of social action," Christians must recognize that justice is "the instrument of love in a world in which self-interest is bound to defy the canons of love on every level."[16]

The implications of Niebuhr's realism are most famously borne out by his rejection of Christian pacifism, a practice on which he and King parted ways.[17] He conceded the theoretical possibility of a nonheretical Christian pacifism, but he observed that the modern form is heretical because "there are no historical realities which remotely conform to it," and "this lack of conformity to the facts of experience [is] a criterion of heresy."[18] Our political leaders should avoid conflict, as well as violence in conflict, but this pragmatic concern is entirely different from an absolute rejection of violence, "in which no concession is made to human sin."[19] Pacifists fail to see, in Niebuhr's view, that "human egotism

[15] Reinhold Niebuhr, "The Christian Witness in the Social and National Order," in *The Essential Reinhold Niebuhr, supra* note 2, at 93, 96.

[16] Reinhold Niebuhr, *Preface to An Interpretation of Christian Ethics* (1956 ed.), 9.

[17] See Chapter 4 for a discussion of King's views on nonviolence.

[18] Reinhold Niebuhr, "Why the Christian Church Is Not Pacifist," in *The Essential Reinhold Niebuhr, supra* note 2, at 102, 104–5.

[19] *Id.* at 107.

makes large-scale cooperation upon a purely voluntary basis impossible," and that "justice can be achieved only by a certain degree of coercion on the one hand, and by resistance to coercion and tyranny on the other hand."[20] As Davison Douglas explains, Niebuhr saw that the "human failure to fulfill the law of love" requires that "society use the coercive power of the state to resist tyranny and evil."[21]

Notwithstanding the practical impossibility of pacifism – and the injustice threatened by its imposition as an absolute principle of Christian morality – the Christian realist should be skeptical toward the government's justifications of violence and coercion. The realist is wary of both the pacifist and the war apologist. Although governments must coerce, "there is an element of evil in this coercion," given the danger that the coercion serves the purposes of the coercing power rather than the community. After all, "Even the most rational men are never quite rational when their own interests are at stake."[22] Niebuhr's explanation captures the thrust of the realist's contribution to the public order: "We cannot fully trust the motives of any ruling class or power."[23]

---

[20] *Id.* at 109.

[21] Davison Douglas, "Reinhold Niebuhr," in *The Teachings of Modern Christianity on Law, Politics and Human Nature*, ed. John Witte Jr. & Frank S. Alexanders (2006), 412, 423.

[22] Reinhold Niebuhr, *Moral Man and Immoral Society* (2002) (1932), 44.

[23] Niebuhr, "Why the Christian Church Is Not Pacifist," *supra* note 18, at 109.

Niebuhr urged caution in trusting those who purported to exercise power in service of love, but he resisted the slide into cynicism toward the law of love itself. He explained, "A realism becomes morally cynical or nihilistic when it assumes that the universal characteristic in human behavior must also be regarded as normative." Even though a person may use her freedom to make herself the center of existence, love – rather than self-love – remains the law of her existence. In other words, a person "can only be healthy, and his communities at peace, if man is drawn out of himself and saved from the self-defeating consequences of self-love."[24] The trick is to ground our conception of justice in the law of love without underestimating the "power and persistence of self-love."[25]

Niebuhr was a significant influence on Martin Luther King. In King's words, "Niebuhr made me aware of the complexity of human motives and the reality of sin on every level of man's existence," including "the glaring reality of collective evil."[26] For both King and Niebuhr, according to Taylor Branch, "Questions about the existence and nature of God seemed to merge with a simpler, more existential question: Is the universe friendly?"[27] As a result of this line of inquiry,

---

[24] Reinhold Niebuhr, "Augustine's Political Realism," in *The Essential Reinhold Niebuhr, supra* note 2, at 123, 130.

[25] *Id.* at 140.

[26] Martin Luther King Jr., *Strength to Love* (1963), 148.

[27] Taylor Branch, *Parting the Waters: America in the King Years 1954–1963* (1989), 86.

King realized "that liberalism had been all too sentimental concerning human nature and that it leaned toward a false idealism."[28] David Garrow concludes that "King's development can easily, accurately and fairly be labeled an increasingly Niebuhrian evolution."[29]

Unlike many of his fellow Protestants who rejected the fundamental premises of liberal theology, Niebuhr "was really criticizing liberalism from within, seeking to curb its excesses, not rejecting its engagement with this world and efforts to reform it."[30] Maintaining a critical stance without disengaging from the rough and tumble of worldly affairs gave him credibility with a committed social activist such as King, especially on the issue of race. Given Niebuhr's belief in the reality of self-love and the corresponding resistance to relinquish power and privilege, he knew that African Americans would need to overcome their oppression by non-violent force, which Niebuhr, like Gandhi, "understood as having more in common with war than with pacifism."[31]

This ran counter to the dominant idea within liberalism at the time about American society's struggle with race. Gunnar Myrdal's hugely influential book *An American*

---

[28] Martin Luther King Jr., *Strength to Love* (1963), 148.

[29] David J. Garrow, "The Intellectual Development of Martin Luther King, Jr: Influences and Commentaries," in *Martin Luther King Jr. and the Civil Rights Movement*, ed. John A. Kirk (2007), 39, 48.

[30] David L. Chappell, *A Stone of Hope: Prophetic Religion and the Death of Jim Crow* (2005), 27.

[31] *Id.* at 28.

Dilemma: The Negro Problem and Modern Democracy[32] predicted that racist practices would gradually yield to our creed of equality as more Americans became enlightened and honest about racism.[33] The problem was that if liberals believed that racism was on its way to extinction naturally, there was little motivation for them to take action.[34] Liberals confirmed Niebuhr's criticism that "modern man has an easy conscience" given the fact that "Christian conceptions of the sinfulness of man" have fallen out of favor.[35] Fortunately, the black civil rights community did not think like Myrdal and other liberals of the time. According to David Chappell,

> Whereas Myrdal and the liberals were optimistic about human development, especially about human institutions, the intellectuals of the civil rights movement stood out for their rejection of this world and its natural tendencies. They were conspicuous for their unwillingness to let social processes work themselves out and for their lack of faith in the power of education and economic development to cure society of oppressive evils. In their thinking, they were more akin to the Hebrew Prophets, Frederick Douglass,

---

[32] Gunnar Myrdal, *An American Dilemma: The Negro Problem and Modern Democracy* (1944). The book was even cited in Brown v. Board of Education. *See* 347 U.S. 483, 495 n. 11 (1954).

[33] Chappell, *supra* note 30, at 37.

[34] *Id.* at 42.

[35] 1 Reinhold Niebuhr, *The Nature and Destiny of Man: A Christian Interpretation* (1941), 23.

and the Reinhold Niebuhr of 1932–44 than they were to mainstream liberals.[36]

King was optimistic about the arc of history, but his optimism was not the sort that allowed him to sit back and watch society's natural tendencies work themselves out over time. King credited Niebuhr's work for helping him see liberalism's sentimentality and false idealism. Particularly problematic was the notion that education would eventually eradicate racism through intellectual enlightenment, given the unavoidable fact that "reason is darkened by sin."[37] As such, humans have an uncanny ability to "use our minds to rationalize our actions," and thus liberals need to recognize that "reason by itself is little more than an instrument to justify man's defensive ways of thinking."[38] As he explained in an interview, "The most pervasive mistake I have made was in believing that because our cause was just, we could be sure that the white ministers of the South, once their Christian consciences were challenged, would rise to our aid."[39] King also resisted the opposite pull of focusing exclusively on humanity's capacity for evil, and he labored to keep the capacities for both good and evil in clear view.[40] King knew that the capacity for good

---

[36] Chappell, *supra* note 30, at 45.

[37] Martin Luther King Jr., "Pilgrimage to Nonviolence" (1960), in *A Testament of Hope, supra* note 3, at 35, 36.

[38] *Id.* at 36.

[39] "Playboy Interview: Martin Luther King Jr." (1965), in *A Testament of Hope, supra* note 3, at 340, 344–5.

[40] "Pilgrimage to Nonviolence," *supra* note 37, at 36.

made his struggle for civil rights possible, but the capacity for evil made the struggle necessary.

Of course, King did not pick up these themes solely from Niebuhr. King's commitments were shaped directly by the black Baptist Church in which he was raised; Niebuhr's realist language was useful to King to the extent that it furthered "a tradition of prophetic resistance to the corrupt tendencies of this world."[41] It should be no surprise, then, that "Niebuhr is the thinker King takes most often into his public statements."[42] Taylor Branch notes that King, in private, described Niebuhr "as a prime influence upon his life," as Niebuhr "touched him on all his tender points, from pacifism and racism to sin."[43] In Chappell's estimation, "what makes King a world-historical figure is his Niebuhrian pessimism about human institutions and his Niebuhrian insistence that coercion is tragically necessary to achieve justice."[44]

This is not to suggest that King wholly embraced Niebuhr's worldview. King himself recalled that, even as a student at Boston University, he "came to see that Niebuhr had overemphasized the corruption of human nature," and that this "pessimism concerning human nature was not balanced by an optimism concerning divine nature."[45] In

---

[41] Chappell, *supra* note 30, at 47.
[42] *Id.* at 53.
[43] Branch, *supra* note 18, at 87.
[44] Chappell, *supra* note 30, at 53.
[45] Martin Luther King Jr., *Stride Toward Freedom: The Montgomery Story* (1987), 82.

other words, according to King, Niebuhr "was so involved in diagnosing man's sickness of sin that he overlooked the cure of grace."[46] Ira Zepp describes King as disagreeing with Niebuhr's "views of pacifism, his suspicion of reason, his pessimism concerning human nature, and his criticism of utopian communities."[47] That said, Niebuhr's influence led King to espouse a "realistic pacifism" through which he saw pacifism "not as sinless but as the lesser evil in the circumstances."[48] King came to believe that "the pacifist would have a greater appeal if he did not claim to be free from the moral dilemmas that the Christian non-pacifist confronts."[49]

In terms of the law, King's realism led him to see a role for the state's coercive power. He reminded listeners that "morality cannot be legislated, but behavior can be regulated," and that "judicial decrees may not change the heart, but they can restrain the heartless."[50] At the same time, law cannot overcome the alienating power of sin. While human law can produce justice, only a higher law produces love.[51] The laws of society cannot reach the "inner attitudes, genuine person-to-person relations, and expressions of compassion" through which the law of love is expressed.[52]

---

[46] *Id.*

[47] Zepp & Smith, *supra* note 3, at 156.

[48] Martin Luther King Jr., The *Autobiography of Martin Luther King, Jr.*, Clayborn Carson ed. (2001), 27.

[49] *Id.*

[50] Martin Luther King Jr., "The Ethical Demands for Integration," in *A Testament of Hope, supra* note 3, at 124.

[51] *Id.* at 123.

[52] *Id.*

Nevertheless, just as Niebuhr insisted that earthly power must be exercised in (admittedly imperfect) service of love, King lamented the tendency to conceive of love and power as opposites, "so that love is identified with a resignation of power, and power with a denial of love."[53] Power is not to be shunned by those concerned with love, for the oppressed "only realize deliverance when they have accumulated the power to enforce change."[54] To avoid the mistake of philosophers (such as Nietzsche) who have rejected love and the mistake of many Christian theologians who have rejected power, King highlighted the need to realize "that power without love is reckless and abusive, and love without power is sentimental and anemic." Power, at its best, "is love implementing the demands of justice, and justice at its best is power correcting everything that stands against love."[55] Power and love must be exercised in tandem.

II. Lawyers as Realists

So what does Christian realism have to say to lawyers? At first glance, lawyers may appear to have already internalized realism's lessons. As noted previously, lawyers do not

---

[53] Martin Luther King Jr., *Where Do We Go from Here: Chaos or Community?* (1967), 247.

[54] Martin Luther King Jr., "Black Power Defined," in *A Testament of Hope*, *supra* note 3, at 303.

[55] Martin Luther King Jr., *supra* note 53, at 247.

trust themselves to judge the moral worthiness of the client's objectives or the moral acceptability of the fallout from the pursuit of those objectives. Consider the Model Code of Professional Responsibility's instruction that a client is entitled "to seek any lawful objective through legally permissible means,"[56] or the Model Rules of Professional Conduct's explanation that "lawyers usually defer to the client regarding concern ... for third persons who might be adversely affected" by the representation.[57] As Stephen Pepper puts it, "for access to the law to be filtered through the disparate moral views of each individual's lawyer does not appear to be justifiable."[58]

The legal ethics scholar Brad Wendel has recently provided one of the more thoughtful and sustained defenses of the view that a lawyer's own moral convictions represent a potentially dangerous addition to the lawyer's work. Rather than portraying the lawyer's obligation as being directed toward the client's interests, as the standard conception of lawyering traditionally characterizes it, Wendel defines the lawyer's obligation of loyalty as being owed to the law itself. This permits Wendel unabashedly to condemn the Department of Justice lawyers who justified torture and the Vinson & Elkins lawyers who facilitated Enron's demise;

---

[56] *ABA Model Code of Prof'l Resp.* EC 7–1.

[57] *ABA Model Rules of Prof'l Conduct* 1.2 cmt. 2.

[58] Stephen L. Pepper, *The Lawyer's Amoral Ethical Role: A Defense, a Problem, and Some Possibilities*, 1986 AM. B. FOUND. RES. J. 613, 618.

their culpability, under Wendel's view, lies in their manipulation (and ultimately perversion) of the law. If lawyers are obligated to push the legal boundaries to the limit in order to maximize their client's stated interests, it becomes markedly more difficult to criticize the DoJ and Enron lawyers provided that there was some remotely colorable legal argument supporting their position. Wendel can more comfortably criticize lawyers whose arguments, while perhaps colorable, are not a good-faith interpretation in keeping with the spirit of the legal norm in question. As such, Wendel's approach might help the legal profession shake its myopic focus on client interests, which is often at the expense of the common good. It remains to be seen, though, whether replacing an exclusive focus on client interests with an exclusive focus on the law goes far enough.

Wendel explains that "the ethical value of lawyering is located in the domain of politics, not ordinary morality."[59] The political justification of lawyering does not spring from a cynicism about the very existence of justice or the public interest, but from the fact that we disagree about those concepts, and that disagreement is why we need law in the first place.[60] Wendel, in a sense, puts a political emphasis on the realist perspective: as fallen human beings, we cannot conclusively figure out what "the good" is or reach perfect consensus about its content. The law represents our best

---

[59] Brad Wendel, *Lawyers and Fidelity to Law* (2010), 2.
[60] *Id.* at 210.

efforts to arrive at a workable understanding about what the good requires in particular contexts. For lawyers to substitute their own judgments for that understanding is to ignore the realism-driven lessons on which the rule of law is built.

Wendel defines the "standard conception" of the lawyer's work as consisting of three principles: the principle of partisanship (the "lawyer should seek to advance the interests of her client within the bounds of law"), the principle of neutrality (the "lawyer should not consider the morality of the client's cause, nor the morality of particular actions taken to advance the client's cause, as long as both are lawful"), and the principle of nonaccountability ("If a lawyer adheres to the first two principles, neither third-party observers nor the lawyer herself should regard the lawyer as a wrongdoer, in moral terms").[61] He tweaks the definition by substituting "legal entitlements" for "interests" under the principle of partisanship. As such, lawyers are "better analogized to political officials than to ordinary moral agents,"[62] and when a lawyer facilitates injustice by manipulating the law, "the proper basis for ethical criticism is the failure to exhibit fidelity to law, not the resulting injustice."[63] Using a famous example from debates about legal interpretation, Wendel explains how fidelity to law should shape a lawyer's interpretation of a statute prohibiting "vehicles in the park":

[61] *Id.* at 6.
[62] *Id.* at 8.
[63] *Id.* at 9.

While we may be unsure whether the statute prohibiting vehicles in the park applies to a baby stroller, a jeep on a war memorial, or an ambulance rushing to the aid of a heart attack victim in the park, we do know that if the statute means anything, it means you cannot drive a souped-up sports car through the park.... Waterboarding is the souped-up sports car of the prohibitions on torture. If one's legal conclusion is that causing someone to experience the physical sensation of imminent death is not torture, then something in that argument has gone off the rails.... This approach to ethical criticism takes seriously the internal point of view of a lawyer participating in the craft of making and evaluating legal arguments. It is not an external critique, on the grounds of the wrongfulness of torture in ordinary moral terms. That is the distinctive perspective of the ethics of fidelity to law.[64]

Because lawyers contribute to the common good by supporting a system that makes cooperation and coexistence in a pluralistic society possible, they should "regard the legal system, and their client's legal entitlements, as creating reasons that override considerations that would otherwise apply to persons not acting in the same professional capacity."[65]

As a Christian realist, King might have expressed concern about the dangers that could accompany Wendel's focus on the client as a citizen to the extent that it obscures a view of the client as a person. Wendel quotes John Rawls's

[64] *Id.* at 15.
[65] *Id.* at 10.

explanation of liberalism approvingly: "The philosophical conception of the person is replaced in political liberalism by the political conception of citizens as free and equal."[66] The wholesale adoption by the legal profession of this Rawlsian understanding might actually exacerbate the profession's existing tendency, as discussed in Chapter 3, to introduce an overly narrow conception of the client into the representation. The move from personhood to citizenship is not costless.

For example, Wendel discusses the hypothetical scenario of a $5,000 loan between two neighbors: Borrower and Lender. Borrower's business flourishes as a result of the loan while Lender falls on hard times and now is desperate for money to pay medical expenses. Borrower could easily repay the loan, but he instead instructs his lawyer to file a motion to dismiss the suit based on the fact that the statute of limitations has expired.[67] Wendel acknowledges that failing to repay a loan is cheating, but "pleading the statute of limitations feels different, somehow, because the defense to the claim for repayment is part of a system that has been established to adjudicate the legitimacy of the obligation." We cannot simply assume that the debt is justly owed, Wendel reasons, because "that is exactly what the legal system needs to determine." We have established certain procedures that determine whether a debt is legally enforceable, and one of

[66] *Id.* at 23 (quoting John Rawls, *Political Liberalism* [1993], 380).
[67] *Id.* at 27–8.

those procedures prescribes a time limit for bringing the claim. Whether or not there are good moral reasons for the Borrower to repay the debt, those reasons "have only limited relevance to what the lawyer is permitted or required to do on behalf of her client."[68] For the lawyer to refuse to assist the Borrower in establishing his legal entitlement to avoid the debt (through the invocation of the statute of limitations) "would be to deprive a client of that very thing for which the role of lawyer is constituted."[69]

Helping the Borrower avoid the debt under these circumstances may be consistent with the Borrower's entitlement as a citizen, yet at the same time be contrary to her well-being as a person. Further, to the extent that the Borrower's well-being as a person is closely connected with the legal system's resolution of his dispute with the Lender, the Borrower's personhood, not just citizenship, is wrapped up with the work of the lawyer. Wendel is concerned that, if a lawyer advises a client not to do something because the lawyer believes that it is morally wrong, the lawyer is displaying "a kind of arrogance or disrespect for competing viewpoints," but also is committing a "political wrong, in light of the social value of the framework for cooperation created by the law."[70] I agree that proceeding with the statute of limitations defense is ultimately the client's call (and the lawyer's call, in turn, is whether she can represent the

---

[68] *Id.* at 28–9.
[69] *Id.* at 128.
[70] *Id.* at 36.

Borrower in carrying out this strategy), but there is a danger if the strictly political terms by which Wendel has justified the lawyer's role serves to marginalize the lawyer's agency in raising the moral dimension of the client's decision. What if, instead of encountering the client only as a citizen with legal entitlements, the lawyer encountered the client as a person who possesses both legal entitlements and an interest in doing right by her neighbors? If our realism is founded on an authentic view of the human person, would our legal advice need to make space for the client's nature as a social being who is accountable to others?

Wendel has a ready response to this critique, citing Isaiah Berlin's admonition "to be extremely wary of any claim to political legitimacy and authority that is founded upon a claim that the rulers have accurately discerned the 'true' nature of their subjects."[71] It is not apparent why or how Berlin's caution would extend to lawyers, even if we concede Wendel's characterization of lawyers as essential participants in the system by which we effectuate the political resolution of our social disagreements. As long as there is a functioning marketplace of lawyers, the authority wielded by any individual lawyer is necessarily limited by the availability of alternative avenues by which to protect the client's legal entitlements; and as long as the lawyer's introduction of interests beyond legal entitlement occurs in the context of

---

[71] *Id.* at 55.

moral counseling, rather than moral imposition, the authority of the lawyer's moral claims is limited by the dialogical nature of the encounter.

Wendel does not object to moral counseling per se, though he views that function as tangential to the lawyer's core function. He explains that, though "there is nothing wrong with discussing with the client whether the client's objectives are prudent, the lawyer's central role is to evaluate whether the client is legally entitled to pursue some objective."[72] Admittedly, few clients are eager to retain a lawyer who gives great moral advice but lacks legal knowledge. Technical proficiency is the floor below which a competent lawyer cannot fall, and such proficiency requires sound advice on the law. But legal and moral considerations do not exist in separate hermetically sealed worlds. If the client, as a social being, desires to act consistently with her nature by doing right by others, in some instances that desire will only find real-world traction through the counsel of an expert who both knows the law and is sensitive to the relationship between a given legal entitlement and the interests of others. Wendel is correct that the lawyer's interpretation of legal directives should be made in a spirit of fidelity to the law, but he may be overestimating the extent to which legal interpretation makes up the entirety of the lawyer's service to the client or contribution to the common good.

[72] *Id.* at 56.

King might also resist Wendel's portrayal of the moral duties we owe to those outside our most intimate circles of friends and family. According to Wendel:

> We owe strangers a duty to refrain from harming them in particular ways, but not a duty to help them become better people, or even to help them to avoid becoming morally corrupt themselves. We owe different obligations to family members and close friends, but these are owed in virtue of the shared history and reciprocal vulnerability that characterizes those relationships. Most lawyer-client relationships, on the other hand, are arm's length economic transactions.[73]

Speaking to Tom Shaffer's emphasis on the importance of moral counseling,[74] Wendel notes that many of Shaffer's examples "involve lawyers and clients who are members of the same tightly knit community, in which other kinds of bonds exist, independent of the lawyer-client relationship." In those cases, any obligation – or even "strong reason" – to offer moral counseling is better located in the fact that the lawyer and client are also friends, neighbors, or coreligionists. Outside these extenuating circumstances, Wendel argues, the lawyer has no greater obligation to provide moral counseling than any other participant in an arm's length economic transaction.[75]

---

[73] *Id.* at 142.

[74] *See* Introduction pages 10–11, *supra.*

[75] Wendel, *supra* note 92, at 142.

Wendel may underestimate the extent to which strong reasons to offer moral counseling may arise from the lawyer-client relationship itself, rather than from independent relationships between the individuals occupying the roles of lawyer and client. King's consistent emphasis on our membership in an "inescapable network of mutuality" does not easily lend itself to bright-line distinctions between relationships to which moral engagement is intrinsic and those for which it serves as an afterthought. (That is not the same as suggesting that every relationship creates identical duties of care.) In the context of some representations, the provision of technically competent legal advice will both effectuate the client's legal entitlements and fully capture that client's relevant interests. But if every human being is a social creature and moral subject, the lawyer will regularly confront scenarios where the language of legal entitlements does not exhaust the scope of the client's relevant interests. Because the lawyer may be best positioned, by virtue of her training and experience, to help the client discern the relationship between the moral and the legal dimensions of a proposed course of conduct, sometimes a duty of moral engagement may flow directly from the nature of the lawyer-client relationship.

But that does not mean that the lawyer or client operates on a blank slate. The law provides, in most instances, a robust normative background that the lawyer is bound to respect. That lawyers disregard their legal obligations is not newsworthy; what might go unnoticed is the possibility that the degree of disregard is a function of the lawyer's own pride and perception of power. For example, researchers have found that companies represented by elite law firms are less likely to comply with Securities and Exchange Commission (SEC) disclosure requirements.[76]

Grounding the lawyer's role in fidelity to law – that is, the client's legal entitlements – or in fidelity to the client's interests, as traditionally understood – that is, the interests as articulated by the client herself, without meaningful input from, or moral reflection facilitated by, the lawyer – tends to marginalize the role of relationships in legal practice. If the law represents the political community's best efforts to determine our relational obligations to one another, lawyers may simply proceed by its terms without delving into the often-messy implications that a legal option may hold for real-world relationships. Similarly, if the client's interests are presumed to be a fixed, predetermined set of marching orders, the lawyer's moral engagement with the matter is over before it begins. Both possibilities excuse the lawyer from entering into more than an arm's length transaction with the client or from bringing into focus the human

---

[76] Preeti Choudhary, Jason D. Schloetzer, & Jason D. Sturgess, *Top-Tier Law Firms and Corporate Disclosure: Evidence from Regulatory Noncompliance*, at 2 ("We document that 39 percent of firms fail to comply with mandatory 12b-25 disclosure rules. In addition, we find robust evidence that firms who retain a top-tier law firm are less likely to comply.") (http://ssrn.com/abstract=1656984)

dimension of the potential costs imposed by a legally permissible course of conduct. Acting on a realist impetus, lawyers may not trust themselves to explore the client's values and their connection with the representation's real-world consequences more fully without subverting the client's desires in favor of their own.

The danger with this mindset, though, is that it can exacerbate the lawyer's existing tendency toward isolation and self-reliance, an affliction that can, in the end, compromise both the lawyer's fidelity to law and the client's best interests. Human fallibility has driven the case for restraining lawyers' moral activism in their relationships with clients but has been largely absent from discussions about lawyers' relationships with each other. In both contexts, though, our fallen condition should be a caution *against* pulling back from meaningful and mutually supportive relationships. To hold otherwise misconstrues the lessons of Christian realism.

Consider the case of John Gellene, a bankruptcy partner at the white-shoe New York law firm of Milbank Tweed. In the course of representing the Bucyrus-Erie Company in its Chapter 11 bankruptcy, Gellene filed a sworn declaration that was supposed to list all of his firm's connections to the debtor, creditors, and any other parties in interest.[77] One of the parties in interest was South Street Funds, an investment group that held $35 million in senior secured notes and

---

[77] *U.S. v. Gellene*, 182 F.3d 578 (7th Cir. 1999).

leasehold interests. South Street was managed and directed by Greycliff Partners, an investment entity consisting of the financial advisers Mikael Salovaara and Alfred Eckert. Gellene failed to disclose the fact that Milbank was currently representing South Street, Greycliff, and Salovaara. In fact, Gellene had billed work to Greycliff and South Street on the same day that he filed a second declaration omitting them as parties in interest with whom his firm had any connection. The court ultimately awarded Milbank nearly $2 million in fees and expenses for the Bucyrus bankruptcy.

Another party to the proceeding discovered Milbank's conflicts of interest – and Gellene's concealment thereof – after the matter had concluded. The party filed a motion seeking disgorgement of Milbank's fees. Gellene did not respond to the motion. Weeks later, when his partners became aware of the motion and asked about it, Gellene lied and said that a response was not yet due, even though the deadline had passed. He even altered the motion to conceal the date on which it had been filed. Eventually, in a dramatic and tearful breakdown, Gellene admitted to his partners that he had lied.

Gellene was charged with two counts of knowingly and fraudulently making a false material declaration in the Bucyrus case, and one count of using a document while under oath, knowing that it contained a false material declaration. Gellene admitted that he had used bad judgment in concluding that the representations did not need to be disclosed, but he insisted that he lacked fraudulent intent.

The jury returned guilty verdicts on all three counts, and he was sentenced to fifteen months in prison and fined $15,000. Given the felony conviction, he was automatically disbarred. The bankruptcy court subsequently ordered Milbank to return the $1.8 million based on Gellene's false statements.

In the deepest and most nuanced account of Gellene's fall from grace, Milton Regan notes that commentators usually speculate that Gellene was either an "aberrant partner with a weakness for cutting corners," or else a fall guy who was pressured by his firm to conceal a conflict in order to secure a nearly $2 million fee.[78] In other words, the problem stemmed either from Gellene's own character flaws or from his vulnerability to the influence of a corrupt organization.[79] Regan devotes himself to expanding our understanding of the challenges faced by large firm lawyers, which "requires a richer account of how character and circumstance interact in daily practice."[80]

For our purposes, what stands out is the degree to which the competitive pressures of large firm life magnified the perfectionist and self-reliant tendencies already exhibited by Gellene (and many other lawyers), increasing the likelihood that he would isolate himself from relationships of support and accountability. As for firm structure, one key shift has been from lockstep compensation to merit-based compensation,

[78] Milton C. Regan Jr., *Eat What You Kill: The Fall of a Wall Street Lawyer* (2004), 6.

[79] *Id.* at 6.

[80] *Id.*

meaning that associates and partners are all competitors for a limited pool of resources.[81] A permanent state of competition, not job security, is the hallmark of the modern large law firm. The focus on competition increases the pressure to achieve favorable results in a given matter. Further, the competition proceeds through constantly shifting teams assembled for discrete projects, then disassembled and reconstituted in different forms for the next project.[82] Lawyers may work together intensely on a specific project, but that does not mean that they have a long-term working relationship.

Gellene's own personality contributed to the problem. As it is for many lawyers, much of his self-worth was based on his intellectual ability, as he admitted.[83] Regan observes that Gellene is hardly unique among lawyers in this regard, as studies suggest that individuals who choose to go to law school have an unusually high need for academic achievement,[84] and thus may have an unusually high need to compete.[85] Tying one's self-image so closely to intellectual achievement carries some costs, of course, including the burden of perfectionism. Gellene admitted that he was afraid to admit mistakes for fear that others would no longer believe he was brilliant. He explained that he felt that he "had to be

---

[81] *Id.* at 7.

[82] *Id.* at 8.

[83] *Id.* at 295 ("Not just for my adult life but before that.... I've been recognized as a person with gifts of my intellect and my ability to deal with problems.").

[84] *Id.*

[85] *Id.*

perfect because that is where I've gotten my view of myself. That is where I've gotten satisfaction. That's where I've tried for better or for worse to have meaning in my life."[86]

In light of this self-image, Gellene was reluctant to seek help from others, and he pushed himself hard, taking on several demanding matters at once. His approach to work, as Regan describes it, "posed the constant threat of isolation."[87] Again, this threat is a reality for many lawyers. Regan reports studies showing that lawyers "may be especially prone to be highly self-critical and anxious about performance, as well as to project an image of self-containment that eschews assistance from others."[88] Further, those who stake their identity on achievement "may channel their insecurity into even greater efforts at control, rather than rely on others for support."[89] For example, although Gellene had passed the New York bar exam, he had been unwilling to take the time away from work to complete the required paperwork for admission. As years went by, it became more and more difficult for him to admit that he was not admitted to the New York bar. As Gellene stated, "As time went on it got more and more absurd and I could not stand up and say, I did something stupid," and "I could not say it to myself and I could not say it to others so I hid it."[90]

[86] *Id.* at 296.
[87] *Id.* at 298.
[88] *Id.*
[89] *Id.*
[90] *Id.* at 299.

These personal traits do not adequately explain Gellene's lies to the bankruptcy court, however. He was not trying to save himself from embarrassment, at least at the outset – he was trying to deceive the court.[91] His willingness to deceive the court, though, was tied to his drive to succeed, to win the competition, to refuse to permit legal "technicalities" to stand in the way of achieving the objective. And his ability to succeed stemmed, at least in part, from his adeptness at justifying apparent breaches of the applicable rules. Regan explains:

> Research suggests that those who advance in the tourna-ment-like environment of large organizations tend to share certain characteristics. They are able to quickly grasp the rules of the game – to "get a sense of the prevailing metric and outperform their peers on it." They tend to be adept at rationalizing questionable behavior when it's necessary to accomplish their objectives. Their skill in doing so is enhanced by an ability to minimize or bracket the moral sig-nificance of the situations that they encounter. This enables them to approach decisions pragmatically, less fettered by a sense of categorical constraint. Tournament survivors thus exhibit the flexibility necessary to move from one competi-tion to another with a minimum of psychological friction.[92]

Donald Langevoort makes a similar point, explaining that success in competitive organizations "is skewed in the

[91] *Id.* at 302.
[92] *Id.* at 303.

direction of rewarding those who are highly focused at the business of competing, which of necessity means the cognitive ability to block out concerns – like difficult ethical problems – that are likely to be distracting."[93] An individual attorney's competitively oriented cognitive "flexibility" takes on a new dynamic in the group context. A team of lawyers will frequently "assume a competitive posture that both builds cohesion among group members and generates hostility toward outsiders," which "makes it more likely that the group will construct a distinctive moral universe that guides its members' judgments about right and wrong in the context of the project."[94] Whenever the high stakes and looming deadlines of a matter can create a sense of crisis, the ability of group members to justify their behavior is especially great.[95]

Legal ethicists are wise to incorporate the fallible nature of lawyers into their traditional justification of the lawyer's role. But they may be overemphasizing one dimension of that fallibility while largely disregarding other dimensions. Prudent concern for the client-directed nature of legal representation should not be allowed to obscure the importance of moral engagement between lawyer and client. No lawyer has a monopoly on moral truth so as to justify silencing the client or subverting the rule of law. The potential for moral

---

[93] Donald C. Langevoort, *The Organizational Psychology of Hyper-Competition: Corporate Responsibility and the Lessons of Enron*, 70 GEO. WASH. L. REV. 968, 971 (2002).

[94] Regan, *supra* note 78, at 349.

[95] *Id.*

engagement to be abused, though, does not change the need for engagement. King's realism always brought to light aspects of our life together that we may prefer to ignore; for the legal profession, one such aspect is the fact that technically proficient legal advice will not always serve the client's interests fully.

At the same time, our fallen human condition is relevant to the lawyer's work. Indeed, our fallen condition may tend to reveal itself among people who are drawn to the practice of law differently than it does in others. Lawyers' tendency to define themselves by their intellectual achievements, their perfectionism, and their drive to win can foster unhealthy isolation, an avoidance of vulnerability, and a fear-driven self-reliance. Large law firms have realized the awesome profit-maximizing power unleashed by building a permanent competition among highly driven individuals who are afraid to fail. For reasons reflected in the travails of John Gellene, Joseph Collins,[96] Enron,[97] and others, it is not at all clear that unleashing this power serves either the rule of law or client well-being. Instead of accounting for the reality of lawyers' fallen nature, some aspects of modern legal practice may capitalize on that fallen nature in the pursuit of short-term interests. For both lawyers and clients, ignoring the reality of our social nature is, in the end, a costly proposition.

[96] *See* Chapter 2, *supra*, at text accompanying notes 45 to 47.
[97] *See* Chapter 2, *supra*, at text accompanying notes 33 to 44.

III. Christian Realism and the Human Person

A fundamental problem facing the legal profession is that the skeptical side of realism is as far as our modern understanding of lawyering gets, but it is not as far as Niebuhr went. There are many lawyers who can wax eloquent about the abstract intricacies of justice who nevertheless lack a personal commitment to bringing about its achievement in the here and now. And they might even style this lack of commitment as a sort of Christian realism. However, in Niebuhr's work, the elusiveness of justice does not excuse Christians from seeking it. As noted earlier, Niebuhr never used his realism to excuse hopelessness or inaction. He championed realism as an impetus to take responsibility for "a tolerable justice" in this world, even though ultimate justice would have to wait until the next.

One reason why Niebuhr's realism did not weaken his commitment to justice is that his realism had a firm foundation and was not simply teetering on the abyss of a bottomless skepticism. Niebuhr's realism meant, quite obviously, that his worldview was grounded in reality. And that worldview presumed, of course, that there is a reality. As a realist, Niebuhr emphasized the importance of grounding our worldview on an accurate understanding of the human person, including the social and transcendent dimensions of human nature. We are not freestanding bundles of legal interests waiting to be maximized; we are relational in that human nature entails our "fulfillment in the lives of others."

The legal profession, particularly the field of legal ethics, lacks a vision of the nature of the human person. A healthy skepticism about lawyers' ability to check their own self-interest when faced with a vulnerable client too often becomes an unhealthy and unhelpful cynicism about the possibility of a discernible, much less articulable, human nature, as though a politically constructed notion of citizenship is sufficient to understand the clients on whose behalf we labor. Pushing human nature to the margins of the conversation creates several problems, including the fact that it depletes the profession of resources to talk meaningfully about problems arising from the current wrenching changes that it is currently undergoing. Putting the social nature of the human person in focus may help conceptualize the nontechnical dimension of legal practice in a way that reconnects the profession with a richer understanding of how lawyers can contribute to human well-being, not just to the maximization of a single client's legal interests.

Right now, not much is in focus regarding the professional distinctiveness of lawyers, though. As explored in Chapter 2, as competitive pressures push law firms toward more economically efficient practices, those efficiencies can make the attorney-client relationship more difficult to distinguish from other provider-consumer transactions. Clients are pushing for these measures in order to reduce transaction costs, but they may alter the nature of the attorney-client relationship in the process, with the attorney becoming less of a trusted personal adviser and more of a fungible source of technical competence. Making the provision of legal services more efficient by subjecting it to the same market forces faced by other types of service providers is not necessarily a bad thing. Indeed, from the public's perspective, higher prices may be the most obvious legacy of lawyers' success in using their "professional" status to justify their exemption from market competition. But if market trends hollow out the trust-centered nature of the attorney-client relationship, will the lower prices reflect the true cost of the shift? This is a tough question for lawyers to grapple with, much less to answer, for if our profession lacks an understanding of the human person, it is much more difficult to articulate why we should care about the marginalization of personal relationships in legal services.

Christian realism couples a belief in our fallen nature with a belief that imperfect approximations of love (in the form of justice) still matter. Lawyers are capable of entering into relationships with their clients, centered on certain understandings that flow from our shared human nature. One such understanding is that our clients themselves are social beings who are accountable to other social beings.

As noted, Niebuhr consistently returned to the bedrock principle that love is the law of life. This love is not a function of individual sentiment, for it "must be enthroned as yet the final standard of every institution, structure and system of justice."[98] It is also unmistakably social. Niebuhr cautioned against a "Christian pessimism" that tempts Christians to abdicate responsibility toward social tasks, such as "raising the level of their social imagination and increasing the range of their social sympathies."[99]

Reacting against what he saw as the excessive optimism of "social gospel" Christians, Niebuhr focused on the fact that "sinful man must achieve tentative harmonies of life which are less than the best," and which fall short of the law of love's demands.[100] He thus tended to spend more time exploring humanity's failure to abide by the law of love than he did exploring the substance of the law of love itself. As a result, it can be difficult when reading Niebuhr to decipher the particular implications of love's normative reality for our everyday lives. He provides some hints, as when he explains that for a modern community to achieve a tolerable justice, its members must "sharply distinguish between their interests and the demands which God and the neighbor make upon them."[101]

---

[98] Reinhold Niebuhr, "The Christian Witness in the Social and National Order," in *The Essential Reinhold Niebuhr, supra* note 2, at 93, 99.

[99] Reinhold Niebuhr, "The Christian Church in a Secular Age," in *The Essential Reinhold Niebuhr, supra* note 2, at 79, 86.

[100] Reinhold Niebuhr, "Why the Christian Church Is Not Pacifist," in *The Essential Reinhold Niebuhr, supra* note 2, at 102, 106.

[101] Reinhold Niebuhr, "The Christian Witness in the Social and National Order," in *The Essential Reinhold Niebuhr, supra* note 2, at 93, 100.

The social nature of the human person came into sharper relief in the work of Dr. King. For King, as discussed in Chapter 3, the language of personalism amplified the social implications of Christian realism. Given the structure of the universe, "the self cannot be self without other selves," and "I cannot reach fulfillment without thou."[102] Niebuhr embraced at least this dimension of personalism, writing that

> only by a voluntary giving of life to life and a free interpenetration of personalities could man do justice both to the freedom of other personalities and the necessity of community between personalities. The law of love therefore remains a principle of criticism over all forms of community in which elements of coercion and conflict destroy the highest type of fellowship.[103]

Even when a person exercises her freedom to make herself the center of her existence, love rather than self-love remains the law of her existence "in the sense that man can only be healthy, and his communities at peace, if man is drawn out of himself and saved from the self-defeating consequences of self-love."[104] Self-love is not limited to the individual, of course. Speaking about the seemingly intractable

---

[102] Martin Luther King Jr., *Where Do We Go From Here: Chaos or Community?* (1967).

[103] Reinhold Niebuhr, "Why The Christian Church Is Not Pacifist," in *The Essential Reinhold Niebuhr, supra* note 2, at 102, 114.

[104] Reinhold Niebuhr, "Augustine's Political Realism," in *The Essential Reinhold Niebuhr, supra* note 2, at 123, 131.

problem of American race relations, Niebuhr framed it as a "dilemma of validating the humanity of man despite the strong tribal impulses in his nature."[105] If we can break our pride and recognize our own limitations, we can "see the truth in others' views and simultaneously [gain] 'a sense of gratitude in the experience of release from self.'"[106]

Tribal impulses are familiar ground for the legal profession, even as the profession struggles to account for the lawyer's fallen nature. For example, the profession forbids the attorney from accepting certain representations that create conflicts of interest, even if there is no showing of actual harm to the client. We do not want lawyers to put themselves in a position where their own interests will tempt them to give less than zealous representation to the client. The profession does not let the lawyer say, "But I'm a strong-willed, self-disciplined person who can rise above my own interests and serve my client!" No, the profession says, the will to power can never be adequately checked, so we will do it for you. Niebuhr might be proud, as far as it goes.

The problem, at the level of professionwide regulation, is that this healthy skepticism is often insufficient to overcome the profession's devotion to the economic interests of lawyers.

---

[105] Reinhold Niebuhr, "The Struggle for Justice," *New Leader* 47 (July 6, 1964): 11 (quoted in Douglas, *supra* note 21, at 431).

[106] Berg, *supra* note 9, at 1595 (quoting 2 Reinhold Niebuhr, *The Nature and Destiny of Man: Human Destiny* 115 (Scribner Library ed. 1964) (1943)).

In 2009, when the American Bar Association relaxed its rule governing conflicts of interest in a way that now permits a lawyer representing a plaintiff in a lawsuit to be hired by the defendant's firm in the middle of the suit,[107] the ABA defended the rule as a prudent acknowledgment of lawyer mobility and urged critics to trust firms' ability to screen effectively. The curious fact is that the ABA had considered this proposal several times in the past, but in the midst of the worst economic downturn in years in the legal profession, the profession made it substantially easier for lawyers to get hired even when a conflict would traditionally have prevented it. Reasonable people can find good-faith reasons to support the change – for example, that the size and global scope of firms have dramatically deepened the impact of rigid disqualification rules – but given the timing, Niebuhr might also notice an inordinate self-love moving the levers of power.[108]

The law of love espoused by King and Niebuhr tells us something about a client's well-being, but it also tells us something about a lawyer's responsibilities toward the client. As argued in Chapter 1, lawyers who love act as subjects, not as objects. In other words, love makes a lawyer an active participant in a dynamic relationship, not a passive

---

[107] *See ABA Model Rules of Prof'l Conduct* R. 1.10.

[108] ABA President Carolyn Lamm even defended the amendment as "particularly important for the employment prospects of those whose careers are affected by the recession." Carolyn Lamm, *Staying On Message*, ABA JOURNAL, January 2010, at 8.

vessel or conduit for client demands. A lawyer "drawn out of himself" gives voice to his client, to be sure, but a lawyer who loves is more than a mouthpiece. A lawyer who loves cares about the client in a way that does not presume to equate the client's well-being with the maximization of her independence and autonomy. In loving the client, the lawyer's own being is involved, and thus the lawyer's devotion to the client's well-being will inescapably implicate the lawyer's beliefs regarding human nature and the conditions on which human flourishing depends.

Christian realism's contribution to the work of the attorney is to keep human fallibility in view, both to check the attorney's own inclination toward prideful usurpation of client prerogatives, and to avoid an unduly optimistic view of the positive law's capacity to capture and reflect the considerations needed for real human flourishing. The attorney's own fallen nature makes fidelity to law vital, but the limitations of lawmaking make an exclusive focus on legal entitlements inadequate. Viewed through the lens of realism, the client's interests are nuanced and complex. The client as person transcends the client as citizen.

Both King and Niebuhr saw law's power to serve as a needed bulwark against the tendency of inordinate self-love to produce alienation and disconnection in the human condition. The starting point for the attorney-client relationship should not be the assumption that the client wishes to maximize her own legal interests without accounting for her social commitments and obligations. The importance of acknowledging the social dimension of a client's nature (and correspondingly, her well-being) is not limited to headline-grabbing cases. When a client asks his lawyer to help negotiate the settlement terms of his divorce, decide how aggressively to interpret applicable environmental regulations, comply with arguable disclosure obligations in a real property sale, or write a hostile letter to the opposing counsel, the lawyer has a choice. She can start from one of two premises: (1) that the client's interests should be defined narrowly in terms directly traceable to the client's immediate and tangible benefit; or (2) that the client's interests include an account of her decision's impact on those with whom she is in relationship. The Christian realist lawyer will not push the client toward certain results – to do so would be to ignore both the client's dignity and the lawyer's fallibility – but she will avoid assumptions about the client's nature that defy reality, including the social nature of the human person.

The realist's awareness of the corrupting power of excessive self-love means that skepticism is necessary. Blind deference to the justice of "the system" is never in order. Realist lawyers in the molds of Niebuhr and King know love should not shun power and power should not shun love. Lawyers shun power when they abdicate responsibility for justice to a professional interest group. They shun love when they equate justice with rights and forget that rights are the means for restoring just relationships. Lawyers must account for a fallen world in our understanding of our professional roles. A lawyer cannot ignore the power dimension of legal practice or the profession's capacity to dress up its own interests as the public interest. Realist lawyers take to heart Niebuhr's caution that privileged groups engage in pervasive self-deception and consistently identify their own interests as universal.[109]

The realist lawyer cannot defer to the American Bar Association for a proper accounting of reality, much less for an account of how the law of love can be reflected in our pursuit of justice. It depends on the lawyer herself to take reality seriously. Christian realism takes an unflinching view of the fallen person, but lawyers are missing the point if they conclude that the fall totally obscures the person. The flight from relationships – both ours and those of the client – is a flight from reality, and from realism.

---

[109] Reinhold Niebuhr, *Moral Man & Immoral Society* (2002) (1932), 117.

Conclusion

It may be fruitful to revisit the conversation between Martin Luther King Jr. and my students who prioritized cleverness over their own moral intuition when they offered strained justifications for Nazi scientists to experiment on concentration camp inmates. Put simply, King would ask them to remove the professional blinders that allowed them to use the concept of role to deny what they held to be true. He would ask them to reflect on their own commitment to the value of human life and ask whether that commitment is simply an off-the-rack item to be picked up or put down as circumstances warrant, or whether it represents the recognition of moral truth, rather than a self-directed moral preference. In other words, King would remind them of what they already know.

Nevertheless, King would help them bring inchoate intuitions into relief by giving them language that captures the commitment. First, for students tempted to equate their vindication of human dignity with their facilitation of the client's individual autonomy, King offers a caution: dignity as autonomy may provide a minimum threshold, but it does not represent dignity's full reach. As reflected in the conversation that has unfolded in bioethics in the decades since King's death, human dignity opens the door to substantive conversations about what we share as human beings, and how those commonalities should shape our relationships, both private and professional. King teaches my students to see dignity as a quality of human interaction to be measured by our willingness to honor our mutual vulnerability, not just as an intrinsic but undefined property of the human person, to be deployed solely as the justification for maximizing individual autonomy. My students' commitment to the human dignity underlying King's ministry provides an orientation toward connecting the "is" of the human condition with the "ought" of moral truth, but the content of both the "is" and the "ought" is further fleshed out by the other foundational tenets of King's worldview.

Second, King's explanation and practice of agape challenge my students to live out their social natures by recognizing their accountability to the good of their clients. Because agape is an active love that seeks out the good of the client, however, a lawyer who aspires to agape will need to rediscover – or discover for the first time – her own status as a moral subject. Lawyers are not mouthpieces; they are partners in an inescapably moral endeavor, and agape requires them to work for their client's well-being, which will not always be coextensive with the maximization of the client's legal interests. Agape does not impose, but it cannot shirk from proposing a course that reflects cognizance of the client's nature and extralegal commitments. If my student becomes a corporate lawyer with an expertise in mergers and acquisitions, for example, she will ensure her ongoing technical competence, but she will also be willing to ask bigger questions about the wisdom of a proposed action. Even if she is not the only person at the table inclined to ask such questions – though depending on the organizational culture, she might be – she may be the only person who can discern and articulate the connections between the legal and extralegal concerns or explain the law's imperfection in pursuing the human values that are implicated by the client's decision. The ensuing conversation is not about the lawyer trying to assuage her conscience, but about the lawyer authentically serving her client's well-being by practicing agape.

Third, while agape's call for lawyers to embrace their status as moral subjects precludes a lawyer from ignoring her client's nature, King's personalism provides some of the content to that nature. Personalism teaches lawyers not to presume that their clients exist as atomized individuals with strictly self-regarding interests. We are social creatures, and thus the viability and vitality of human relationships are a key component of our well-being; they provide the tableau against which our normative aspirations should be formed. Few will deny the premises of personalism, but most of us fail to live out its implications. King calls us to close the gap between our abstract conception of our social nature and the on-the-ground isolation and marginalization that mark the modern human condition. Lawyers can use the authority of rights to increase our isolation or to repair breaches in the human community. King's civil rights work was a powerful example of the latter. The Catholic Church's lawyers, laboring to minimize their client's financial liability no matter the nonfinancial (and overlooked financial) costs, exemplify the former. My students should not disavow their devotion to a particular client's interests, but they should remain open to a broader conception of those interests. If my student develops a family law practice, will she direct her client to ask for the maximum share of marital property permitted by statute, or will she encourage the client to consider how the legal resolution of the marriage will shape the relationships that will emerge from the divorce? Clients may reject the implications of personalism, but lawyers should not assume that rejection as the starting point for the representation.

Fourth, King helps my students understand justice, and the lawyer's potential role in securing justice, as something more than access to law. The restoration of relationships provided the ends of King's work, but it also provided the means. The beloved community cannot be built on violence or hatred, which degrades the human person in light of our relational natures. So the first time my student receives a "nasty-gram" letter from opposing counsel, hopefully she will have a broader view of the stakes represented by her response: the tone and substance of her communications, even with a hostile counsel, are not just tools in a contest over ego or power or gamesmanship. They are examples of the daily steps we take toward either building or tearing down relationships. If my student counsels employers on the ubiquitous contracts that limit an employee's postemployment ability to work in the same field, she will not view the employee as an object to be controlled, but as a subject whose legitimate need to earn a livelihood must be balanced with the employer's legitimate need to protect its standing in the market. The relevance of our social nature to our conception of justice does not extend only to relationships of physical presence – after all, the employer may never see that former employee again – but to relationships of accountability. Justice asks, Have you done right by this person? The means and ends of justice are inextricably linked.

Fifth, King's Christian realism helps my students account for the dangers of their own human pride without abdicating their responsibility to speak the truth to clients. Fidelity to law is an important professional value and can be a valuable bulwark against the lawyer's overreaching, but fidelity to law does not provide a sufficiently robust vision of the lawyer's role given that the client's interests are not fully captured by the law's terms. Expecting the lawyer to focus exclusively on the client's legal entitlements to the exclusion of her broader interests, however, replaces a holistic view of the client as person with a one-dimensional view of the client as citizen. If my student becomes a legal aid lawyer, she will have to be vigilant against the pride that can lead to paternalism, especially when working with clients who are already marginalized on account of poverty. At the same time, the lawyer cannot abandon her own status as a moral subject committed to the client's well-being; acting as a mouthpiece often disserves the client. Instead, my student must invest herself in cultural competency, learning enough about her client and the client's background to reach across the sociological barriers of poverty, race, religion, or national origin that often separate lawyer and client in these contexts. The complexities of human reality should not lead my student to retreat from relationship in favor of an arm's length emphasis on technical proficiency; instead, the complexities should motivate my student to invest her whole self, including her technical proficiency, in a real relationship of mutual understanding with her client.

Skeptics will insist that, in many cases, none of this will make any difference because the attorney's legal expertise will give her no extralegal insight that the client does not already possess. Bush administration officials, we presume, knew that the validation of torture amounted to a utilitarian view of human dignity. Ken Lay and Jeffrey Skilling probably recognized that Enron's push-the-envelope legal strategy was part of a broader high-risk strategy to conceal the ventures that would ultimately bring down the company. My student's client probably knows that walking away with the earnest money when the home buyer loses his job and cannot close the deal will cause the buyer significant hardship and may be difficult to justify morally, especially if the client has another buyer lined up quickly enough to avoid any financial loss. In these cases, when there is not a distinctly legal angle to the moral dimension of the problem posed by the representation, what is there for the lawyer to say?

Such a scenario was hardly foreign to King. We need to remember that he wrote his letter from a Birmingham jail cell to an audience of white clergy. We can presume that they were well educated in the Christian moral tradition. Nevertheless, King quoted Jesus Christ, the prophet Amos, the apostle Paul, Martin Luther, and John Bunyan in justifying his willingness to protest segregation in Birmingham.[1] King was not telling his readers something that they did not already know. The white Christian clergy of Birmingham knew the moral truths proclaimed by King, but it was convenient and comfortable for them to deny what they knew. The truth teller's role is not always to inform, but to remind. As David Luban puts it, cases of "intense moral disagreement are rarer than a different sort of case: one in which

---

[1] *See* Martin Luther King Jr., "Letter from Birmingham City Jail" (1963), in *A Testament of Hope: The Essential Writings and Speeches of Martin Luther King Jr.*, ed. James M. Washington (1986), 289.

the moralistic lawyer and the client largely agree in their moral values but differ because the client simply doesn't want scruples to get in the way of a favorable outcome."[2] The lawyer's acquiescence facilitates the client's own cognitive dissonance, whereas the lawyer's proactive moral engagement "may break the spell."[3]

To state it in practical terms, what would a truth-telling role for lawyers have looked like in the events leading up to the financial collapse of 2008? Assume that both Goldman Sachs and its lawyers knew, or should have known, that the bank was contributing to economic instability by packaging troubled assets (including subprime mortgages) as securities and selling them to investors, even while the bank itself was betting that those assets would fail. Upon concluding that the practice was legal, was there anything left for the lawyer to say? To be sure, the lawyer who seeks to walk in King's footsteps need not (indeed should not) preach or scold. It is neither in the lawyer's business interests nor in keeping with agape to mount a moral high horse in communicating concerns that go beyond the question of legal permissibility. But that does not make the extralegal concerns immaterial to the client's interests, broadly understood. The lawyer could help Goldman Sachs draw connections between legal interests and human interests, explaining the mechanisms

---

[2] David Luban, *The Inevitability of Conscience: A Response to My Critics*, 93 CORNELL L. REV. 1437, 1448 (2008).
[3] *Id.* at 1449.

of securities laws, but also exploring the values represented therein – in this case, minimizing and making risks transparent to investors. The recent debates preceding and following the enactment of the Dodd-Frank Act, which aims to regulate the securitization practices that contributed to the collapse more strictly, reflect the complexity of this area and show how far behind the learning curve Congress remains in trying to maintain its competence to regulate.[4]

Lawyers can help the client see the law's inadequacy but still keep the law's aim at the center of the conversation with the client. Sometimes the lawyer's explanation will speak to the client's economic bottom line or the client's tolerance of risk. At other times, the explanation may be based on a belief that the client shares the human interests that the law is struggling to encompass. After hearing his firm's securitization strategy compared to "selling a car with faulty brakes then buying an insurance policy on that car," the Goldman Sachs chair, Lloyd Blankfein, admitted to Congress that the firm's "behavior is improper"[5] and expressed regret for the losses caused to the investing public. The apology, if sincere, suggests that the bank's interests were not fully captured by the terms of legal permissibility or financial profit. Even if the client's response to the lawyer's cautionary explanation

---

[4] Dodd-Frank Wall Street Reform and Consumer Protection Act, Pub. L. No. 111–203, § 929P(b), 124 Stat. 1376 (2010).

[5] CBS News, "Bankers Defend Actions to Congress" (January 13, 2010) (available at http://www.cbsnews.com/stories/2010/01/13/business/main6091377.shtml) (accessed October 4, 2011).

is "I already know that," that does not make the conversation superfluous. The lawyer's articulation of the human interests implicated by a decision and protected imperfectly by law sends a powerful signal to the client that these are important considerations. The signal might even be enough for the client to grant herself permission to include them as relevant factors in the decision.

Then again, it might not. In some cases, the outcome of the case will look exactly the same. Jeffrey Skilling might have kept creating off-balance-sheet entities to hide Enron's true financial condition, no matter how thoughtful and well-meaning the advice he received from counsel. Further, in some cases, the attorney-client conversations will not look any different, even if the attorney has endeavored to take all of King's lessons to heart. Sometimes my students will have a routine slip-and-fall case, or patent prosecution, or home sale where extralegal issues never arise. In those cases, technical competence may prove to be enough to see the lawyer through.

Even those cases, however, will still look different to my students who are handling them even if they do not look different to the casual observer. If my students take King's lessons to heart, they will give an added measure of personal accountability to their work. This accountability will not always be susceptible to measurement through malpractice liability or disciplinary proceedings. It is a broader accountability that aims to reconcile the picture of the human person that arises from the way they approach their work as lawyers with the picture of the human person that they believe to be accurate. Sometimes the reconciliation may occur through the attorney's selection of cases, or through the attorney-client dialogue, or through the care the attorney bestows on the various relationships that make up her professional life. In all cases, the attorney will contribute a robust conception of her own moral agency. King warns my students not to abdicate their personal responsibility for justice; they can work for it by contributing to the important work of institutions, but that work cannot exhaust the lawyer's responsibility.

I have yet to suggest how these lessons are to be imparted to my students. Alas, a direct conversation between King and my students cannot happen; my students are stuck with me. So how do I convey these lessons? Aside from the obvious (making a point to assign "Letter from Birmingham City Jail"), I am more careful about laying a foundation before attempting a conversation about the lawyer's work that goes beyond the ethics rules or fiduciary duty law. Years ago, when I started class with that hypothetical about scientific researchers in Nazi Germany, I was expecting my students to reject the presumptions they carried about the nature of the lawyer's role – that is, that the role justifies behavior that would ordinarily be deemed immoral – without giving them resources to reflect upon those presumptions. Now I first assign them the case of *Buck v. Bell*, in which the Supreme Court upheld the state practice of forcibly sterilizing women who were deemed mentally incompetent. The students squirm at Justice Holmes's pronouncement that "three generations of imbeciles are enough,"[6] but they struggle to articulate their discomfort in the language provided by the law. We then read about human dignity through the lenses provided by a diverse group of authors, including John Paul II, Immanuel Kant, John Stuart Mill, and Peter Singer. My hope is not that they arrive at some consensus regarding human dignity; my hope is that they realize that there is something to talk about when we talk about human dignity. If our intuition tells us that forced sterilization violated Carrie Buck's dignity, can we put that intuition into language that would be accessible to our client if we represented the warden of the mental institution where she lived? If the language is available, can we justify our failure to use it?

Incremental pedagogical changes like this may be (I hope) part of a broader realization that professional formation requires more than technical competence. Joseph Singer notes that "the ability to make sophisticated arguments about justice and morality is a skill all lawyers need."[7] And yet, in his classes at Harvard Law School, he finds it sorely lacking:

> [S]tudents are mute when I ask them to make or to defend arguments based on considerations of rights, fairness,

---

[6] *Buck v. Bell*, 274 U.S. 200 (1927).

[7] Joseph W. Singer, *Normative Methods for Lawyers*, 56 UCLA L. REV. 899, 904 (2009).

justice, morality, or the fundamental values underlying a free and democratic society. They get out the first sentence: "I have a right to use my property as I see fit," or "I have a right to be left alone." But then they go silent. Their silence is partly caused by their inability to determine what vocabulary to use or how to make the argument. But the underlying reason for this uncertainty is their fear that such an argument is merely a matter of opinion that has no objective basis.[8] They know that others can disagree, and they feel unable to defend their arguments.

More than thirty years ago, Roger Cramton identified one contributing cause of this phenomenon by noting the pervasive disregard of values in the law school classroom. He observed that the law school professor "typically avoids explicit discussion of values in order to avoid 'preaching' or 'indoctrination.'"[9] Judging by a recent report on legal education issued by the Carnegie Foundation for Advancement of Teaching, not much has changed since then.[10] After visiting law schools across the country, researchers concluded that "in the minds of many faculty, ethical and social values are subjective and indeterminate and, for that reason, can potentially even conflict with the all-important values of the

---

[8] *Id.* at 904.

[9] Roger C. Cramton, *The Ordinary Religion of the Law School Classroom*, 29 J. LEG. ED. 247, 256 (1978).

[10] William M. Sullivan et al., *Educating Lawyers: Preparation for the Profession of Law* (Carnegie Foundation for Advancement of Teaching, 2007).

academy."[11] In fact, the view that "it is indoctrination even to ask students to articulate their own normative positions was surprisingly prevalent" in law school.[12]

But, the researchers found, the law school classroom as a morality-free zone is more likely to be confusing than clarifying. The report's authors observe that when first-year law students express confusion about moral and legal obligations, course instructors frequently "tell them that their concerns about fairness or other moral issues are not relevant to legal analysis[,] and [they ask their students] to set aside those concerns."[13] "Besides providing a distorted understanding of the nature of law itself,"[14] professors' reactions are "bewildering rather than clarifying" to students.[15] Instead, the report's authors suggest that the instructor could

> [introduce] a careful discussion of the distinction and relationship between the moral and the legal, illustrate[] something of the breadth of law's concerns, [and thus] deepen students' understanding of the law [on] both the particular legal issues in the case under consideration and the law as a social institution.[16]

Our current practice of professional formation – both in and beyond law school – inculcates powerful moral values that

[11] *Id.* at 133.
[12] *Id.* at 136.
[13] *Id.* at 144.
[14] *Id.*
[15] *Id.*
[16] *Id.*

emanate from the adversarial system, but, by omission, our practices also send strong messages that other moral questions are of marginal importance to the lawyer's work.

Though our awareness of the problem appears to be growing, there are other market and regulatory forces moving in the opposite direction. The cost of legal education and crippling student debt are moral problems of their own, and the changing nature of the legal services market (as discussed in Chapter 2) makes the high-salary assumptions underlying tuition increases increasingly precarious. There is talk of returning legal education to a trade school model, and if an American Bar Association proposal to pare down accreditation requirements becomes reality, a law school may function simply as a more intensive bar preparation course.[17] Making space in law school for the discussion of moral considerations, more client-counseling exercises, and opportunities for individual student reflection is not costless, but the primary obstacle is one of mindset, not money. If we get to the point where we are serious about forming lawyers who can work for the robust sense of justice envisioned by

---

[17] *See* Letter dated March 28, 2011 from Michael A. Olivas, President of the American Ass'n of Law Schools, to Hulett H. Askew, Consultant on Legal Education, American Bar Ass'n (http://taxprof.typepad.com/files/aals-submission-for-april-2–2011-src-open-forum.pdf) (objecting that ABA's proposed revisions to law school accreditation requirements "may well ease financial pressure at law schools, but they may also lead to a 'race to the bottom,' as schools find that they can reduce their offerings and services while still remaining accredited").

King, we have to be equally serious about equipping lawyers for the task.

We must keep in mind, though, that King's call transcends any particular professional role, and so the conversation that his legacy has sparked goes far beyond matters of legal education or professional regulation. King was always cognizant of the law's limits,[18] and this cognizance became more painful near the end of his ministry.[19] The law is not the final embodiment of justice (much less love), for the law cannot coerce the authentic restoration of human relationships. But the law has a role to play. The law can help lay the groundwork for the restoration of relationships, though ultimately the process of restoration requires the willful participation of the human person. In this regard, lawyers have a bigger potential role to play than the law does, for lawyers not only provide access to the law, they can also bring the law's animating purpose and inescapable imperfections into relief, thereby permitting the client a more

[18] *See* Martin Luther King Jr., "An Address before the National Press Club" (1962), in *A Testament of Hope, supra* note 1, at 99, 100 ("It may be true that morality cannot be legislated, but behavior can be regulated. The law may not change the heart, but it can restrain the heartless.").

[19] King "came to a deep and very painful realization, a realization he had had inklings of before, but that never had crystallized: those acts of Congress, no matter how comprehensive, really did very little to improve the daily lives of the poor black people across the rural South." David Garrow, "Reformer to Revolutionary," in *Martin Luther King Jr.: Civil Rights Leader, Theologian, Orator* (1989), 428.

fulsome view of the real human interests implicated by our day-to-day decisions.

Distilling King's legacy into separate intellectual components, as I have in this book, should not detract from the power of his legacy's coherence.[20] His most abiding lesson is the life he offered, practicing love in the service of justice. In the end, King's lesson is about a life lived for others, not in some sense of noble self-denial, but in the stark recognition that "the self cannot be self without other selves."[21] He calls the lawyer to invest in something bigger than herself, which could be disorienting for members of a profession steeped in norms of individual rights and entitlements. Ultimately, though, his call should inspire lawyers, for "the arc of the universe is long, but it bends toward justice."[22] Lawyers willing to learn from King will realize that they can be part of the story.

[20] "[W]e cannot simply categorize and prioritize the significance of one influence over another. Each of them contributes to the overall significance in light of their common ideological assumptions that point back to the inherent goodness of God and hence of humanity created in God's good image. It is this larger tradition, one could reason, that eventually informed the black church's social views, abolitionism's hope, Thoreau's civil disobedience, Rauschenbusch's social gospel, Gandhi's nonviolence, Brightman's Personalism, and even the manner in which King essentially viewed the Christ narrative and its social implications." Richard Wayne Wills Sr., *Martin Luther King Jr. and the Image of God* (2009), 55–6.
[21] Martin Luther King Jr., "Where Do We Go from Here?" in *A Testament of Hope, supra* note 1, at 252.
[22] *Id.*

Index

Index

Index

Index